PHOTOSHOP®

RESTORATION & RETOUCHING

SECOND EDITION

KATRIN EISMANN

New Riders

201 West 103rd Street, Indianapolis, Indiana 46290
An Imprint of Pearson Education
Boston • Indianapolis • London • Munich • New York • San Francisco

Photoshop® Restoration & Retouching

Second Edition

Copyright © 2004 by Katrin Eismann

International Standard Book Number: 0-7357-1350-2

Library of Congress Catalog Card Number: 2002117003

Printed in the United States of America

First printing: July 2003

07 06 05 04 03   7 6 5 4 3 2 1

Interpretation of the printing code: The rightmost double-digit number is the year of the book's printing; the rightmost single-digit number is the number of the book's printing. For example, the printing code 03-1 shows that the first printing of the book occurred in 2003.

Trademarks

For Instructors

This book was built around the techniques that I have taught over the years to the numerous students in my digital and creative imaging classes. I hope that this book can help you teach Photoshop as well, and that the examples and images I have provided will help you learn and demonstrate the concepts and techniques of retouching and restoration. As a teacher, I'm sure you know how much time and work is involved in creating exercises and preparing materials that fulfill all the needs of a classroom. I ask now that you respect my work, and that of the many contributors and imaging professionals whose work I've featured in this book, by not copying pages of the book, distributing any of the images from the web site, or otherwise reproducing the information, even if paraphrased, without proper attribution and permission. Of course, if students own their own copies of the book, they can freely download and use the images from the web site in the classroom.

Warning and Disclaimer

PUBLISHER
Stephanie Wall

EXECUTIVE EDITOR
Steve Weiss

PRODUCTION MANAGER
Gina Kanouse

ACQUISITIONS EDITOR
Elise Walter

DEVELOPMENT EDITOR
Beth Millett

TECHNICAL REVIEWER
Doug Nelson

TECHNICAL EDITOR
Wayne Palmer

PROJECT EDITOR
Jake McFarland

COPY EDITOR
Kathy Murray

INDEXER
Lisa Stumpf

PROOFREADERS
Jessica McCarty
Karen Gill

COMPOSITION
Kim Scott

MANUFACTURING COORDINATOR
Dan Uhrig

INTERIOR DESIGNER
Anne Jones

COVER DESIGNER
Anne Jones

MARKETING
Scott Cowlin
Tammy Detrich
Hannah Latham

PUBLICITY
Susan Nixon

Contents at a Glance

Foreword   xi

Introduction   1

PART I: PHOTOSHOP FOR RETOUCHING

  1 Photoshop Essentials   9

**PART II: CORRECTING TONE, EXPOSURE,
           AND COLOR**

  2 Improving Tone and Contrast   33

  3 Exposure Correction   67

  4 Working with Color   91

**PART III: ESSENTIAL RESTORATION, REPAIRING,
            AND REBUILDING TECHNIQUES**

  5 Dust, Mold, and Texture Removal   137

  6 Damage Control and Repair   165

  7 Rebuilding, Rearranging, and
         Re-creating Portraits   183

  8 Refining and Polishing the Image   223

PART IV: PUTTING THE BEST FACE FORWARD

  9 Portrait Retouching   273

 10 Glamour and Fashion Retouching   325

         Appendix Contributors   353

         Index   357

Table of Contents

1

PHOTOSHOP ESSENTIALS

Working Efficiently with Keyboard Shortcuts	10
Palettes and Custom Workspaces	13
Context-Sensitive Menus	16
Quick Image Navigation	17
Learning the Importance of Layers	18
File Organization and Workflow Issues	21
Before You Begin: A Word to the Wise	29
Closing Thoughts	29

2

IMPROVING TONE AND CONTRAST

Evaluating Image Tone and Previsualizing the Final Image	34
The Importance of Adjustment Layers	37
Mastering Tonality with Levels	38
Improving Image Tone with Levels	39
Curves and Contrast	46
Working with Blending Modes	49
Bringing Out Detail with Screen and Channel Mixer	53
Tricks for Maximizing Adjustment Layers	54
Combining Tonal Corrections	56
Basing Tonal Corrections on Selections	59
The Benefits of High-Bit Data	63
Closing Thoughts	66

3

EXPOSURE CORRECTION

Improving Dark Images	68
Digital Flash Techniques	74
Salvaging Overexposed Images	80
Painting with Light	88
Closing Thoughts	89

4

WORKING WITH COLOR

Color Essentials 92
Identifying a Color Cast 94
Understanding Color Correction with Image Variations 94
Mimicking the Color Darkroom with Color Balance 98
Global Color Correction 99
The Numbers Don't Lie 112
Selective Color Correction 121
Alleviating Extreme Color Problems 124
Correcting Color Temperature Problems 126
Interchannel Color Correction 131
Closing Thoughts 133

5

DUST, MOLD, AND TEXTURE REMOVAL

Dustbusting 101 138
Eradicating Mold, Mildew, and Fungus 141
Reducing Print Texture and Moiré Artifacts 151
Maintaining Image Structure 162
Closing Thoughts 164

6

DAMAGE CONTROL AND REPAIR

Eliminating Scratches 166
Removing Unwanted Elements 168
Repairing Tears, Rips, and Cracks 171
Removing Stains and Discoloration 174
Closing Thoughts 182

7

REBUILDING, REARRANGING, AND RE-CREATING PORTRAITS

Re-creating Backgrounds 184
Finding Suitable Replacement Materials 194
Building a Digital Background Collection 196
Rebuilding a Portrait 201
Bringing People Closer Together 207
Reconstructing Color 210
Alleviating Extreme Color Damage 215
Closing Thoughts 222

8

REFINING AND POLISHING THE IMAGE

Converting Color to Black and White	224
Combining Color and Black and White	236
Toning Images with Color	241
Hand-Coloring a Black-and-White Image	245
Working with Soft and Selective Focus	251
Creative and Vignette Edges	256
Sharpening Filters	259
Closing Thoughts	269

9

PORTRAIT RETOUCHING

Levels of Retouching	274
Developing a Portrait Retouch Strategy	276
Removing Distractions	278
Flattering the Contours	279
Improving Skin Texture	288
Accentuating Facial Features	301
Improving Facial Features	315
Working with Soft and Selective Focus	320
Closing Thoughts	324

10

GLAMOUR AND FASHION RETOUCHING

Devising a Working Strategy	326
The Subtle Digital Beautician	328
Removing the Distractions	328
Complexion, Hair, and Eye Refinement	336
The Digital Diet	343
Glamour Lighting	348
Closing Thoughts	351

APPENDIX

Contributors	353

DEDICATION

For the readers of the first edition: Your many emails, questions, ideas, and suggestions inspired me to write the second edition. Thank you all very much!

Johnnie, I couldn't and wouldn't have achieved any of this without you. Fore!

To the Salttowners: Thank you for the images, memories, and understanding phone calls. Alles Liebe!

ABOUT THE AUTHOR

Katrin Eismann is an internationally respected lecturer and teacher on the subject of imaging, restoration, retouching, and the impact of emerging technologies upon professional photographers, artists, and educators. Her clients include Eastman Kodak, Apple, Adobe, American Film Institute, Professional Photography Association, and the University of California Los Angeles. She received her Bachelor of Fine Arts degree in Photographic Illustration with a concentration in electronic still imaging from the Rochester Institute of Technology. In 2002, she completed her Masters of Fine Arts degree in design at the School of VISUAL ARTS in New York City.

In the future, Katrin would like to take photographs that do not require any color correction, retouching, cropping, dodging and burning, or enhancement of any kind. To learn more about Katrin and to see her creative work, please visit www.photoshopdiva.com. To learn more about the book, *Photoshop Restoration & Retouching*, please visit the book's supplemental web site, www.digitalretouch.org.

ABOUT THE TECHNICAL REVIEWERS

These reviewers contributed their considerable hands-on expertise to the entire development process for *Photoshop Restoration & Retouching*. As the book was being written, these dedicated professionals reviewed all the material for technical content, organization, and flow. Their feedback was critical to ensuring that *Photoshop Restoration & Retouching* fits our readers' need for the highest-quality technical information.

Doug Nelson is a freelance writer living in the St. Louis area. He has been involved with photography since 1968, with computers since 1974, and with digital image editing since 1988. His web site, RetouchPRO.com, is the world's largest online community for retouchers and photo restorers.

Wayne Palmer has had a passion for photography all his life. He has a degree in education from Bloomsburg State College, but his interest in photography kept him in the darkroom as much as the classroom. After graduation he worked for Guardian Photo, Inc. for 13 years in the marketing of photofinishing services on a national level.

Wayne started his own business, Palmer Multimedia Imaging, in 1994, offering custom photographic, videographic, and digital photo restoration services. He has worked with Photoshop since version 3, and previously used Aldus PhotoStyler.

A self-described AV nerd, Wayne enjoys sharing his knowledge of photography, digital imaging, and computers. He teaches Photoshop and Digital Photography in the continuing education department of the Pennsylvania College of Technology and volunteers his time to instruct seniors in computer literacy through the James V. Brown Library.

ACKNOWLEDGMENTS

As many authors have recognized, writing a book initially seems like a secluded undertaking, but the very task of researching and seeking expert insights into any topic changes the process from solitary to collaborative. Over the years, I have learned from countless Photoshop experts, engineers, artists, and students. Many have techniques featured throughout this book. Thank you to Mark Beckelman, Joel Becker, Carrie Beene, Rick Billings, Russell Brown, Shan Canfield, Robb Carr, Jane Conner-ziser, Helene DeLillo, Bruce Fraser, Greg Gorman, Mark Hamburg, Michael Kieran, Sanjay Kothari, Julieanne Kost, Dan Margulis, Bert Monroy, Myke Ninness, Wayne Palmer, Herb Paynter, Marc Pawliger, Andrew Rodney, Jeff Schewe, Eddie Tapp, Chris Tarantino, Laurie Thompson, Greg Vander Houwen, Lee Varis, John Warner, Lloyd Weller, and Ben Wilmore for putting up with yet another email, phone call, or question from me.

Creating a book is an undertaking where more work is done behind than in front of the curtain. My fantastic crew included these people: Elise Walter always understood when I needed just a few more days, Steve Weiss was always ready with a solution, Kathy Murray made me sound as though I know what a dangling participle is, Doug Nelson and Wayne Palmer were my technical editors who kept pushing me to be clearer, Jake McFarland took the raw materials and finessed them through the editing process, and finally I can't believe that Beth Millett let me talk her into filling her little free-time with this update. Beth, I wouldn't and couldn't have done it without you.

Thank you to the numerous contributors who make this second edition so valuable. Readers, photo enthusiasts, and imaging professionals from all around the world are featured in these pages and listed in the "Contributors" appendix. You were all wonderful to work with, generous with your images and techniques, and understanding of my production deadlines. Merci, Vielen Dank, Graçis, and Thank You! In addition, Jeffery Foster allowed me to feature and post images from Ablestock.com. I appreciate the quality of the images and his assistance very much.

Thank you to the numerous readers who emailed since the release of the first edition. I sincerely enjoyed hearing from you, seeing the images you worked on, and reading your questions, which showed me what was unclear or missing in the first edition. A technique that is complicated or poorly explained is worthless, and I listened to your ideas and addressed your questions while preparing this second edition. In fact, calling this book a second edition is not accurate—this really is a brand new book. I reviewed every single technique and substituted many images with better examples. My primary goal was to write a book that readers of the first edition would find valuable enough to purchase and feel they got their money's worth. Please let me know if I accomplished this.

TELL US WHAT YOU THINK

As the reader of this book, you are the most important critic and commentator. We value your opinion and want to know what we're doing right, what we could do better, what areas you'd like to see us publish in, and any other words of wisdom you're willing to pass our way.

As the Publisher for New Riders Publishing, I welcome your comments. You can fax, email, or write me directly to let me know what you did or didn't like about this book—as well as what we can do to make our books stronger. When you write, please be sure to include this book's title, ISBN, and author, as well as your name and phone or fax number. I will carefully review your comments and share them with the author and editors who worked on the book.

Please note that I cannot help you with technical problems related to the topic of this book, and that due to the high volume of email I receive, I might not be able to reply to every message.

Fax: 317-581-4663

Email: stephanie.wall@newriders.com

Mail: Stephanie Wall
          Publisher
          New Riders Publishing
          201 West 103rd Street
          Indianapolis, IN 46290 USA

FOREWORD

Summer, 2003

I grew up looking at the work of great photographers. Their images arrived in our home in magazines and periodicals. Each week we anxiously waited to see what was sure to be new and exciting. Those magical images were frozen in time. They documented and archived great moments of our world and its history. They were exciting, evocative, and memorable photographs.

But times change. With the onslaught of television, advertising, and ultimately the wide-spread proliferation of digital imaging technologies, still images held less and less significance for me personally. Over the past dozen years or so, I had progressively taken to the opinion that traditional photography had become irrelevant.

Not only had the craft of photography been lost, the very aesthetic of the photography that I knew seemed stagnant and stifled. Even worse, the descriptive power of photography was diminished and the ability of a photograph to deliver credible truth and emotional impact was in doubt.

In recent years, two events have changed that opinion.

9/11/01

The first was the events of September 11, 2001. In the earliest hours and days following the attacks, we feared that more than 20,000 individuals had died. At that same time, New York was spontaneously wallpapered with photographs. They were nearly everywhere you turned. At every corner. On every lamp post. Plastered on the sides of buildings, bridges, and construction sites.

The pictures were of the thousands of missing husbands, wives, children, brothers, sisters, and friends. They were posted by families and friends. They were clearly the pictures that were within reach. They were taken directly from their desks, mantles and, no doubt, refrigerator doors.

The images we saw on the streets were enlarged Xerox copies. They were black and white. They were simple snapshots from parties, weddings, and backyard barbeques. Casual glimpses of the most innocent moments. Nothing formal, nothing contrived, most certainly nothing professional. Yet these were some of the most powerful images I have ever seen.

The impact of these photographs was staggering. Even haunting. Because the images were posted along the normal commuting paths of the individuals, depending on the path you chose to travel, you would encounter photographs of different individuals. These were images of the people you would walk past without a moment's notice on a normal day in New York. They were no longer anonymous commuters. They were frozen in place. Their names and addresses printed clearly for us to see. Their families asking our help in finding them.

Suddenly we were not anonymous anymore. These were our neighbors. This was the space we once shared and were still sharing. These were the missing and they were presumed dead, but their photographs allowed them to linger in this world. Through these images, at that moment, we had a last chance to learn their names and understand more about them—and maybe even help. For a time and at an extraordinary moment, New York was an open book.

PHOTOSHOP RESTORATION & RETOUCHING

Another, far more positive event occurred that also restored my opinion of the value of still images. It began shortly after the publication of the first edition of *Photoshop Restoration & Retouching*. It continues today.

I have all the faith in the world in Katrin Eismann. She is an exceptional teacher—passionate, demanding, and inspiring. Nonetheless, I never anticipated the ground swell of response that she would receive from her readers. They pointed in a fresh and powerful way to the inherent meaning and value that a photograph can represent.

The most impressive responses were not from professional photographers. They were certainly not limited to digital imaging artists. The most surprising responses were from the individuals who, for the first time, applied these new skills to images they once thought ruined beyond repair. Their reaction was humbling and amazing.

Like the 9/11 images, most of the restored photographs were of family and friends—loved ones both living and deceased. The passion these individuals felt about salvaging and recovering these images was palpable. The joy they expressed in once again having a precious image was equaled only by the personal accomplishment they felt in restoring the image.

The stories the readers told and the images they sent were sometimes sad, at other times hilarious. All were presented with pride, accomplishment, and appreciation. A wonderful and delightful response to a technical book directed at intermediate users of Photoshop. A reminder to me that the relevance of an image, like beauty, is most often determined by the eye of the beholder.

Today I am far more positive about photography because I have been reminded of how much impact a simple image can have. And, in a world full of images, how precious the smallest print can be.

THE AUTHOR

I know Katrin Eismann better than many people. The first time I heard her speak was more than 10 years ago. She was defining unsharp masking to a class at the Center for Creative Imaging. At that moment, I turned to the guy next to me and told him, "I am going to marry her!" We were married two years later.

Katrin is a classic over-achiever, and she takes everything seriously. Everything. Fortunately, she has developed the ability to distill complex software techniques into digestible, step-by-step screen captures. She does this extremely well and it makes working through her books and her classes a pleasure.

Katrin is extremely generous. She learned early on that no one individual can master all the elements of the complex digital imaging systems. Subsequently, Katrin has always included, referenced, and promoted other imaging artists, teachers, and technicians. This is not common.

Katrin's work with at CCI and with ThunderLizard conferences brought the highest caliber presentations to thousands of avid Photoshop users and photographers. Katrin's insistence on the highest quality and the most up-to-date content was always driven by her concern that her students or the audience get what they paid for: valuable information presented patiently and effectively.

To this day and with this book, the second edition of *Photoshop Restoration & Retouching*, Katrin Eismann has again placed quality and value as the highest priority. Every chapter has been reviewed, rewritten, and updated. This is essentially a new book, with new images and many new techniques.

In this edition, Katrin is working with Doug Nelson, the creator of RetouchPRO.com. Doug's passion for image restoration is well documented. His involvement and his professionalism has ensured once again that *Photoshop Restoration & Retouching* will inspire and educate. You should expect nothing less. You will not be disappointed.

John McIntosh

Chair, Computer Art
School of VISUAL ARTS New York City

INTRODUCTION

THE IMPORTANCE OF IMAGES

A few years ago I was watching a TV news report about a tornado that had flattened a neighborhood near Oklahoma City. As the camera crew neared a family, the interviewer asked, "Did you have a chance to save anything?" The woman sobbed, "The family photos are gone—the wedding pictures, the kids, the photos of the grandkids—all gone." A few years later, I was watching a news report on the fires that swept through Los Alamos, New Mexico. The news team interviewed a couple who had lived in the same home for 30 years. When asked whether they had been able to save anything they replied, "All we took were the photographs." In both instances, the first item these people mentioned were their photographs. Objects without any great financial value, but with tremendous personal value.

Our photographs contain our memories and our legacy, and they connect us to our family and friends. Even if they are cracked, yellowed, or damaged, we don't throw them away. No matter how tattered or faded a photograph is, it still helps us remember and learn about the past. The combination of image, emotion, and memory fascinates me. With the addition of one component to this mixture—Photoshop—you can make faded colors rich again, remove damage, and clean up mold, making images as clear and crisp as the day they were taken. With the skilled use of Adobe Photoshop as presented in this book, you can fight the ravages of time and, more importantly, share the memories with your family and friends.

I started working with an early version of Photoshop 1.0 in 1989, and since 1992 have been teaching digital imaging at workshops and schools around the

world. My students always surprise me with questions, challenges, and examples of taking what I've taught them and going much further than I imagined possible. Take a look at what Sean Melnick, a graduate of the School of VISUAL ARTS in New York City and an imaging professional, started with in **figure 1**. **Figure 2** shows what Sean created, as well as his passion and perseverance to bring the individual pieces together with the careful use of layers, Adjustment Layers, and cloning. For Sean, more important than the actual image was the moment he showed the final print to his grandparents—their eyes lit up as they remembered everyone in the picture. Our photographs are our legacy.

figure 1

figure 2

As you can see by paging through the book, not all the pictures and examples featured in this book are historical. Many of the examples are contemporary—images that were captured with the latest digital cameras or came from leading photo studios. As a photographer, I always try to get the picture right before hitting the shutter, instead of using Photoshop as an afterthought to rescue a bad photograph. In other words, if I can create a better picture by fixing the lighting, hiring a professional makeup artist, or changing camera lenses or position, I'll always opt to make the extra effort to get the picture right in front of the lens.

THE IMPORTANCE OF LEARNING

A few years ago, I decided to start playing golf. I'm athletic, coordinated, love being outside, and very dedicated after I put my mind to a challenge. I figured that with a few golf lessons, I would be able to enjoy an idyllic, relaxing round of golf with my husband John, who has been playing golf for 30 years. Little did I know how much went into a good golf swing—position of the feet, weight distribution, keeping your eye on the ball, hands relaxed yet firm, position of the club head, and that's all before you even start a back swing. It took two years and a lot of golf balls (and some significant frustration) before I even hit the ball solidly. One day, we were playing and I launched the ball with a 7 wood down the fairway and onto the green. I was stunned and remember thinking, "Wow! That's what a good golf swing feels like." Needless to say, I was hooked and, although I still hit plenty of bad shots, it's the good ones that keep me going out and practicing more.

Time and practice—you can't be good at a sport, cook a gourmet meal, or restore an image without it. There will be frustration, anger, and muttering, generally along the lines of "Why do I even bother… this looks terrible…I might as well just stop right now." Please turn off that noisy, no-good critic (who we all have in our heads). Shut the voice down and keep practicing. Just as you learned to master a hobby, sport, or language, you'll learn to master and enjoy Photoshop restoration and retouching.

IS THIS BOOK RIGHT FOR YOU?

This book is right for you if you love images or work with photographs as a dedicated amateur or full-time professional. You may be a historian, photographer, librarian, teacher, multimedia artist, designer, artist, or the grandmother who wants to share the best photos with the rest of the family. This book addresses salvaging historical images and righting the contemporary images that have gone wrong—the missed exposures, the poor color balance, the busy and distracting background, or the inevitable wrinkle, pimple, or extra pounds that just drive you crazy every time you look at that photo.

This book is not for you if you don't have the time, curiosity, and patience to read through the examples, try them out, and then—just as I push my students—take the techniques further by applying them to your own images.

You have three ways to learn the techniques presented in this book:

- By reading the examples and looking at the images.
- By downloading the images from the book's web site, www.digitalretouch.org, and with the book in hand, re-creating my steps.
- By taking the techniques shown here and applying them to your own images. As you work, you'll need to adjust some of the tool or filter settings to achieve optimal results. It is exactly at that moment, when you are working with your own images, that you're really learning how to restore and retouch images.

This is not an introductory book. To get the most out of it, you should be comfortable with the fundamentals of Photoshop, know where the tools are and what they do, and be familiar with common tasks, such as how to activate a layer or save a selection. As mentioned, I've been working with Photoshop for over 10 years, and yet I still learned a lot by writing this book. In fact, I tried to write a book that I would want to buy or that would interest the many intermediate and advanced Photoshop users who are looking for in-depth and challenging learning materials.

THE STRUCTURE OF THE BOOK AND THE WEB SITE

This book is divided into three primary areas:

- Working with tone, contrast, exposure, and color
- Removing dust and mold and repairing damage
- Professional portrait and fashion retouching

In fact, the book is structured in the same way you should work with your images, starting with a brief overview of Photoshop essentials, file organization, and the tools a retoucher needs. It then works through tonal and color correction (the first things to focus on when retouching an image), followed by chapters on dust and damage removal, adding creative effects, doing portrait retouching, and the techniques professional retouchers use in the fashion and glamour business.

Each chapter starts with a brief overview of what will be covered in the chapter. I always start with a straightforward example that leads to more advanced examples. You may be tempted to jump to the more advanced sections right away, but I don't recommend it. My teaching and chapter structure serves the purpose of building up the tools and techniques in which the introductory examples serve as the foundation for the advanced examples. Similarly, the chapters on tonal and color correction serve as the foundation for the portrait and glamour retouching chapters. Do I expect you to sit down right now in the bookstore and read the book from cover to cover? Of course not—you should really pay for it first! Rather, take the book home, page through the chapters so you can see how the book and retouching workflow is structured, and then work your way through the book.

Instead of including a CD with the book, I designed and maintain a supplemental web site where you can download many of the tutorial images featured in the book. Please visit www.digitalretouch.org to download images, view the reader gallery, follow links to additional retouching resources, and to contact me. Each chapter (except for Chapter 1,

"Photoshop Essentials") has 4 to 12 JPEG images that you can download. For those of you with a fast Internet connection (or a lot of patience), I've also included 1–10MB self-extracting image archives for each chapter.

 N o t e

The images on the book's companion web site are for your personal use and should not be distributed by any other means.

Most of the images in the book originated from my or my husband's image and photography collection. Numerous professional retouchers, teachers, photographers, and Ablestock.com have generously shared many of their images and examples, many of which are posted on the web site. Throughout the book, I did use some images from stock CD collections or feature images for which we were not able to procure permission to post the files, and I would be breaking copyright agreements if I posted them on the web. Call me old-fashioned, but I respect International and U.S. copyright laws—the copyright of all images remains with the originator, as noted throughout the book. Please do not email the publisher or me to request images that are not posted. I will not send them to you. You really don't want me to go to jail, do you?

In the cases where I didn't have permission to post specific images on the book's web site, you can use similar images from your own photo albums or collections to follow along. Although you won't have the exact image I am using in the book, the problems being corrected are so universal that I am sure you'll be able to learn the techniques by working with similar images. After all, I'm sure you will be branching out to your own problem files sooner rather than later.

I would love to hear from you. Please email your comments about the book and web site to me at katrin@digitalretouch.org. Show me how you've taken the techniques in these pages and gone further with them. If you send me before-and-after files (please keep them small, 1MB in total) of the retouched image, I'll post them in the reader's gallery. Be sure to include your contact information;

great examples of restoration and retouching may be fodder for the next edition of the book. As I mentioned in the acknowledgments, this second edition would never have come to fruition if it hadn't have been for the many readers who wrote me to ask questions and show me their images.

IS THIS BOOK APPLICABLE TO PHOTOSHOP ELEMENTS?

I've received numerous emails asking me whether this book is worthwhile for a Photoshop Elements user. Photoshop Elements is a terrific program; it includes a surprising number of Photoshop features and is often included with the sale of a scanner or digital camera. My technical editor, Wayne Palmer, calls it, "75% of Photoshop for around $75."

With the difference in price tags, Elements does have its limits, but it is definitely capable of tackling a great number of restoration tasks presented in this book.

First, the limitations:

- Only 8-bit RGB and grayscale color modes are supported.
- Curves, Color Balance, and Channel Mixer are missing from the adjustment options.
- No History snapshot features.
- No Healing Brush.
- No access to channels or quick mask.

Second, the possibilities:

- Supports Adjustment Layers, Adjustment Layer layer masks, and layer Blend Modes.
- Supports the "Use all Layers" feature, which allows you to clone onto an empty layer.
- Most filters are included—sharpening, blurring, and high pass.
- Selections can be saved.
- Supports layer masking—indirectly.
- You do have a History palette and can simulate the snapshot feature by saving your work at different stages as "copy merged" layers.

A reader wrote to me regarding my book and Photoshop Elements. "I am using your book with Photoshop Elements. What your book does that others don't is discuss the reasons for making certain adjustments, and the theory behind making certain adjustments, so I think it is applicable to Elements, but I also have PaintShop Pro and I find it helpful for that as well. There are many books that are highly rated that give the reader examples and exercises, and tell the reader exactly how to make adjustments to suit a specific photo. It's hard to take that info and make it work for the readers in their own photos. For example, a book that tells me to set Unsharp mask for a specific photo to 143, 2, 12 does not help me learn the best way to sharpen my own photos, so I think your book does a good job of explaining much more the theory of retouching, not just the mechanics of correcting a sample photo."

The Hidden Power of Photoshop Elements 2 by Richard Lynch (Sybex, 2003) is the perfect complement to this book if you are using Photoshop Elements.

WHAT IS NOT COVERED IN THIS BOOK

Although this book was an ambitious project from the very start, there is a lot of Photoshop that I do not cover. I concentrated on Photoshop 7.0, which is the latest version. If you are still working with versions 4.0, 5.0, or 6.0, you will still learn a lot from this book, because the most important tools for retouching—layers, Adjustment Layers, and Blending Modes—all go back that far. (And this book probably will still be useful long after the next release of Photoshop.) I do not work for Adobe, but I can highly recommend the upgrade to 7.0. I do not address Photoshop basics; I don't go down the toolbar, which would just bore you to death; and I don't cover complex selections or masking. I concentrated on image restoration and retouching and, with these words, I wish you a lot of fun as you bring back image memories and take your contemporary photographs to a higher level.

Best regards,

Katrin Eismann
katrin@digitalretouch.org
The Big Apple, New York City

Photoshop for Retouching

1

1

PHOTOSHOP ESSENTIALS   **9**

1

PHOTOSHOP ESSENTIALS

Put three people in a room, give them each a computer and 30 minutes, and I bet that they'll each come up with at least three different ways to solve the same Photoshop problem. The variety of approaches that Photoshop allows can at times be frustrating or invigorating, depending on how much you like to explore and experiment. So what separates a casual Photoshop user from a power user? In most cases, it's experience and the ability to visualize the final outcome of the project. To power users, Photoshop is transparent—the interface practically disappears as they work to create the retouched or restored image. For novices, Photoshop can be so overwhelming that they get lost finding tools, commands, and controls. Even though they might get the image done, it will have taken them a lot longer than necessary.

Learning to move quickly through Photoshop helps you be a better retoucher because you can concentrate on the image and not the software. In this chapter, you learn to be more efficient with Photoshop and, in the same vein, be a better Photoshop retoucher by

- Working efficiently with shortcuts
- Using file navigation
- Discovering the importance of layers
- Developing file organization and workflow methods

Restoration and retouching is more than being a fast mouse clicker. Good retouchers understand that the images they are working with are very important to the client, a family member, or the person in the picture. Before you start a retouching project, take a moment to consider that the pixels represent real people and real events—they're more than a collection of dark and light specks of digital information. It's your job to bring back memories from faded, cracked, and damaged originals. This is a weighty responsibility, and keeping that in mind throughout the retouching process helps you see the image with empathy and care.

WORKING EFFICIENTLY WITH KEYBOARD SHORTCUTS

Photoshop was developed from the ground up to be used with two hands: one on the keyboard and one on the mouse. The time you save by using keyboard equivalents to access a tool or command, and to navigate through a file, will make you a more efficient retoucher. Additionally, using the keyboard rather than the mouse reduces the total number of repetitive mouse clicks that can add up to the pain, aggravation, and lost productivity of repetitive-motion injury.

Knowing the keyboard shortcuts to access tools, change settings, and control palettes enables you to concentrate on the image and be a better retoucher. For example, imagine that you're retouching a file and need to access the Clone Stamp tool, increase the brush size, and change the brush opacity to 40%. The manual method involves selecting the Clone Stamp tool, dragging to the brush size required, highlighting the Opacity value, and typing 40. The shortcut-key method entails tapping the letter S, tapping the right bracket to increase the brush size, and typing in the desired opacity with either the numerals on the top of your keyboard or on the extended keypad to the right of your keyboard. It's a much faster way to get the same results!

Photoshop offers numerous methods to navigate through a file and a plethora of documented and undocumented shortcut keys. Do you need to know them all? Of course not. Should you learn how to activate the tools that you'll be using everyday? Absolutely. If you use a Photoshop tool or command three or more times a day, learning its keyboard shortcut saves time and makes sense. Additionally, if you access a filter or sequence of commands more than three times a day, learning how to create an action also is a good idea.

 T i p

Look inside the Photoshop software box. The folded reference card lists the most important shortcuts and key commands you'll need.

For all accounts and purposes, Photoshop is identical on both the Macintosh and Windows platforms. Throughout this book I have used both commands, beginning by the Macintosh command in parentheses followed with the PC command in brackets. For example, undoing the last step would read (Cmd + Z) [Ctrl + Z]. In general, the Macintosh Command (Cmd) key is used where the PC Control (Ctrl) key would be, and you'll find that the Mac Option key maps to the PC Alt key. Control is used on the Mac where the right mouse button is used on Windows.

The following section covers the primary navigational shortcuts and shortcut keys used throughout this book that will help you be a more efficient retoucher. More than 600 useful Photoshop key commands and shortcuts are clearly cataloged in *Photoshop 7 Power Shortcuts* by Michael Ninness (New Riders, 2003).

Learning the most useful Photoshop shortcut keys and navigation techniques takes 15 minutes. To get the most out of the time, go to your computer, launch Photoshop, and open a file that is at least 10MB. The reason I suggest practicing with a 10MB file is that you will really appreciate the ease of navigation when you are working with an image that is larger than your monitor can display (see the section, "Quick Image Navigation," later in this chapter).

The Toolbar

Tapping the appropriate letter on the keyboard activates a specific tool in the Photoshop toolbar. In most cases, the first letter of the tool's name is the letter to tap, such as B for Brush and M for the Marquee tool. Of course, there are exceptions to the first-letter rule, such as J for Healing Brush and V for the Move tool. **Figure 1.1** spells out the letter commands you use to access each tool.

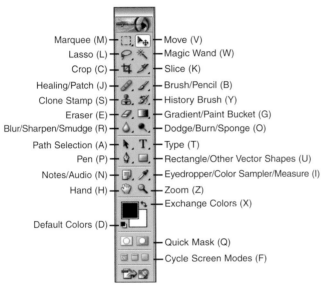

figure 1.1

The Photoshop toolbar with keyboard commands.

 T i p

To see and learn the tool tips, choose Edit > Preferences > General and turn on Show Tool Tips. As you hold the mouse over a tool, Photoshop shows the name and command key as shown in **figure 1.2**.

figure 1.2

Use the Tool tips to learn the most important keyboard quick keys.

As you can see in **figure 1.3**, some tools are nested. For example, the Dodge, Burn, and Sponge tools all share one spot on the toolbar. You can cycle

through the tools by holding the Shift key as you press the shortcut key until you reach the desired tool. **Table 1.1** lists all the nested shortcuts you'll need.

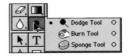

figure 1.3

The Dodge, Burn, and Sponge tool are nested within one another.

If you would rather just press the key (without holding Shift) to cycle through a nested tool, select Edit > Preferences > General and uncheck Use Shift Key for Tool Switch.

table 1.1
Nested Retouching Tools

Marquee	Shift + M cycles between the Rectangular and Elliptical Marquee tools.
Lasso	Shift + L cycles through the Lasso, Polygon, and Magnetic Lasso tools.
Healing Brush	Shift + J cycles through Healing Brush and Patch tools.
Brush and Pencil	Shift + B cycles through the Brush and the Pencil tools.
Clone Stamp	Shift + S cycles through the Clone Stamp and Pattern Stamp tools.
History Brush	Shift + Y cycles through the History and Art History Brush tools.
Eraser tool	Shift + E cycles through the Eraser, Background Eraser, and Magic Eraser.
Gradient and Paint Bucket	Shift + G cycles through the Gradient and Paint Bucket tools.
Sharpening tools	Shift + R cycles through the Sharpen, Blur, and Smudge tools.
Tonal tools	Shift + O cycles through the Dodge, Burn, and Sponge tools.
Path Selection tools	Shift + A cycles through the Path Selection and the Direct Selection tools.
Pen tool	Shift + P cycles through the Pen and Freeform Pen tools.
Annotation tool	Shift + N switches between note or voice annotation.
Eyedropper, Color Sampler, and Measure	Shift + I cycles through the Eyedropper, Color Sampler, and Measure tools.

Saving Tool Presets

How often have you set the Crop tool to 5 by 7 inches or defined a soft-edged, white brush with 5% opacity set to the Painting Mode overlay? Okay—maybe the Crop tool example rings true but trust me, as you delve into fine portrait retouching, the second example of the finely tuned brush will also come in very handy.

Wouldn't it be great if you could just save a library of all the tools you use often and, with a single click, have access to them without having to enter values or percentages ever again? With Photoshop 7, you can do just that. With Tool Presets you can load, edit, and create libraries of tool presets using the Tool Preset picker in the options bar, the Tool Presets palette, and the Preset Manager.

In the following example, I create a useful library of the most commonly used Crop tool settings. Work along and you'll never have to set your Crop tool again.

To create a Crop tool preset:

1. Choose the Crop tool and set the options you want in the options bar, as seen in figure 1.4. In this example, I entered 5 in and 7 in. To use pixels, type px after the numbers; for centimeters, type cm; and for millimeters, type mm after the number. If desired, enter a resolution in the Resolution box. I prefer to leave that blank so I don't inadvertently scale an image as I crop it.

figure 1.4

Determining the settings for the Crop tool.

2. Click the Tool button on the left side of the options bar and click the Create New Tool Preset button (it looks like a little piece of paper) or click on the fly-out menu arrow of the Tool Presets palette (figure 1.5), and select New Tool Preset.

3. Name the tool preset, as shown in figure 1.6, and click OK.

Taking a few minutes to create useful tool presets is a fantastic way to speed up your retouching work. To view and access the tool presets, either click the Tool Preset button on the left side of the options bar or use the Tool Presets palette, as shown in figure 1.7.

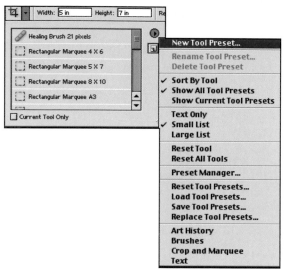

figure 1.5

Accessing the Tool Preset menu.

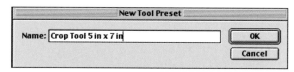

figure 1.6

Naming the preset.

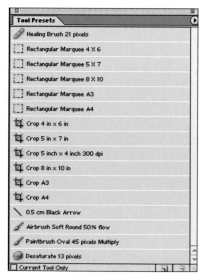

figure 1.7

The Tool Presets palette with all saved tool settings.

Notice that in figure 1.8 the Current Tool Only checkbox is checked in the lower-left corner. This shows only the presets for the active tool, which keeps your list of visible presets a little more manageable.

After creating a series of Tool Presets, make sure to save your presets via the fly-out menu in the Tool Presets palette. You wouldn't want to lose your settings if Photoshop crashes.

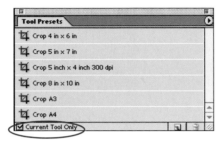

figure 1.8

The Tool Presets palette with only the active tool settings visible.

The Options Bar

Photoshop 5.0 and 5.5 had the Tool Options palette, which showed the various settings and controls for the tool you had currently selected. Since Photoshop 6.0, these options (and many other features) are housed in the options bar. Position the options bar at the top or bottom of your monitor and, to keep down monitor clutter, dock the palettes you use most often into the palette well, as shown in figure 1.9.

When using any painting tool, change the opacity by simply typing the required value; you don't need to highlight the Opacity box. Just type a number from 1 to 9, and the brush opacity or pressure will change to the corresponding value between 10% and 90%. Typing 0 will set it to 100%, and you can set even finer values by quickly typing the precise percentage you want.

To change brush size or hardness, use these shortcuts:

- Left bracket ([) decreases brush size while maintaining hardness and spacing settings.
- Right bracket (])increases brush size while maintaining hardness and spacing settings.
- Shift + left bracket ([) decreases brush hardness while maintaining size and spacing.
- Shift + right bracket (]) increases brush hardness while maintaining size and spacing.

PALETTES AND CUSTOM WORKSPACES

Hiding, showing, and rearranging palette position while working is irritating, inefficient, and worst of all adds unnecessary wear and tear to your mousing muscles. Learning the essential F keys to hide and reveal palettes to creating custom workspaces is helpful to keep the Photoshop interface out of the way, allowing you to concentrate on the image at hand.

The Palettes and Function Keys

Adobe has assigned function keys to the most important palettes (listed in table 1.2). The function keys are the topmost row of buttons on your keyboard and they begin with the letter F; hence, the nickname *F keys*. You can use them to hide and reveal palettes. I keep my palettes either on a second monitor or, when working on a laptop or single monitor system, I'll position the palettes to be as far out of the way as possible. If the palettes are blocking the image, press Tab to hide all the palettes and the toolbar. Press Tab again to reveal all the palettes and toolbar, or press F keys to reveal individual palettes. Press Shift + Tab to hide the palettes while keeping the toolbar visible.

figure 1.9

Palette Well

The options bar reflects the controls of the active tool and includes the palette well, where you can place often used palettes.

table 1.2
F Keys to Show and Hide Palettes

Brush palette	*F5*
Color palette	*F6*
Layer palette	*F7*
Info palette	*F8*
Actions palette	*F9*

Not every palette has a function key. Docking palettes that don't have a function key with palettes that do will give you access to every palette quickly. For example, dock the History and Actions palettes together and then use F9 to open the Actions palette, and click the History palette tab to bring it to the forefront.

Taking a few moments to arrange the palettes and learn the function keys is similar to setting up your workspace in a traditional studio: brushes go over here and camera equipment goes over there. Position the palettes in relation to how often you use them, with the more important ones—Layers, Channels, and Info—close at hand.

Palette Tips

- When working with a single monitor workstation, have as few palettes open as possible.
- Decide on an ideal palette placement for your workflow. This saves time when hiding and showing palettes, because they will reappear exactly where you positioned them. Save this workspace with a logical name so you can recall it easily later.
- Press the Tab key to hide and show all palettes and the toolbar at once.
- Shift + Tab hides all palettes while keeping the toolbar on screen.
- Pull unnecessary nested palettes out of their groups and close them. For example, the Navigation palette is redundant if you use the navigational tips discussed later in this chapter. If you separate and close it, it won't pop up with the other docked palettes.
- In case you close a palette and you forget to use the F key to make it appear again, use the Window menu to select the palette you want to see.
- Create actions to assign custom F-key commands to your most often used workspaces to recall them even more quickly than using the Window Workspace menu.

- When creating a workspace for the File Browser, the workspace will note the exact folder you accessed with the File Browser at the time. This can be very useful when you are working with the download folder for digital camera files.

Workspace Settings

Photoshop has long had the option to save your current palette locations upon quitting (go to Edit > Preferences > General and check Save Palette Locations). Every time you launch Photoshop, move palettes, and quit Photoshop, the new palette positions are saved, which may or may not be the best settings for retouching work. New in Photoshop 7 is the ability to save and recall any number of custom workspaces that you can customize for specific tasks—all of which will save time and reduce frustration.

Setting up and saving custom workspaces that reflect the task at hand is well worth the effort. For example, I have one workspace set up for tone and color correction (where all I need to have visible are the Layers, Channels, and Info palettes, a workspace for using the File Browser (see figure 1.10), and one for creative image editing on my dual monitor system, which places all palettes on the secondary monitor to free up the primary monitor for images, as seen in figure 1.11). And, if you share your computer, different users can have their favorite workspaces without disrupting anyone else's workspace and workflow.

figure 1.10

A workspace dedicated to using the File Browser.

figure 1.11

Using two displays enables you to reserve one for the work in progress and one for the palettes and tools.

 N o t e

The File Browser is a new Photoshop 7 feature. It provides a quick way to navigate your image folders. Use it to preview, rotate, rename, and open files within Photoshop. You can specify which thumbnail size the File Browser uses, and it displays a wealth of information about your files in the metadata on the lower-left side of the window, without having to open each image. By default, the File Browser is a tab in the palette well, but you can also use File > Browse or (Shift + Cmd + O) [Shift + Ctrl + O] to access it. I find the File Browser especially useful after downloading digital camera files I want to edit, organize, and rename.

To create a custom workspace:

1. Arrange and size your palettes as desired.

2. Select Window > Workspace > Save Workspace.

3. Name your workspace and Photoshop will save the workspace setting file into the Adobe Photoshop 7 Settings > Workspace folder.

4. After creating additional workspaces, you can access different workspaces by selecting one from the Window > Workspace > menu.

Adobe also included Delete Workspace and Reset Palette Locations in the Window > Workspace menu. Reset Palette Locations can be very handy if you can't locate a palette or simply want to return to the default Photoshop palette position.

 The Workspace View

Your monitor is your worktable: keeping it organized and neat will pay off with time saved and frustration reduced. Learning to use every bit of your monitor's real estate can make a small monitor seem a lot larger than it really is and make a large monitor seem even more expansive.

- Take advantage of your monitor's real estate by working in either Full Screen Mode with Menu Bar or Full Screen Mode. Tap F to cycle through the viewing modes.

- Consider working with a two-monitor system. This requires either a special "dual-head" video card or the installation of a second video card. (If you install a second card, you'll need to specify a primary monitor in your system settings.) Because you won't be doing any critical color correction or retouching on the second monitor, it can be less expensive—or even used.

- When cleaning up files, work at 100% or 200% view to see every pixel.

- Create a second view. Select Window > Documents > New Window, and position this second view so that you can reference it as you retouch. This is incredibly useful when retouching an image of a person's face, because you can zoom in on an image detail on the primary document and simultaneously keep an eye on how retouching the details is impacting the overall image (see figure 1.12).

© Ablestock

figure 1.12

CONTEXT-SENSITIVE MENUS

Every Photoshop tool includes context-sensitive menus that you access by (Control + clicking) [right-clicking] directly on the image. These menus give you tremendous control over each tool. Rather than going through the menu of every tool here, I suggest you open an image and go through the context-sensitive menus of each tool. In exchange for that, I'll review the most important context menus you should be aware of. For some tools, the context-sensitive menu will change depending on the state of the tool or file at the time. For example, notice the difference of the context-sensitive menu for any selection tool with and without an active selection (as shown in figures 1.13 and 1.14, respectively) and after using a filter (as seen in figure 1.15).

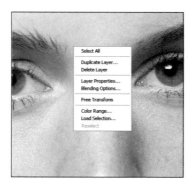

figure 1.13

Context-sensitive menu for any selection tool without an active selection.

figure 1.14

Context-sensitive menu for any selection tool with an active selection.

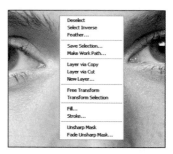

figure 1.15

Context-sensitive menu for any selection tool with an active selection after applying a filter.

Brush Context and Controls

While you are using the painting, toning, and sharpening tools, (Control + clicking) [right-clicking] brings up the window to edit brush size quickly, as shown in figure 1.16. (Shift + Control + clicking) [Shift + right-clicking] brings up the Painting Modes (see figure 1.17).

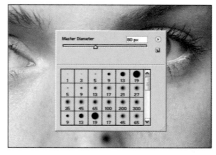

figure 1.16

The context-sensitive menu for brushes allows you to select size and brush type quickly.

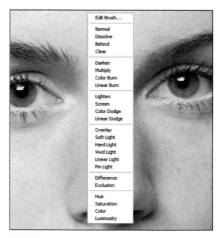

figure 1.17

Accessing the Painting Modes.

With the Healing Brush, (Control + click) [right-click] to access the Healing Brush's specific brush settings menu (**figure 1.18**). Pressing (Shift + Control + click) [Shift + right-click] lets you choose your source as well as Blend Modes, as you see in **figure 1.19**.

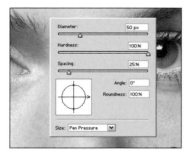

figure 1.18

The context-sensitive menu of the Healing Brush.

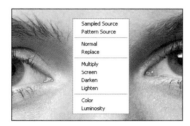

figure 1.19

As the context-sensitive menu reveals, Healing Brush uses fewer Blending Modes.

Toning Tools Context-Sensitive Menus

While you are using the Dodge and Burn tools, (Shift + Control + clicking) [Shift + right-clicking] enables you to change the tonal range affected (see **figure 1.20**). The same keyboard shortcut quickly accesses the Sponge tool's saturate/desaturate mode.

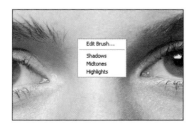

figure 1.20

The context-sensitive menu of the Dodge and Burn tools.

Magnifying Tools Context Menus

Use the context-sensitive menu of the Zoom tool to quickly see the image at useful views (see **figure 1.21**).

figure 1.21

Using the context-sensitive menu of the Zoom tool is one way to quickly zoom in and out of a file.

QUICK IMAGE NAVIGATION

Moving through a file and zooming in and out quickly are essential skills for an efficient retoucher. Critical retouching is done at a 100% or 200% view (as shown in **figure 1.22**), which means that you are seeing only a small part of the entire file. Zooming in and out of a file allows you to see how the retouched area is blending in with the entire image.

Use any one of the following techniques to navigate through a file.

To go to 100% view to see the full resolution of the file:

- Double-click the Zoom tool (magnifying glass) in the toolbar.
- (Cmd + Option + 0) [Ctrl + Alt + 0]. *Note:* That's a zero, not the letter O.
- (Space + Control + click) [Space + right-click] and drag down to Actual Pixels.
- Type 100 in the zoom percentage window in the lower-left corner of the file and press the Enter key.

To see the entire image:

- Double-click the Hand tool.
- (Cmd + 0) [Ctrl + 0]. *Note:* Again, this is a zero, not the letter O.
- (Space + Control + click) [Space + right-click] and drag down to Fit on Screen.

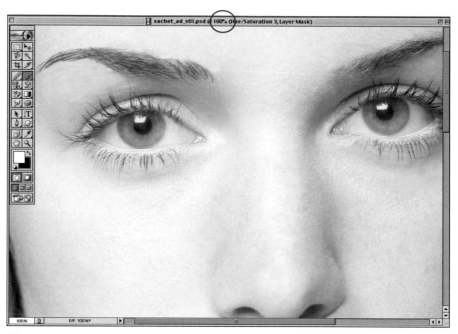

Figure 1.22

Professional retouchers work at 100% or 200% view.

To zoom in on a specific area:

- (Cmd + Space) [Ctrl + space] and drag over the area you want to zoom into.

To pan through an image:

- On both Macintosh and PC, holding down the space bar converts any tool (except the Type tool, if you are actively entering text) into the Hand tool, which enables you to pan through an image. This works only if the image is larger than your monitor can display.

You can review an image that will not fit entirely on your monitor using only the keyboard. Starting in the upper-left corner, these shortcuts will adjust the viewing area one screen width or height at a time:

- Tap the Home key to jump to the upper-left corner.
- Tap the End key to jump to the lower-right corner.
- Tap Page Down to move down one full screen.
- Tap Page Up to move up one full screen.

- Tap (Cmd + Page Down) [Ctrl + Page Down] to move one screen width to the right.
- Tap (Cmd + Page Up) [Ctrl + Page Up] to move one screen width to the left.

If all these navigational tips are starting to get jumbled, remember that you don't need to sit down and memorize them all at once. Just learn the ones you use all the time—including the most often-used tools. Learn also how to hide and show palettes and you'll be working like a power user in no time.

LEARNING THE IMPORTANCE OF LAYERS

With the introduction of layers in Photoshop 3.0, Adobe truly entered the world of professional image enhancement. For a retoucher, layers are the most important feature in Photoshop, and throughout this book you will be working with eight different types of layers:

- Background layer: This is your original data and should be treated as carefully as your original prints or film. Never, ever retouch directly on the Background layer. It should remain as pristine as the day you scanned it. Do I sound adamant about this? You bet. The Background layer is your reference, your guide, your before and after. Do not touch it. To maintain the Background layer's integrity, either duplicate it or do a Save As to back up the original file before undertaking any color correction, retouching, or restoration.

- Duplicate layers: Duplicating any layer by dragging the layer to the New Layer icon creates an exact copy, in perfect registration, on which you can work and retouch without affecting the original data. Use the shortcut keys (Cmd + J) [Ctrl + J] to duplicate a layer quickly.

- Copied layers: Many times you don't want or need to duplicate the entire Background layer because you need only a portion of a layer to work on. In those cases, select the part of the image you want to use and select Layer > New > Layer via Copy or press (Cmd + J) [Ctrl + J]. Photoshop copies and pastes the selection onto its own layer and keeps the newly created layer information in perfect registration with the original data.

- Adjustment Layers: Introduced with Photoshop 4.0, Adjustment Layers enable you to apply global and selective tonal and color corrections. You use them extensively in Chapters 2, 3, and 4 to do tonal, exposure, and color corrections.

- Empty layers: Photoshop represents empty layers with a grid pattern. Think of these empty layers as a clear sheet of acetate on which you paint and clone without affecting the pixel data of the layers underneath.

- Neutral layers: Photoshop doesn't show the Blending Mode neutral colors of white, gray, or black when used in combination with specific layer Blending Modes. We'll be using neutral layers to apply subtle and dramatic tonal improvements throughout the retouching process.

- Fill layers: Fill layers enable you to add solid, gradient, or patterned fills as a separate layer. The solid color fill layer is useful when you are coloring and toning an image.

- Merged layers: As the number of layers increases, it is often easier to work on a Work in Progress (WIP) layer, which is a flattened layer created with all visible layers you have been retouching. To create a merged layer with image information, follow these steps:

  1. Select the topmost layer in the layer stack.

  2. Add a new layer by clicking the New Layer button on the Layers palette.

  3. Hold down (Option) [Alt] and select Layer > Merge Visible from the Layers palette or from the Layers palette fly-out menu. Please note: You have to hold (Option) [Alt] the entire time until Photoshop merges all of the visible layers. Or use the super secret Command key combination (Cmd + Option + Shift + N) [Ctrl + Alt + Shift + N] to add a new layer and then (Cmd + Option + Shift + E) [Ctrl + Alt + Shift + E] to merge all visible layers to the active layer.

The best aspect of layers is that they all (with the exception of the Background layer) support layer masks, Blending Modes, opacity and fill changes, and Advanced Blending Options—features you'll be working with throughout the book to retouch and restore images.

Layer Naming and Navigation

Layers enable you to build up a retouch. In many cases, a retouching project can take 5, 10, 20, or more layers to finish. Relying on the generic Photoshop name such as *Layer 1* or *Layer 1 copy* to identify layers is a sure way to be confused and frustrated as you try to find the layer you need to work on. It only takes a split second, but naming your layers as you build up a retouch enables you to identify and activate the correct layer quickly and easily.

Look at the difference between the two layer stacks in figure 1.23. The layers on the left have generic names, and the layers on the right have useful names. Which would you rather work with? Additionally, the context-sensitive menu of the Move tool gives you instant access to all the layers at the pointer position that have pixel information. As shown in figure 1.24, (Control + clicking) [right-clicking] shows all layer names that have pixel information at the exact point where the mouse is. Best of all, you can then drag down to a specific layer name and activate it—even if the Layers palette is not open at the time.

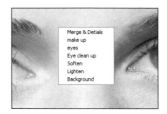

figure 1.24

The context-sensitive menu of the Move tool shows you the layers at the cursor position that have pixel information at the cursor location.

Working with Layer Sets

In Photoshop 7, you can create up to a total of 8,000 layers and layer effects, something that requires a way to organize and manage layers more efficiently. Layer sets, shown in figure 1.25, are folders in which you can place related layers. The folders can be expanded or collapsed, the layers can be moved around within the set, and layer sets can be moved around within the layer stack.

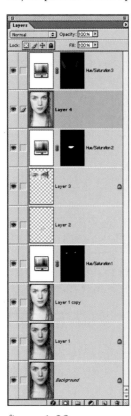
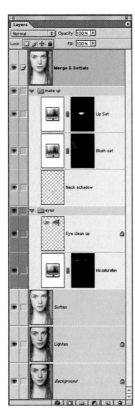

figure 1.23

The generic layer names in the palette on the left won't help you find your way through a complex retouch, but the ones on the right prove that naming your layers is a good habit to adopt.

To name a layer, simply double-click the existing name in the Layers palette and type a meaningful name. It only takes a split second to name a layer, and it will save you countless minutes of frustration.

© John Warner Photography

figure 1.25

The many layers you create when retouching become much more manageable when they are grouped as layer sets.

There are two ways to create a layer set:

• Select New Layer Set from the Layers palette menu, name the layer set, and then drag the desired layers into the set.

• Link all the layers you would like in a layer set, and then select New Set from Linked in the Layers palette menu. All the linked layers will be placed into the newly created layer set.

There are three ways to delete a layer set:

- Drag the layer set to the trash can on the Layers palette to delete the entire layer set without showing a warning dialog box.

- Select Delete Layer Set from the Layers palette menu. The dialog box in **figure 1.26** then gives you choices to cancel the operation, delete the set, or delete the set and the set's contents.

- (Cmd + drag) [Ctrl + drag] the layer set to the trash can to delete the layer set folder without deleting the contents of the layer set. The layers in the set remain in the document in the order they appeared in the set.

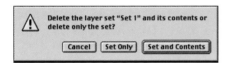

figure 1.26

You can delete the set (the folder) or the set and the contents.

You can color-code layers to identify layer relationships quickly and lock layers to prevent accidental edits to image data, transparency settings, and layer position. All in all, organizing, naming, or color-coding layers and layer sets takes only a moment, but it can save you a lot of time in hunting and searching for the layer you want to work on.

Creating and using consistent layers and layer set naming conventions is imperative if you want to create an efficient workflow. If you work with a partner, on a team, or as part of a production workflow, you'll especially need to use layer names. Imagine that you're working on a complicated retouching project and for some reason, you can't come to work to finish the retouch. If the layers are well named, someone else on your team will be able to open the file, find the layers that need additional work, and finish the project. However, if the layers are all over the place, not named, or not in layer sets, it will take a while for someone else to simply figure out where to begin. In the worst-case scenario, a very important layer might be ruined or deleted. Enough said—name your layers!

Flattening and Discarding Layers

I'm a conservative Photoshop retoucher with a large hard drive. I don't throw away layers unless I know that they are absolutely wrong or unnecessary. Keep all production layers with a file because you'll never know whether a mask or tidbit of information from a layer will be useful later in the project. By clicking the eyeball in the view column on the left side of the Layers palette, you can turn off a layer whenever you like. I flatten an image after doing a Save As and only as the very last step before sending a file to the printer or taking a file into a page layout program.

FILE ORGANIZATION AND WORKFLOW ISSUES

Taking a few moments to organize your folders and files helps you work more efficiently by saving you time searching for files and projects, and it also reduces the likelihood of deleting important files. For each project I work on, I create a Master Folder, and in that folder I make three folders—Scans, WIP (Work-in-Progress), and Finals (see **figure 1.27**). As you can imagine, the scans go into the Scans folder and those originals are not changed. The Work-in-Progress folder contains all the layered files and versions of the retouch in progress. The third folder is where only flattened, sized, and sharpened files go. The Finals folder contains only one version of the final file and not files that are obviously not completed, such as "retouch_3_little_better_like_it_more_I_think_maybe_4b.tif."

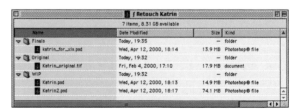

figure 1.27

Keep your working files organized as shown here.

Note

Although I work in a Macintosh environment, I exchange files with printers and clients who use PCs, which means that I have to take those systems into account. I make it a habit of keeping filenames as short as possible, without spaces, odd characters such as /*, or punctuation, and I always have Photoshop add the three-letter file extension to the file when saving. Because you can tell Photoshop to add the extension automatically, there isn't any reason for Macintosh users not to use it. The PC system adds the file extension without this Preferences setting, so PC users don't need to worry about this detail.

The Retouching Workflow

Each retouching project is unique, requiring a sensitive eye and sympathetic mouse. Of course, each retoucher is just as unique, and over time you will devise your own retouching workflow.

The primary steps in my retouching workflow are shown here:

1. Assess the original: Study the original and identify the problems or areas that need enhancement, repair, or replacement. Never lift the mouse without first taking a few minutes to identify the character of either the image or the person in the photograph.

2. Input: Scan or photograph the original. Use a professional service bureau if you don't have the capability to input the original. For additional information on image scanning, go to www.digitalretouch.org and download Scanning & Resolution.pdf in the "Additional Information" section.

3. Develop a strategy: Make a plan to outline the steps to do the retouch. Start with the big problems—exposure, color, and contrast—and then move on to repairing problems, such as dust, mold, and scratches, or removing lines,

wrinkles, or blemishes. Make notes on paper or on the file, as described in Chapter 10, "Glamour and Fashion Retouching." The structure of this book reflects my retouching strategy; it starts with the big problems and then moves into ever-finer nuances of restoration and retouching.

4. Retouch: Do the planned retouch. As mentioned, work on a duplicate of the original scan and use layers to build up your work.

5. Output and deliver: Make a print and deliver the file to the client.

6. Archive: Make a backup of all files involved in a project. Burning a CD is an inexpensive and reliable method to make backups. I recommend burning two identical disks and storing them separately. Use an asset management program, such as Canto Cumulus or Extensis Portfolio, to organize your files and backups.

Tip

The invisible step 7 is to collect payment from the client in exchange for the completed work. Professional retoucher Wayne Palmer says, "I keep all originals until the client has paid for the job. That way I have something of value, which often motivates the client to pay more quickly."

The Retoucher's Workplace

Your retouching studio or work area is a place you'll be spending a lot of time, so it makes sense to invest the time and money to make it as comfortable and productive as possible. You do not need to remodel your home or build an addition; I'm just suggesting you consider a few improvements that can make your workplace a nicer and more efficient place to be.

Environment and Lighting

The retouching environment should be a quiet area away from distractions and foot traffic. Paint the walls a neutral gray and set up the lighting so that there aren't any reflections showing in the monitor. In **figure 1.28**, you see a retouching work area that is built into a corner. The L-shaped configuration enables the retoucher to get a lot of work done without having to get up and down to make a scan or print. As you can see in **figure 1.29**, the daylight balanced GTI Graphic Technology lightbox (www.gtilite.com) and 5,000° Kelvin task lamp (www.ottlite.com) provide an area to study originals. To make the retouching area more focused, keep your bookkeeping, paperwork, and business phone on a separate desk.

figure 1.28

My *retouching area, with both Macintosh and Windows equipment.*

figure 1.29

Controlled lighting is essential when evaluating prints and slides.

Furniture

It always amazes me that people will spend thousands of dollars on computer equipment and then put it all on a cheap folding table that wobbles and bows in the center under all the weight. Even worse than those are some of the rickety chairs people sit in to work on the computer. After a few hours they wonder why their necks or lower backs are so sore. I prefer a chair with armrest support—and as Wayne Palmer points out, "If you use a chair with arms, the arms must be able to slide under the desk. If the chair's arms keep you away from the desk, you have to reach for the keyboard and mouse. After a few hours of this, you will develop muscle aches."

A good table without harsh edges, preferably one that angles down to where your arms rest on the table, and a chair with lower-back and arm support are essential retouching equipment. Just think of it; over the course of a few years, you'll probably replace your computer a few times. How often do you need to replace a good working table and professional chair? Not very often, so making the investment in good furniture will pay off in health and well being for years to come.

Speaking of health, you should know that uninterrupted, intensive computer use can be bad for your eyes, back, wrists, and more. But it doesn't have to be if you watch your posture, vary your computing activities, and take frequent breaks. An important tip for retouchers is to use these frequent breaks to focus your eyes on something in the distance. For more information about steps you can take to make your work area and work habits as healthy as possible, visit www.healthycomputing.com.

As Patrick O'Connell wrote to me, "Over the course of a week, I spent about 25 hours restoring this image (**figures 1.30** and **1.31**), and if there's a secret to it at all, I'd say the key was to realize when I was starting to get tired and sloppy, and quitting for the day." You need to take breaks and return to your work with a fresh eye.

figure 1.30

Before image restoration.

figure 1.31

After image restoration, which included taking breaks.

Computer Equipment

Adobe has done a fantastic job in developing and releasing Photoshop for both Macintosh and Windows. So does it matter which computer platform you use? Yes, it does. It should be the operating system that you're most comfortable with. My first computer experience was on a Mac, and since then I've come to appreciate its interface, operating system, and how easy it is to maintain. On the other hand, for every one person who prefers a Mac, I'm sure there are many, many people who swear by Windows. Photoshop is Photoshop is Photoshop. The few differences in Photoshop on a Mac or Windows are not going to alter the skills and techniques you need to know to do retouching magic.

Spending money on computer equipment requires research and planning. If you are about to build a workstation for Photoshop work, consider these variables:

- CPU speed: The higher the speed, the faster the computer. Be careful to watch the internal bus speed as well; the fastest CPU will not produce the performance increases you expect if the internal bus speed is slow.

- RAM: Photoshop is a RAM-hungry program, and the more you have allocated to Photoshop, the better it will run. How much RAM do you need? As much as you can afford! Photoshop prefers three to five times the amount of RAM as the size of the image file you're working on. Take into account that often you'll have more than one image open and that as you add layers and use History, your RAM requirements will increase. So how much is enough? Take your average image size and multiply it by five, and then use that figure as your starting point. Adding more RAM to a machine is the easiest way to increase Photoshop performance.

Tip

You can see how efficiently your computer system is running by selecting Efficiency from the status bar found at the bottom of the document window. A reading of less than 100% tells you that the functions you are performing are being written to the scratch disk, which is always slower than working in RAM.

- Hard drive space: This is a classic "bigger is better" proposition as long as you are choosing from the highest-performance drives. Photoshop wants fast hard drives to write data to when it runs out of RAM, so given the choice, go with speed over excessive gigabytes.

- Scratch disk: The scratch disk is free hard drive space that Photoshop uses as temporary memory after it fills the RAM with image processing. The scratch disk needs to be at least

twice the size of the RAM allocated to Photoshop and, more importantly, the space needs to be contiguous; that is, a scratch disk needs to be unfragmented and free of clutter. You can set up partitions on your drive to keep certain areas from being fragmented, or you can use additional software to optimize your drive over time. If you have more than one hard drive, use one for Photoshop and your image files, and the other for your scratch disk.

- Monitor: This is the visual component of your system, and no matter how fast or sexy your CPU is, if you are not happy with the image your monitor produces, you will not be happy with your workstation. A good monitor will outlast one to two upgrades of your CPU. The only limitation on the effective life of a monitor is the accuracy of the color it produces—something which is usually in the three-to-five year range.

If you choose a traditional CRT display, 17 inches is minimum and 21 inches is desired. Be careful to match the size of monitor to the amount of video RAM installed in your computer. You must work with millions of colors. Flat-panel LCD displays are much easier on your eyes but harder on your pocketbook.

Tip

To have two monitors running on the same computer, your computer needs to be able to support a second video card or replace your existing card with one that supports dual display. Install the new card and use the control settings to determine which monitor will be your primary monitor. You can just drag images and palettes back and forth between them.

To use one monitor on two computers: IOGEAR makes a switcher to run up to four computers with one monitor, keyboard, and mouse. Macintosh users will need to purchase an additional adapter from IOGEAR that makes the pin conversion possible.

- CD or DVD-ROM: This is a usability and compatibility issue. In either case, make sure that you have a writeable, not a read-only, CD or DVD drive. In most instances, a write-able CD will be the most practical and usable media to make backups and create disks for your clients.

- Pressure sensitive tablet: An absolute must. A pressure sensitive tablet lets you work with a stylus, and it feels just like working with a pencil or brush. The harder you push, the thicker the stroke. Wacom is the leader in this technology, and their progressive improvements with these devices continue to be impressive. Wacom tablets range in size from miniature (4×5 inch) to huge (12×12 and larger). Most photographers work best with the smaller (6×8 inch tablets). On my desktop system, I work with the Wacom Cintiq, which is a pressure-sensitive monitor (shown in **figure 1.32**) and when I travel, I never leave home without my portable 4×5 inch Wacom tablet and Apple Powerbook.

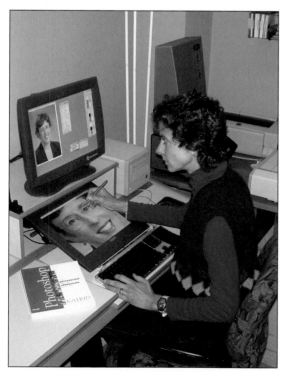

figure 1.32

Katrin retouching a portrait on her Wacom Cintiq pressure sensitive display.

Tip

To decrease reflections and distractions, build a monitor hood with black quarter-inch foamcore board, as shown in **figure 1.33**, or visit www.photodon.com to purchase monitor hoods.

figure 1.33

A homemade monitor hood cuts down on reflections.

- Back-up or archive system: This is another critical issue as you take on more and more work. You should always back up your work as well as your system settings. This is a personal discipline that will make you feel very smart when you need the backup or very stupid if you did not back up your files. Temporary backup of your work is best accomplished to an external (or additional) hard drive. Fire-wire drives can be an extremely fast media for backups. Archiving is best done with remov-able media, such as CD-Rs or DVD disks.

- Scanners: Look at the originals you will be scanning; if most of them are prints, purchas-ing a good flatbed scanner makes sense. If the majority of your work stems from film origi-nals, a film scanner would be a better choice.

It is difficult to make a general recommenda-tion on scanners because they vary from very poor to very good and from cheap to expen-sive. Most retouchers have a mid-level flatbed scanner that is capable of scanning 11×17 inch prints. Look for a scanner that captures at least 10 bits of data, and keep an eye on the optical resolution of the scanner—it should be 600 pixels per inch or higher.

Alternative Input Options

Having a service bureau or professional photo lab do scanning and printing for you can be a good alternative, especially when you're just starting out and need to stagger your equipment expenses. Working with a service bureau also gives you access to high-end equipment and services that you may need only once in a while.

- Copy work: In many cases, antique originals are too large, too fragile, or too three-dimensional to scan with a standard film or flatbed scanner. In figure 1.34, you see medium-format and 35 mm black-and-white copy negatives that will be scanned in for the retoucher to clean up. The additional example in figure 1.35 shows how Wayne Palmer needed to restore a series of antique photographic images that were mounted inside convex, glass bowl frames. Because the originals were three-dimensional, he couldn't just lay them on a flatbed scanner, so he made copy slides and scanned those.

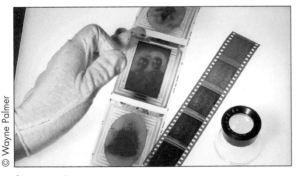

figure 1.34

Working with copy negatives can be a high-quality and cost-effective way to input sensitive originals.

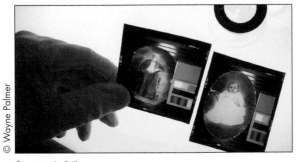

figure 1.35

It's the unique challenges that make the job interesting. The originals were mounted inside convex glass bowls.

- Professional digital cameras: As digital cameras get both better and cheaper, they are becoming a great input option. Numerous professional museums and historical collections are working with high-resolution scanning cameras, such as the Better Light 6000 or 8000, to digitize their sensitive artwork and archives. Figures 1.36 and 1.37 show an example from the Dallas Museum of Fine Art, which is using the Better Light 6000 to catalog fine art.

figure 1.36

Professional digital cameras offer incredible resolution and color fidelity when inputting artwork.

figure 1.37

Close-up view of painting.

- Prosumer digital cameras are now a viable copying solution. $800 to $2,500 can buy a 3 to 6 megapixel digital camera capable of very respectable resolutions. Look for one that can capture uncompressed RAW files and compare their highest non-interpolated resolution (the most important feature for copy purposes). **Figure 1.38** shows Wayne Palmer's copystand with a Nikon 990. (Notice how he tilted the tintype to reduce the reflections bouncing off of the silvery surface.) Depending on the image size required, Wayne will shoot copy files with either the Nikon 990, Canon D10, or 35 mm or medium format film.

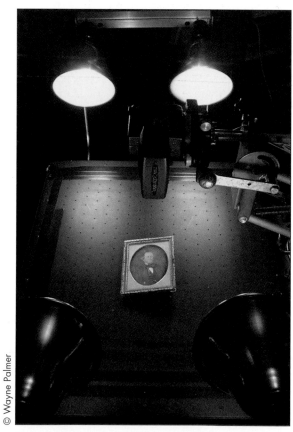

© Wayne Palmer

figure 1.38

A *professional copystand and a consumer-level digital camera.*

- Printers: The quality of inkjet printers is skyrocketing while the costs are nose-diving. Issues to consider before buying a printer include the size of the prints you need and how long the prints will last once you've printed them. Henry Wilhelm does extensive research on inkjet print permanence, and you can read the latest up-to-date information at www.wilhelm-research.com. Also visit www.inkjetmall.com and www.piezography.com to see the technology and inks that Jon Cone is developing to make absolutely stunning black-and-white prints that rival the traditional black-and-white, silver-gelatin darkroom print.

- Additional software: As you do more and more retouching, you may want to consider investing in software that can help you file, track, organize, and most importantly find your files (such as Canto Cumulus or Extensis Portfolio). Other purchases to consider include color management packages, such as the GretagMacbeth EyeOne Pro and production and special effects filters. For color management information, visit Andrew Rodney's web site at www.digitaldog.net and www.adobe.com.

BEFORE YOU BEGIN: A WORD TO THE WISE

Photoshop is a powerful tool that can either work wondrous magic or wreak havoc on image data. To ensure the best results in your restoration, always start with the best image data possible:

- Professional photographers always shoot more than one exposure of an image. Although the exposure difference may seem minimal, believe me, starting with a properly exposed piece of film or digital file will minimize many a headache.

- Start with the best digital data possible. Investing in a quality scanner is something you will seldom regret. If your scanner captures high-bit data, take advantage of it as discussed in the in Chapter 2, "Improving Tone and Contrast," in the section "The Benefits of High-Bit Data."

- Always work on a copy of your original scan.

- Use Adjustment Layers as described throughout the book. (You'll find a concentration of examples in Chapters 2, 3, and 4.) Because you can double-click an Adjustment Layer to open it for further finessing, you have much more control and freedom with your tonal, contrast, and color changes.

CLOSING THOUGHTS

The one thing that no computer, book, or class can give you is the passion to practice, learn, and experiment with the skills and techniques it takes to be a good retoucher. Retouching is more than removing dust or covering up a wrinkle here or there. Retouching enables you to give someone cherished memories that have faded with the print. Retouching and restoration is a fantastic hobby and a challenging profession, so let's dive in and get to work.

Correcting Tone, Exposure, and Color

II

2

IMPROVING TONE
AND CONTRAST   33

3

EXPOSURE CORRECTION   67

4

WORKING WITH COLOR   91

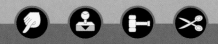

2

IMPROVING TONE AND CONTRAST

If you had a choice of walking into two unfamiliar rooms—one with the lights on and one without lights—which one would you choose? Unless you're a horror film aficionado, I imagine you'd choose the room with the lights. Working with the tonality and contrast of an image is similar to lighting a room to influence the atmosphere. Finessing the lights and darks of an image can transform a flat, uninteresting photograph into an image that pops off the page and is a pleasure to look at.

Adjusting an image's tone and contrast is a very important step to bringing an image back to life. Although it may not be as sexy or dramatic as replacing a person's head or removing a bothersome telephone pole, adjusting an image's tone and contrast with Levels and Curves is an essential skill.

In this chapter, you'll work with grayscale images and learn to

- Evaluate an image's tonality
- Use Levels to improve highlights and shadows
- Use Curves to adjust image contrast
- Use Blending Modes to save time
- Share Adjustment Layers to save effort
- Apply selective tonal improvements to specific image areas

EVALUATING IMAGE TONE AND PREVISUALIZING THE FINAL IMAGE

Taking a moment to evaluate the tone of an image is tremendously important. In that moment, you should identify the tonal character of the image and imagine what the image should look like after you're finished editing it. This technique, called *previsualization*, was developed by the black-and-white photographers Ansel Adams and Edward Weston. By imagining the final image, you create a goal to work toward. For example, in Photoshop you open a dark file. Your previsualization would be, "I want the image to be lighter." Having a visual goal in mind helps you stay focused and not get distracted with the many options that Photoshop offers.

An image's tonal character can be light, dark, or average, also called *high-key*, *low-key*, or *medium-key*. Subject matter and how much light was in the original scene determine the tonal character of the image. If you're not sure which tonal-type image you're looking at, viewing the image histogram (Image > Histogram) or a Levels histogram can be a helpful aid.

A *histogram* is a graphical representation of the pixels in the image, plotting them from black (on the left) to white (on the right). The greater the number of pixels in the image at a specific level, the taller the histogram is at that point. Knowing this, you can look at the histogram of any image and can tell where the majority of the pixel information falls.

As seen in figure 2.1, the high-key image histogram is bunched to the right because the image is primarily made up of lighter pixels. The low-key histogram falls more to the left because the image is primarily made up of darker pixels (see figure 2.2). The medium-key histogram is spread out, with most of the information falling in the middle (see figure 2.3). Of course, there are images that defy labels as illustrated in figure 2.4, in which the histogram's two clumps reveal an image with a split tonal personality.

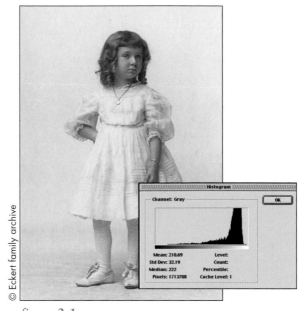

© Eckert family archive

figure 2.1

Although the little girl has dark hair, the majority of the image is very light, making this a high-key image.

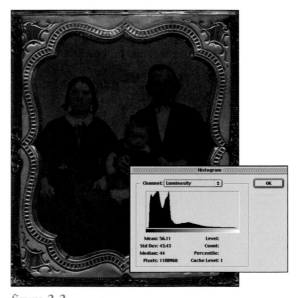

figure 2.2

This dark tintype is an example of a low-key image.

figure 2.3

This image has a full tonal range, from the dark shadows to the light areas of the church.

figure 2.4

Photographed in the late afternoon, the lower part of the image is in shadow and the upper part is in sunlight. This image has low-, medium-, and high-key areas.

When editing the tones, it is helpful to recognize which tonal type of image you're working with so you don't apply extreme tonal corrections. For example, if you are working with a high-key image in which the histogram is biased to the right, it wouldn't make any sense to try to force the tonal character of the image into the shadows (the left side of the histogram). By becoming familiar with what the tonal values represent—the shadows, midtones, or highlights of an image—you'll learn which areas of the histogram need to be adjusted to either lighten or darken the image.

I'm often asked whether there is an ideal histogram shape, and the answer is "No." The image's tonality and character determine the ideal histogram shape. So don't worry if a histogram seems biased to one side or the other; just keep an eye on the histogram as an aid when editing the tonal values.

 N o t e

When you are working with grayscale images, the Image > Histogram and the Levels dialog box are identical. When you are working with color images, the two dialog boxes show different histograms. With color images, the Image > Histogram is showing either the luminance or the individual R,G,B information, while the Levels dialog box is showing the RGB channel composite and the individual R,G,B channels.

Assessing Tone with the Measuring Tools

Evaluating the image on a calibrated monitor in a controlled viewing environment (see Chapter 1, "Photoshop Essentials," for recommendations on setting up a studio) is essential when retouching. If you are unsure about your monitor or your visual assessment of an image, rely on the Eyedropper, Color Sampler tool, and the Info palette when working on a file to evaluate and measure image tone and to track changes as you work. The Eyedropper is a digital *densitometer* (a fancy word for the measuring tool) that you can move throughout the image to measure tonal and color values. The Color Sampler tool is nested with the Eyedropper tool on the toolbar. Keeping your eye on the Info palette is an essential habit while editing tone, contrast, and color.

Select the Eyedropper tool and set the sample option to 3 by 3 Average, which also sets the sampling size of the color sampler tool to the same size. In the Info palette, set the first read-out options to reflect the actual image data and the second read out either to suit your own personal preferences or to reflect your final output. For example, if you are going to use offset printing, your second read out would be CMYK. Photographers that are familiar with the Zone System prefer to use grayscale (K) to read the black tonal-output values.

Tracking Tonal Changes with Color Samplers

Color Samplers are four lockable probes you can tack onto an image, enabling you to keep your eye on specific areas during the image editing process. The Color Sampler tool is nested under the Eyedropper on the toolbar and uses the same sample sizes as the Eyedropper. With the Color Sampler tool active, clicking in your image attaches up to four samplers. Each sampler is numbered and has a corresponding area in the Info palette display. You can move any sampler at any time, as long as the Color Sampler tool is active.

These four Color Samplers can be used to measure and track shadows, midtones, highlights, and a fourth tone of your choice. In **figure 2.5,** I'm using four samplers to track image highlights, shadows, and midtones, but Color Samplers can do something even better. While you're adjusting tonal values, the Color Samplers provide a before and after read out in the Info palette (see **figure 2.6**).

Color Samplers automatically disappear when you select other tools and reappear when the Eyedropper tool is activated again.

figure 2.5

Using the Color Samplers to track tonal values is a good habit to develop, and each sampler has its own read out on the Info Palette.

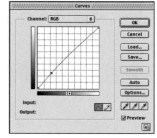

figure 2.6

While making a change (such as in the Curves dialog box), the Color Sampler read out shows you the value before a tonal adjustment on the left and the value after the tonal adjustment on the right.

 N o t e

To remove Color Samplers, (Option + click) [Alt + click] them with the Eyedropper tool, or drag them off the image area, or (Control + click) [right-click] and select Delete from the context-sensitive menu, or click the Clear button in the options bar to remove them all at once.

Using a Stepwedge

To help understand how specific tonalities will look on the print, I use a digital stepwedge, as seen on the left side of **figure 2.7**. A *stepwedge* is a target that goes from black to white in exact increments. Photographers and printers have been using them for years as an objective reference to see and measure how tones are captured, displayed, and reproduced.

The numbers on the little boy are the points at which I measured the values in the image. By keeping my eye on the Info palette set to grayscale, I can envision how dark or light the print will be. The highlight on the shoulder will print at 10% (a very light gray), his forehead will be a medium light gray, the trees in the background form a tonal frame around the boy at 50%–80% (medium to dark gray), and the dark tree trunks will have a 90% value.

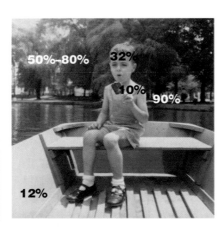

figure 2.7

Using a 21-step stepwedge to see how light and dark tonal values are is helpful in visualizing and understanding the tonality of a print.

ch2_stepwedge.jpg

ch2_printcalibrator.jpg

 N o t e

Make your own stepwedge using the Gradient tool. Start with a new 1×10 inch, grayscale, 300ppi image. Select the black to white gradient, and make sure that Dither is unchecked in the options bar. Hold Shift while drawing the gradient across the entire width of the file. Select Image > Adjustments > Posterize > 21 to create a perfect 21-step stepwedge.

THE IMPORTANCE OF ADJUSTMENT LAYERS

Whether you work with Levels or Curves or any of the other supported image-adjustment features, I insist (yes, insist) that you use Adjustment Layers, one of the very best features in Photoshop. Introduced with Photoshop 4.0, Adjustment Layers are nondestructive layers that enable you to make, change, and refine tonal and color adjustments as many times as needed without altering the underlying layer's original data until you choose to apply them by flattening the image. Adjustment Layers apply the adjustment math on top of the pixel information, which makes them a fantastic tool to experiment, refine, redo, and learn from tonal and color adjustments.

Use Adjustment Layers when working with Levels, Curves, Color Balance, Hue/Saturation, Selective Color, Channel Mixer, Invert, Threshold, and Posterize. I don't recommend using Brightness/Contrast because working with Levels and Curves offers better control and uses more sophisticated mathematics to apply the tonal changes. The benefits offered by working with Adjustment Layers include the following:

- They allow you to make tonal corrections without changing or degrading the source image data until you flatten the image.

- They support opacity. By lowering the Adjustment Layer's opacity, you reduce the strength of the tonal or color correction.

- They support Blending Modes. Blending Modes mathematically change how layers interact with the layer below them. They are a great aid in retouching because they allow you to improve image tonality quickly.

- They are resolution independent, allowing you to drag and drop them between disparately sized and scaled images.

- They include layer masks with which you can hide and reveal a tonal correction with the use of any painting tool.

- They are especially helpful when making local tonal, contrast, and color adjustments to parts or smaller areas of an image.

- If you don't like an adjustment, just throw the offending Adjustment Layer into the Layers palette trash and start over.

MASTERING TONALITY WITH LEVELS

Working with Levels enables you to influence three tonal areas of an image: the shadows, midtones, and highlights. You can use the sliders and the black-point or white-point eyedroppers to place or reset black or white points (see **figure 2.8**). The gray eyedropper is not available when you are working with black-and-white images; it is used to find neutral points in color images. Often, you can make an image pop right off the page just by setting new white and black points and moving the midtone gamma slider (to the left to lighten or to the right to darken the image).

Auto Function controls

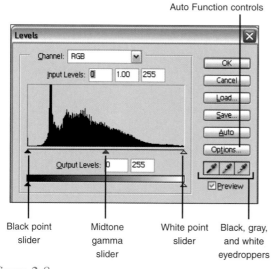

Black point slider Midtone gamma slider White point slider Black, gray, and white eyedroppers

figure 2.8

The Levels interface.

The most important Level controls to enhance image tone are these:

- Eyedroppers: Use the eyedroppers to set white and black points for both black-and-white and color images and the neutral gray eyedropper to define a neutral tone in color images.
- Sliders: Use the highlight and black sliders to remap the black and white points. You

prompt Photoshop to remap the points by moving the relevant slider to the area of the image that contains the majority of the light or dark information.

- Auto button: Use the Auto button to prompt Photoshop to set a light point to white and a dark point to black. You can configure the way Photoshop determines which points to look at by clicking the Options button directly underneath Auto.

- Options button: Prior to Photoshop 7, I didn't use or recommend the Auto Color Correction feature. However, Photoshop 7 adds a new Options dialog that lets you control how Auto works. The Auto Color Correction features are identical in Levels and Curves and very useful for color correction, as discussed in Chapter 4, "Working with Color."

To get the most out of Levels, you need to set the black and white target values before beginning. This process, called *targeting*, tells Photoshop which values to use for black and white. By targeting the highlight and shadow value for your printing process and paper combination, you ensure the image will stay within the reproducible range.

1. Open the Levels dialog box and double-click the white eyedropper. A Select Target Highlight color label appears above the color picker (see **figure 2.9**).

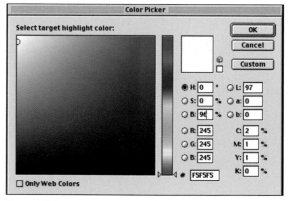

figure 2.9

Setting the white target color to 96% ensures that you retain a slight tonality in the whitest part of your image.

2. For printing to an inkjet printer, use the HSB scale and set the white target color to 96% brightness, or RGB 245, 245, 245, and click OK. For printing to offset, use the CMYK values of 5 C, 3 M, 3 Y, and 0 K.

3. Double-click the black eyedropper and set the shadow target color to 5% on the HSB scale, or RGB 12, 12, 12, as shown in figure 2.10; click OK.

By setting the white target color to 96% you will hold slight tonality in your whitest whites, and the black target color 5% will hold shadow information in the darkest parts of the image.

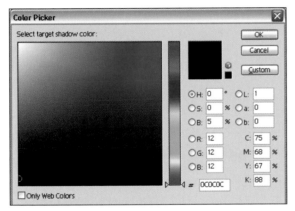

figure 2.10

The 5% black target color setting maintains shadow information in even the darkest areas of the image.

The generic 96% highlight and 5% shadow values are a safe place to start to avoid printing highlights without tone (paper white) or shadows that are so dark with ink that you can't see any detail in them.

IMPROVING IMAGE TONE WITH LEVELS

In the following exercises, you use Levels to rescue muddy or low-contrast originals to transform them into black-and-white images that are a pleasure to look at because the tones extend across the entire dynamic range from black to white. These exercises use single-channel monochrome (black-and-white) images. You can use the following techniques on color images only if you work on the composite channel (the primary histogram) and don't venture into tweaking the individual color channels. Color correction is best done by working with individual channels, as you'll learn in Chapter 4.

Working with the Black and White Point Sliders

This original image, from 1906, is badly faded, as you can see in figure 2.11. The areas which should be white have gotten darker and the shadows are not a rich black, which reduces the contrast and makes the print tonally flat and unattractive. After scanning it on a flatbed scanner, I used the following technique to darken the shadows and clean up the highlights. The corrected image (figure 2.12) has snap to it.

figure 2.11

figure 2.12

ch2_faded.jpg

1. Add a Levels Adjustment Layer by clicking the Add Adjustment Layer icon at the bottom of the Layers palette and selecting Levels from the desired type from the menu (**figure 2.13**) or select Layer > New Adjustment Layer > Levels and click OK.

figure 2.13

Adding the Levels Adjustment Layer via the Layers palette.

2. Move the white point slider just to the inside of where the lightest image information begins, as shown on the right side of the histogram (see **figure 2.14**).

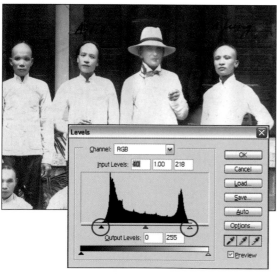

figure 2.14

Moving the white and black sliders to improve image contrast.

3. Move the black point slider until it falls just inside the area of darkest image information, as you see on the left side of the histogram in the figure.

4. Click OK to accept these changes.

When working on your own images, after adjusting the tonal range with Levels, you may want to continue the retouching process.

 C a u t i o n

Dragging the white or black sliders too far into the white or black area of the histogram may clip important information to pure white or pure black. Evaluate the image and the image histogram to see where the image information falls, and take care not to clip it with extreme moves of the Levels sliders.

Working with the Midtone Slider

The image in **figure 2.15** was taken in Shanghai in 1906. In addition to using the white and black point sliders, as in the preceding technique, here you also use the midtone gamma slider to lighten the image. When working with faded images, using the black and white point sliders to add contrast is a good starting point. If, after using them, the image is too dark, adjust the midtone slider to the left to lighten the image; or if the image is too light, move the midtone slider to the right. **Figure 2.16** shows the improved image.

ch2_faded2.jpg

1. Add a Levels Adjustment Layer.

2. Move the highlight slider to the area of lightest image information, as shown on the right side of the histogram in **figure 2.17**.

3. Move the black point slider to the area of the darkest image information, as you see on the left side of the histogram in the figure.

4. Now, move the midtone gamma slider to the left to lighten the image. The amount you move the midtone gamma slider depends on the original image and how much lighter you want the image to be.

BEFORE

figure 2.15

Finding the White and Black Points

The image shown in figure 2.18 is from the early 1900s. The little girl in the picture is my grandmother. The image is flat, faded, and its corners are missing. After using the black and white eyedroppers and the midtone gamma slider in Levels, I've added contrast and snap to the image, as you see in figure 2.19.

AFTER

figure 2.16

BEFOR

figure 2.18

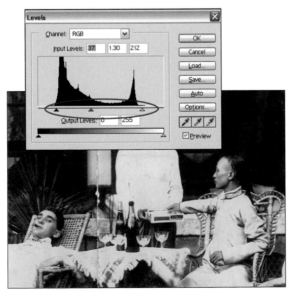

figure 2.17

After adjusting the white and black points, move the midtone gamma slider to the left to lighten the image.

AFTER

figure 2.19

N o t e

There isn't a magic formula when adjusting tonal information. How much lighter or darker you make an image depends on the condition of the original image and your subjective interpretation of how the final image should look. In some cases, a darker image may better reflect the original scene, and in other cases, a tonally lighter approach may be more appropriate.

There are many instances where you might not be sure where the black or white point of an image is. You can use a temporary Threshold Adjustment Layer to find the white and black points and use Color Samplers to pinpoint those exact spots for reference while adjusting tone.

ch2_threshold.jpg

1. Add a Threshold Adjustment Layer.

2. The image is now reduced to two tones— black and white—as shown in **figure 2.20**.

figure 2.20

The Threshold Adjustment Layer splits the image into black or white.

3. To find the black point, move the slider all the way to the left and then slowly move it back to the right until you see black clumps, as shown in **figure 2.21**. Ignore the two bottom corners because they are just the lid of the scanner and are not true image information.

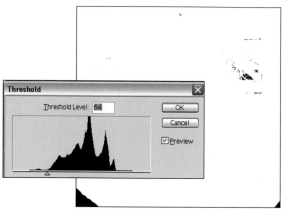

figure 2.21

To find the black point, drag the slider to the left side of the Threshold histogram.

4. Click OK and use a Color Sampler to tack a marker right on top of the black clump. Notice when the Threshold dialog box is active, the Eyedropper becomes the active tool. Simply Shift + click your image to change the Eyedropper tool to the Color Sampler tool to add the reference tack.

5. To find the white point, double-click the Threshold Adjustment Layer icon on the Layers palette to reopen the Threshold layer. Or if the Threshold is still active, move the slider all the way to the right. Then move the slider to the left until you see white clumps, as illustrated in **figure 2.22**. As with the black point location, ignore areas that are not part of the image, such as the edge of the print.

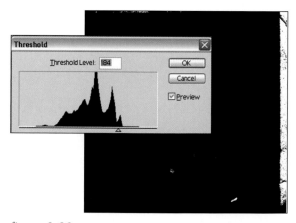

figure 2.22

To find the white point, drag the slider to the right side of the Threshold histogram.

6. Click OK and add a Color Sampler as a tack right on top of the clump of white.

7. Turn off or throw away the Threshold Adjustment Layer and you'll see that the image hasn't been affected but that the samplers are showing you exactly where the black and white points should be placed, as shown in **figure 2.23**.

White point   Black point

figure 2.23

After turning off the Threshold Adjustment Layer, the Color Samplers show you exactly where the black and white points should be placed in the image.

8. Now add a Levels Adjustment Layer and use the Color Sampler tacks as reference points in setting the true black and white points. Activate the white eyedropper and click once where the tack is referring to the lightest area of the image and repeat with the black eyedropper to click the black reference tack.

 T i p

While working with Levels, you can get an on-the-fly view of where the image detail begins and ends. Press (Option) [Alt] while dragging the white or black output slider to toggle to a temporary threshold view.

Working with Levels Eyedroppers

When working with historical images or photographs in which you don't have personal knowledge of the tones or color, you can use your visual memory to improve tone. **Figure 2.24** shows a formal portrait that lacks the needed contrast. My estimations of the black-and-white prints resulted in the much-improved image shown in **figure 2.25**.

© Eckert family archive

BEFORE

figure 2.24

AFTER

figure 2.25

⊕⊳⊱ **ch2_profile.jpg**

1. Add a Levels Adjustment Layer.

2. Click the white eyedropper, and then click an area that needs to be reset to white. In **figure 2.26** I'm resetting the shoulder of the woman's dress. By clicking the area that should be white, Photoshop will remap and redefine the tonal information to change the dingy gray to pure white.

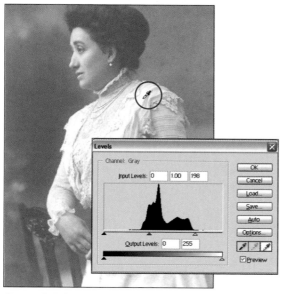

figure 2.26

Use the white eyedropper to identify where the new white point should be.

3. Click the black eyedropper, and then click an area that needs to be reset to black. In **figure 2.27**, I'm darkening the area in the woman's hair. Just as the white eyedropper remaps white, the black eyedropper defines and remaps the darkest tones. Using the eyedropper approach is both effective and simple—a winning combination.

4. If setting the black or white point made the image too contrasty, use the black or white point sliders to lessen the contrast. If the image becomes too bright, move the Levels histogram highlight slider to the right to reduce the brightness. As seen in **figure 2.28**, by moving the black point slider from 82 to 68, the shadows are lightened.

figure 2.27

Use the black eyedropper to deepen the dark areas of the image.

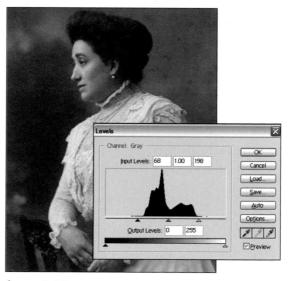

figure 2.28

Moving the slider to 68 produces lighter shadows.

5. If the image is still too light or too dark, adjust the midtone gamma slider. To lighten an image, move the midtone gamma slider to the left. To darken a light image, move the midtone gamma slider to the right.

N o t e

If you click an area that isn't representative of white in your image, other lighter tones will be forced to white and you could end up losing information that may be important. If you click an area with any Levels or Curves eyedropper and don't like the results, press (Option) [Alt] to change the Cancel button to Reset and click. This will return the file to its initial state.

Output Levels

A properly adjusted image can print values from rich blacks to clean whites on a printer and paper combination that can handle a wide tonality. If your highlight values are getting blown out to paper white or the shadow information lacks tonal differentiation, you can use the Output levels in the Levels dialog box to reduce the range of the tones and bring the print within the gamut of your printer. Entering new values under Output Levels, either by moving the sliders or entering numbers in directly, will compress all the tonal values in your image to print within the new high or low values you specify.

For example, when I print this image (see **figure 2.29**) onto glossy paper on a dye sublimation printer, I can see that the whites are too bright. Look at the stem of the glass, especially where it meets the liquid. Instead of showing detail, it displays pure white or the paper itself. Adding a Levels Adjustment Layer and reducing the Output Levels highlight to 240 per image, as shown in **figure 2.30**, brings the file within the limit gamut range of that paper and printer combination.

Using the Output feature, a Levels Adjustment Layer enables you to target the file for a specific printer without permanently changing the image information. If you plan to print that same file with a different printer or paper, either turn the Levels Adjustment Layer off or adjust it to match the gamut of your printer and paper.

© Ablestock.com

figure 2.29

The original image has been blown out and the light areas are too white.

figure 2.30

When the Output Levels highlight is adjusted, the image regains the needed tonality.

CURVES AND CONTRAST

After you're comfortable working with Levels, Curves is the next tool to add to your Photoshop repertoire. The advantage of Curves is that it gives you 16 points to influence the tonal values of an image, whereas Levels allows you just three (highlight, midtone, and shadow points).

The Curves dialog box enables you to work with either 0–100 dot percentages or 0–255 tonal values. Click the small triangles circled in **figure 2.31** to toggle between the two. From my experience, people with prepress experience prefer the 0%–100% scale, while photographers prefer the 0–255 scale—the same values used in Levels. The 0–255 scale places the highlights on the shoulder (upper part) of the curve and the shadows on the toe (lower part) of the curve. This is how a photographer reads film curves and why I prefer to use the 0–255 scale. The 0%–100% values are mapped exactly the opposite, with the highlights at the bottom left and the shadows at the upper right.

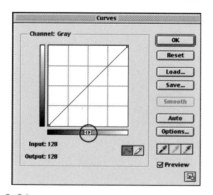

figure 2.31

You can choose to work in dot percentages or digital values by clicking the small triangles.

When you add a point to the curve and move it, you are changing the relationship between a pixel's input to output value. For example, if you increase the midpoint 128 value, you're telling Photoshop to remap the 128 values to a higher value, and the image will get lighter. If you are working with the 0–100% scale, moving the 50% point down will also lighten the image.

The best aspect of Curves is the control you have over the many points of tonal information. With Curves, you can quickly enhance image contrast by applying a classic S-curve (described in the next section), or you can spend more time with the interface and use bump points to bring out selective tonal details, as we'll do in "Bringing Out Detail with Curves."

Increasing Contrast with Curves

Figure 2.32 shows another family heirloom that has aged significantly. The image lacks contrast, and the highlights, such as in the father's shirt and baby's jumper, are too gray. I used Curves to deepen the shadows and lighten the lighter areas. Applying an S-curve enabled me to quickly add the pop needed, as shown in **figure 2.33**.

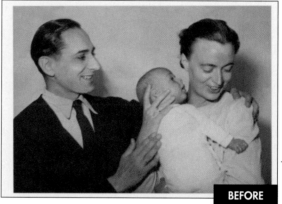

figure 2.32

figure 2.33

ch2_BWfamily.jpg

T i p

(Option + click) [Alt + click] in the curves grid to toggle between a 4×4 quarter tone and 10×10 increment grid.

Click the icon at the bottom right of the Curves dialog box to toggle between larger and smaller display sizes.

1. Add a Curves Image Adjustment Layer.

2. Move the mouse into the image and (Cmd + click) [Ctrl + click] a light area of the image that needs to be made lighter. This automatically adds a handle on the Curves graph. In this example, I selected the infant's white jumper and (Cmd + clicked) [Ctrl + clicked] to add a handle point to the Curve, as shown in figure 2.35.

figure 2.35

While in the Curves dialog box, pinpoint a light area of the image that needs to be made lighter.

3. In the Curves dialog box, click the point and move it up to lighten the image highlights.

4. (Cmd + click) [Ctrl + click] a dark area that needs to be darker. This automatically adds a handle on the Curves graph. In this example, I used the gentleman's dark sweater as my shadow point.

5. Click the point and move it down to darken the shadows. **Figure 2.36** shows the Curves dialog box after my adjustments.

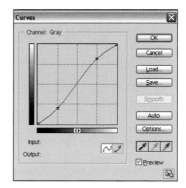

figure 2.36

The Curves highlight and shadow points control image contrast.

When using Curves, keep an eye on the Info palette as you are adjusting contrast and tonal values. You don't want to force the dark areas so far down that they become pure black. Conversely, try to keep some details in your highlights, so don't force whites to 0%. The only values that should be completely white are specular highlights, such as reflections on chrome bumpers.

C a u t i o n

When using Curves to increase contrast, there is always a trade off. Adding contrast in one area takes tonal information away from another. Therefore, making adjustments that are too radical can lead to posterization in the flat areas of the curve.

T i p

Use the mouse to select a handle in the curve and then use the arrow keys to make fine changes in position. When you use the Shift key, the arrow keys will make larger changes. Use (Cmd + Tab) [Ctrl + Tab] to cycle from point to point on a curve.

Bringing Out Detail with Curves

The original image in **figure 2.37** is faded but still salvageable. I used Curves to open up the midtones and highlights, deepen the shadows, and target the blacks and whites for printing, as shown in **figure 2.38**. Lightening both the highlights and midtones accentuates the sunny day and focuses attention on the little boy. By darkening the darker tones, such as the trees (visually less important image areas), I am framing the little boy, which draws the viewer's eye to him.

figure 2.37

figure 2.38

ch2_icecream.jpg

1. Add a Curves Adjustment Layer.

2. (Cmd + click) [Ctrl + click] an area that needs to be made lighter or to which you want to draw attention. In this instance, I used the boy's forehead to lighten the skintones. As you can see in **figure 2.39**, the entire image became lighter.

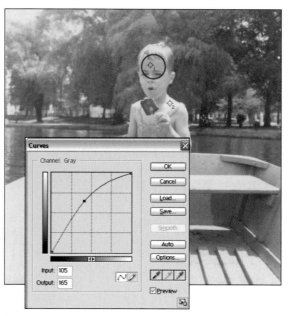

figure 2.39

Starting with the boy's face—the most important image area—I lightened the image to reduce the muddiness and darkness and to draw the viewer's eye to the face.

3. (Cmd + click) [Ctrl + click] a dark tree trunk in the image background to add a handle on the Curves graph. Lower the values of the trees as shown in **figure 2.40**.

4. Notice the Info palette read out: The highlights on the boy's collarbone are now at 4%, a value that will print very close to paper white, without any tonal detail. To reduce the brightness of the highlights while maintaining the effect of the increased contrast, (Cmd + click) [Ctrl + click] the brightest highlight near the collarbone and lower the highlight value to drop the brightest highlight back to 7%, as shown in **figure 2.41**.

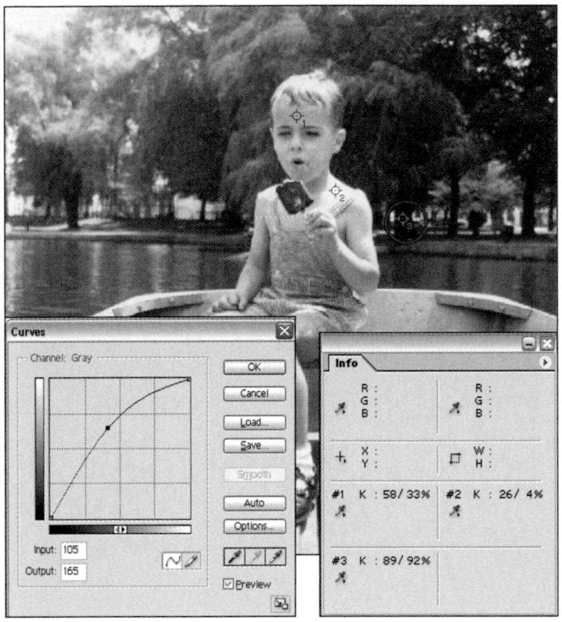

figure 2.40

Darkening the background adds pleasing contrast and tonally frames the boy with trees.

figure 2.41

Reducing the brightness of the highlights ensures that the lightest areas will print with tonality and detail.

5. After adjusting the image contrast, take a moment to look at the image with a fresh eye. Notice where your eye goes in the image. In this case, my eye kept falling to the side of the boat, in the lower-left corner. To selectively reduce the changes made, paint onto the mask of the Adjustment Layer with a 20%–25% black soft-edged brush, as shown in **figure 2.42**. Wherever you paint with black on the Adjustment Layer layer mask, you are hiding the adjustment.

figure 2.42

Painting black onto the Curves Adjustment Layer layer mask reduces the contrast and brightness in unimportant or distracting image areas.

WORKING WITH BLENDING MODES

Every Photoshop layer, including Adjustment Layers, supports Blending Modes, which influence how a layer interacts with the layers below it. This happens on a channel-by-channel basis so Blending Modes can in some instances simultaneously lighten and darken. For retouching work, Blending Modes simplify and speed up tonal correction, spotting, and blemish removal. In Photoshop 7, Adobe rearranged the Blending Modes into functional groups, as labeled in **figure 2.43**.

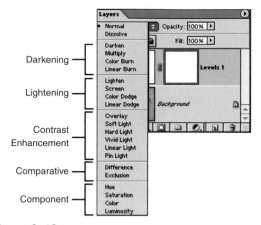

figure 2.43

The Blending Modes are organized into functional groups.

With the following exercises, you'll work with the most important Blending Modes to solve tonal problems:

To darken image information:

- All of the darken modes darken when using colors more than 50% gray.

- Darken allows only the darker areas to be visible.

- Multiply darkens the entire image and is useful to add density to highlights and midtones. It is especially useful for overexposed or very light images.

- Color Burn darkens the dark tones and colors without affecting whites.

- Linear Burn darkens, but unlike multiply, linear burn will clip values and it has a stronger darkening effect than either multiply or color burn.

To lighten image information:

- All of the light modes lighten when using colors less than 50% gray.

- Screen lightens the entire image. Use it to open up/lighten dark image areas and to bring out tonal information in underexposed images.

- Color Dodge, the opposite of Color Burn, lightens light tones and colors and has no effect in dark image areas.

- Linear Dodge lightens. Unlike Screen, Linear Dodge will clip and it has a stronger lightening effect than either Screen or Color Dodge.

To increase image contrast:

- Overlay, Soft Light, and Hard Light Blending Modes lighten the lights and darken the darks, because they are a mixture of Multiply and Screen. All three are useful to boost image contrast. Of these three, Hard Light adds the most contrast, Soft Light adds the least contrast, and Overlay is the average of the three. They are all useful, and I usually try all three when adding contrast to see which one is the most effective Blending Mode for the task at hand.

- Vivid Light combines Color Dodge and Color Burn.

- Linear Light combines Linear Dodge and Linear Burn.

- Pin Light is a combination of Lighten and Darken.

The best thing about working with Blending Modes is that they are completely reversible, allowing you to experiment to achieve the desired result. To access the Blending Modes, use the pull-down menu in the Layers palette, as shown in **figure 2.43**.

Using Multiply to Build Density

As soon as you see a very light or very faded image, you should be thinking *Multiply*. The Multiply Blending Mode works as though you are sandwiching two slides over one another. Imagine that you're standing in front of a window and have a slide in each hand. Now place the two slides over one another and look through the slides—the results will always be darker. By using the Multiply Blending Mode on the Levels Adjustment Layer, you are doubling the tonal density of the image. **Figure 2.44** shows a print that has not fared well over the years. To restore it to the image you see in **figure 2.45**, we need to build up overall density to strengthen the image.

figure 2.44

BEFORE

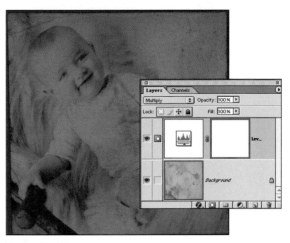

figure 2.46

Setting an Adjustment Layer to Multiply automatically adds density.

In extreme examples such as this one, you can continue improving the image tone by either

- Duplicating the Levels Adjustment Layer to increase density even more. If one Adjustment layer isn't enough, but two is too many, try adjusting the opacity slider on the second one.

- Double-clicking the Levels thumbnail icon in the Layers palette and adjusting the sliders by bringing in the black and white point sliders to where the tonal information begins, as shown in **figure 2.47**.

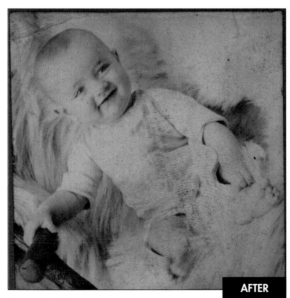

figure 2.45

AFTER

⊕◿⊱ **ch2_fadebaby.jpg**

1. Add a Levels Adjustment Layer and, without changing any settings in Levels, click OK.

2. In the Layers palette, change the Blending Mode to Multiply. **Figure 2.46** shows how the image becomes darker.

3. In many cases, adding a Multiply Levels Adjustment Layer is enough to build up enough image density to create a pleasing image.

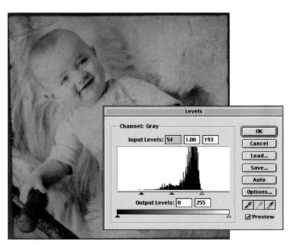

figure 2.47

Adjust the black or white points on the Levels Adjustment Layer to improve image tonality.

Note

Deciding which method to use—duplicating the Adjustment Layer, finessing the Levels sliders, or in some cases duplicating the Adjustment Layer and changing its Blending Mode to Soft Light— to add contrast and lighten the highlights is a matter of experimentation and experience. No one can look at an image and say, "I need to do A, B, and C and use these exact values." Keep in mind that the more you experiment with these techniques, the more experience you will gain and the more options you'll have to improve images.

Adding Contrast with Hard Light

Overlay, Soft Light, and Hard Light are great Blending Modes to add contrast to an image. In **figure 2.48**, the original image is very badly faded and the soldier is barely recognizable. Using the Hard Light Blending Mode with a Levels Adjustment Layer enhances this image quickly and easily (see **figure 2.49**).

1. I added a Levels Adjustment Layer and clicked OK when the Levels dialogue came up.

figure 2.48

figure 2.49

2. In the Layers palette, I changed the Blending Mode to Overlay, then Soft Light, and then Hard Light to see which one adds the most contrast and improves the image the best.

3. In this example, I set the Blending Mode to Hard Light and then double-clicked the Levels Adjustment Layer and adjusted the shadow, midtone, and highlight sliders, as shown in **figure 2.50**.

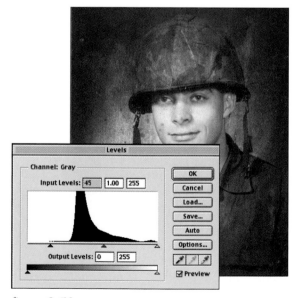

figure 2.50

Adjusting the Levels sliders in addition to using the Hard Light Blending Mode.

BRINGING OUT DETAIL WITH SCREEN AND CHANNEL MIXER

Think of Screen Blending Mode as the reverse of Multiply. Instead of darkening everything, Screen lightens everything. Imagine a slide projected onto a screen. Now project another slide on top of it. The image will always be lighter.

This can be used to great advantage with very dark originals, such as the one in **figure 2.51**. The woman on the right is a Native American princess, so it was very valuable to the owner. The paper base has yellowed and darkened so much it's hard to make out any detail at all. The Screen Blending Mode brings much of the contrast back to the image, as shown in **figure 2.52**.

When I face extreme tone or color problems, I always check the individual color channels to see whether I can identify the problem. To see the channels, open the Channels palette and click each channel (red, green, or blue) or use (Cmd) [Ctrl] with 1, 2, or 3 to see the red, green, and blue channels, respectively. (Cmd + ~) [Ctrl + ~] returns you to RGB with all channels being displayed. In this example, the blue channel has practically no image information at all, as you can see in **figure 2.53**.

Red channel

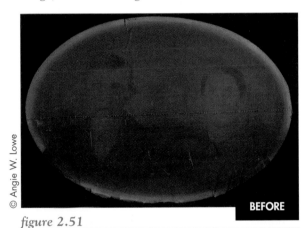

© Angie W. Lowe

BEFORE

figure 2.51

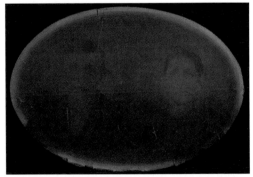

Green channel

AFTER

figure 2.52

🌐▷⤢ **ch02_princess.jpg**

Blue channel

figure 2.53

Looking at the individual channels can often help identify what is causing extreme problems.

To lighten this detail while maintaining the character of the original, use a Channel Mixer Adjustment Layer with the Screen Blending Mode.

1. Keeping in mind that the red and the green channel contain the most image information, add a Channel Mixer Adjustment Layer. Channel Mixer uses sliders to blend each of a source image's color channels into a new output channel. The strong color cast in this image is not part of the essential image information, and by using Channel Mixer in monochrome mode by checking the Monochrome option, you can quickly remove detrimental color problems.

2. Because the red and green channels have the best image information, move those sliders to the right to increase the amount that they are adding to the image. I used 90% red and 60% green, as shown in figure 2.54. Click OK.

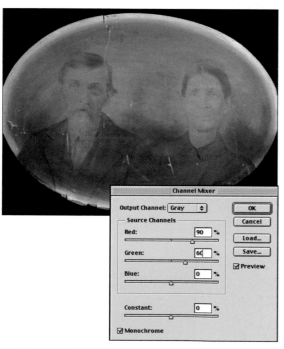

figure 2.54

Adjusting the Channel Mixer sliders to create an image with the good channel information, while ignoring the severely damaged blue channel.

3. Change the Blending Mode of the Channel Mixer Adjustment Layer to Screen, which allows some of the original color character of the image to show through. (For additional information on working with the Channel Mixer, see Chapter 8, "Refining and Polishing the Image.")

TRICKS FOR MAXIMIZING ADJUSTMENT LAYERS

You can move and share Adjustment Layers between documents by using the Move tool to drag them from one open document to another. The files don't have to be the same size or dimension—meaning you can make a tonal correction on one file and just drag it over to another file, and Photoshop will apply the same improvement to the second file. Use this drag-and-drop technique when you have a number of similar corrections to make to similar originals.

On one project, I had to retouch a series of images that were taken at the same time and stored together and, consequently, they all had faded in a similar manner. After scanning in the originals, I opened one representative image and used a Curves Adjustment Layer to improve the contrast. Then I opened the other files and just dragged the initial Adjustment Layer over to them, which applied that correction to all the subsequent files. Of course I looked at each image and tweaked the corrections where needed, but by using this technique, I was done with the job in no time flat. Please see Chapter 4 for a dramatic example of quick-and-easy color correction with shared Adjustment Layers.

Saving and Loading Adjustment Settings

If you need to correct a lot of images with similar tonal problems, saving and loading the Adjustment Layer settings can really speed up your work. Additionally, if you use Actions to automate your workflow, you can open and adjust many images without breaking a sweat.

1. Create the appropriate Adjustment Layer and click Save (see **figure 2.55**).

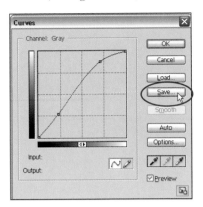

figure 2.55

Clicking the Save button saves the setting so you can use it again.

2. Save the settings into a folder.

3. With the second image active, add a Curves Adjustment Layer and click the Load button.

4. Navigate to find the saved settings and click Open to apply the change. As you can see in **figure 2.56**, all three images are quickly corrected by loading the Curves correction file.

Saving Adjustment Layers

The only problem with saving the settings of Adjustment Layers is that any Blending Modes and Opacity settings used are not saved with the adjustment settings file. This is, of course, a drawback to a Blending Mode aficionado like me. In the following example, I boosted the contrast of the image with a Curves Adjustment Layer set to Soft Light at 50% Opacity, as shown in **figure 2.57**. To use these settings later, I saved the Adjustment Layer in a separate, empty Photoshop file from which I can drag and drop the Adjustment Layer whenever I need it.

1. To save the adjustment settings with the Blending Mode, select the Adjustment Layer and select Duplicate Layer from the Layers palette menu.

figure 2.56

Three identically corrected images.

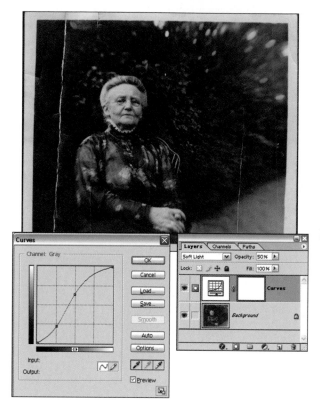

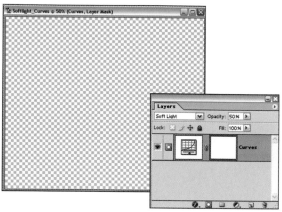

figure 2.59

The resulting file saves layer settings such as Opacity and Blending Modes that would otherwise be lost.

4. Save this file into a folder just as you would any Photoshop document. To conserve drive space, you can crop the Adjustment Layer file down to almost nothing.

5. After opening the file, use the drag-and-drop method to add this Adjustment Layer, complete with Blending Mode, Opacity values, and adjustments, to any file.

figure 2.57

Saving the Curves Adjustment Layer would not have saved the other layer options that I used to fine-tune this image.

2. Make sure to set the destination to a new document, name the file, and click OK (see figure 2.58).

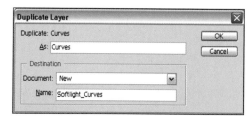

figure 2.58

Setting the destination.

3. This creates a Photoshop document, as shown in figure 2.59. As you can see from the Layers palette, the Blending Mode and Opacity settings have been preserved.

COMBINING TONAL CORRECTIONS

So far, you've seen numerous examples of improving tone with Adjustment Layers, in which correcting the tone or contrast problem used one type of Adjustment Layer, but you can expand your Photoshop repertoire by combining numerous types of Adjustment Layers. Here is a well-done example that illustrates the use of applying several Adjustment Layers to restore tone and contrast to a very faded and discolored original (see figure 2.60) to create the rich image shown in figure 2.61.

Often an image is so dark and discolored that I simply don't know which problem to take care of first. In this example, the passage of time has compressed the tonality of the original and added an unpleasant orange color cast. Try the following technique to clear up both problems with one adjustment.

© Thomas Liptak

figure 2.60

figure 2.61

🌐 ⚐ **ch2_fadedfamily.jpg**

To expand the overall tonality and to remove the strong color cast, Thomas Liptak used a Levels Adjustment Layer and, interestingly enough, he worked on the individual color channels, which cleared up the color cast in three very easy steps.

1. Create a new Levels Adjustment Layer.

2. Activate the red channel by clicking on the pull-down menu (Cmd + 1) [Ctrl + 1] and move the highlight levels slider to where the majority of the highlight information begins and the shadow slider to where the majority of the shadow information is (see **figure 2.62**).

figure 2.62

Adjusting the red channel information.

3. Select the green channel (Cmd + 2) [Ctrl + 2] and move the shadow and highlight sliders, as shown in **figure 2.63**.

figure 2.63

Adjusting the green channel information.

4. Select the blue channel (Cmd + 3) [Ctrl + 3] and move the individual highlight and shadow levels sliders to where the majority of the information begins, as shown in **figure 2.64**. As you can see, both the extreme color cast and the darkness has been removed very well and very easily.

figure 2.64

Adjusting the blue channel information.

5. After removing the darkness and color cast, Thomas continued to finesse this image closer to its original black-and-white state with a Channel Mixer Adjustment Layer, as shown in **figure 2.65**. Upon careful examination, you'll notice that the image still maintains a slight tonality because Thomas used the Channel Mixer sliders on the red and blue channels to balance the image while maintaining a hint of color.

Thomas has created an excellent black-and-white image, one that utilizes the fullest possible tonal range without sacrificing details. In fact, it's almost too good, too clean, and too contrasty—almost too contemporary. To restore a feeling of history without sacrificing tonality, Thomas added a subtle Color Balance Adjustment Layer to restore a bit of the "antique" coloration (see **figure 2.66**).

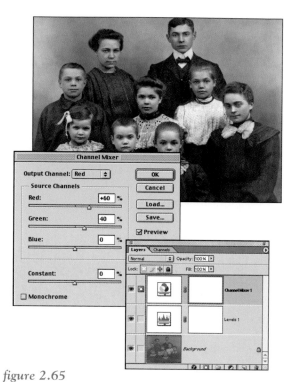

figure 2.65

The Channel Mixer Adjustment Layer helped to neutralize the print ever so subtly.

figure 2.66

Restoring some of the antique look with a Color Balance Adjustment Layer.

BASING TONAL CORRECTIONS ON SELECTIONS

We have applied tonal changes to the entire image (global changes), but many times you just want to improve a specific part or area of a file (local changes). That is when you need to start thinking and working selectively. In this section, you use Photoshop's selection and painting tools to control where the changes take place. Selective changes can start with either an active selection or with a global Adjustment Layer.

The shadow areas in figure 2.67 are too dark. When I make a selection and then add an Adjustment Layer, Photoshop knows to change only the actively selected area, as seen in figure 2.68. Even better than that, after you've clicked OK to the tonal correction, the Adjustment Layer is a small black-and-white version of the selection. Photoshop has created a mask—wherever it is black, the adjustment doesn't take place, while the effect shows through the white areas. The best thing about this technique is that you can use any type of selection tool that you are comfortable with, from the Magic Wand tool to the Color Range command, to create the initial selection.

1. Make a selection of the tonal areas that you want to enhance. In this example, I used Select > Color Range set to Shadows, as shown in figure 2.69, to create the active selection, and then accepted the selection by clicking OK.

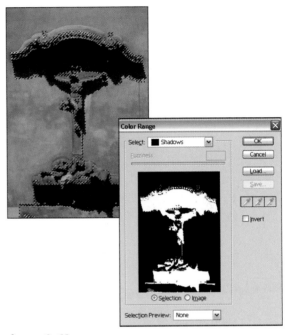

figure 2.69

Using Color Range to select the shadows.

2. Add a Curves Adjustment Layer. Notice that in figure 2.70 Photoshop automatically creates a mask for the Adjustment Layer using the selection (look at the thumbnail in the Layers palette). Where the mask is black, no tonal correction will take place. Where the mask is white, the tonal adjustments you make will take place.

3. Adjust the Curve to open the shadows, as shown in figure 2.71. In some situations, you may want to experiment with Blending Modes to accentuate the adjustments. In this case, Screen is an effective choice.

© Katrin Eismann

BEFORE

AFTER

figure 2.67   *figure 2.68*

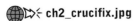 ch2_crucifix.jpg

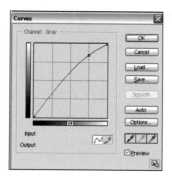

figure 2.70

Adding a Curves Adjustment Layer when a selection is active creates a mask to control where the tonal adjustments are made.

figure 2.71

The edited Curve.

figure 2.72

A harsh transition can lead to a tie-dye effect along tonal differences.

figure 2.73

Softening the layer mask with Gaussian Blur.

4. If you notice distinct or abrupt tonal changes like the one circled in **figure 2.72** after applying a change, use the Gaussian Blur filter on the layer mask to create a transition from black (no change) to white (change), as shown in **figure 2.73**.

Multiple Masked Adjustments

One of the greatest benefits of working with Adjustment Layers is the ability to use the layer mask to control exactly where the image improvement takes place. Additionally, you can stack up many separate Adjustment Layers with masks to fine-tune an image with tremendous control and flexibility.

Take a look at figure 2.74. As Ken Crost wrote to me, "The original image was from 1922, but all I had to work with was a copy print which seemed to accentuate all of the defects even more." Now look at the fantastic restoration Ken completed by carefully masking out the individual elements, as shown in figure 2.75. Ken used a one- to two-pixel feathered Lasso to select the individual image elements he wanted to lighten or darken. Because he added an Adjustment Layer, the selection was transferred to the layer mask, which controlled exactly where the change took place.

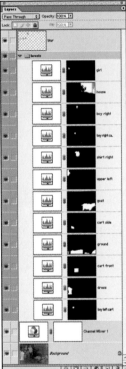

figure 2.74

The original image was not only more than 80 years old, it was also a copy print.

figure 2.75

The layer masks control exactly where the tonal changes take place.

Using Selections to Enhance Dynamic Range

Photos with a wide dynamic range have more tonal information for the viewer's eye to enjoy. By opening up tonal detail in the darker areas of an image, you can create rich images that are reminiscent of the classically printed black-and-white photographs without changing the overall contrast. This technique works best in photos where the brightest areas still retain detail. **Figure 2.76** shows the original photograph of a frozen waterfall—the shadows are very dark. In **figure 2.77** the shadows have been opened up and the tonal balance is broader and visually more interesting.

© David Bryant

BEFORE

figure 2.76

AFTER

figure 2.77

⊕▷< **ch2_icefall.jpg**

1. Select just the luminosity by pressing (Cmd + Option + ~) [Ctrl + Alt + ~](that "~" is a tilde—the squiggle next to the numeral 1). On keyboards that don't have a tilde key, you can load the image luminosity by (Cmd + clicking) [Ctrl + clicking) on the RGB composite icon in the channel palette, as shown in **figure 2.78**.

figure 2.78

(Cmd + click) [Ctrl + click) on the RGB composite icon to select the image luminosity, and then click the Save selection as channel button.

2. Create an Alpha channel based on your selection by clicking on the Save Selection as Channel button on the channel palette. It's always a good idea to save complex selections as Alpha channels.

3. Return to the Layers palette, choose Select > Deselect, and then duplicate the Background layer by dragging it over the New Layer icon.

4. Load the saved Alpha channel by choosing Select > Load Selection and selecting the channel as circled in **figure 2.79**. Click OK.

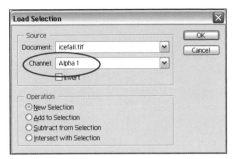

figure 2.79

Loading the Alpha channel as a selection.

5. Add a layer mask to the duplicate layer. A mask based on your highlights selection is automatically created. You want to affect everything *except* the highlights, so press (Cmd + I) [Ctrl + I] to invert the layer mask.

6. Change the Blending Mode of the duplicate layer to Screen. This will open up only the shadows and increase dynamic range as seen in figure 2.80.

7. Duplicate the Screen layer to strengthen the effect if desired.

figure 2.80

Invert the layer mask and set Blending Mode to Screen. Duplicate to intensify effect.

THE BENEFITS OF HIGH-BIT DATA

The only problem with my love affair with Adjustment Layers is that Photoshop 6 and 7 do not support working with Adjustment Layers on 16-bit-per-channel images—which are also referred to as *high-bit* or *high-bit depth* files. The highest possible number of shades of gray that a standard 8-bit grayscale file can contain is 256. An RGB image uses three channels and is a 24-bit image. A CMYK image uses four channels and is often referred to as a *32-bit image*. Oddly enough, this doesn't mean that the CMYK file contains more shades of gray, because each channel is still made up of a maximum of 256 shades of gray.

For very critical, high-quality tonal and color correction, 256 shades of gray per channel does not offer you a lot of room to change tone and color. Working with high-bit data—files that contain more than 256 shades of gray per channel (see table 2.1)—gives you more tonal values to change the tonal and color character of an image.

table 2.1

Bit-Depth per Channel	Shades of Gray
8-bit	256
10-bit	1,024
12-bit	4,096
16-bit	16,384

If you work with scanners or digital cameras that capture high-bit data, I recommend you take advantage of the additional tonal information high-bit data provides. Perform the tonal and color corrections and cleaning up dust on the high-bit file before converting to 8-bit data.

Figure 2.81 shows you the histograms for two images. The image on the top was scanned at 8-bit, and the image on the bottom was scanned at 16-bit; otherwise, the two scans are identical.

© Katrin Eismann

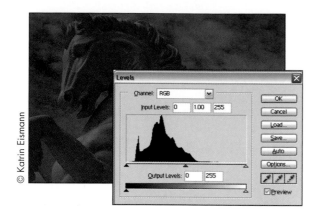

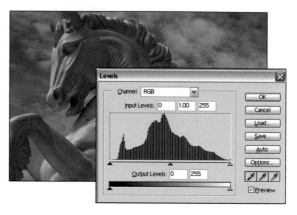

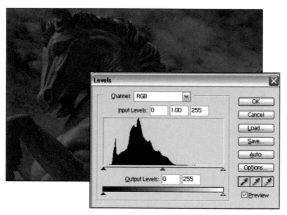

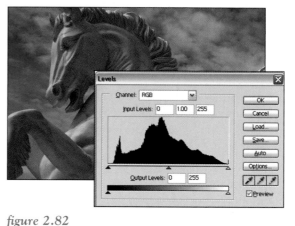

figure 2.81

Before tonal changes, the 8- and 16-bit histograms are identical.

figure 2.82

After tonal changes, the histograms show that the 16-bit image withstood the adjustment far better than the 8-bit image.

After bringing the files into Photoshop, I made the identical Levels adjustment to apply the same tonal and color correction to both files. The top histogram in **figure 2.82** reveals the tonal decimation to the 8-bit file. Where the white spikes occur in the image, tonal information is missing. In the high-bit file at the bottom of **figure 2.82**, the same changes improve the file, and the histogram shows that I still have plenty of data to work with. Ideally, you want to avoid leaving white gaps in the histogram because image areas with white gaps may band or posterize when printing.

Don't Try to Trick Photoshop

Trying to trick Photoshop into thinking it is working with a high-bit file by converting an 8-bit scan to 16-bit, applying changes, and then converting back to 8-bit doesn't work. This voodoo maneuver is a waste of time. Tricks like that don't improve the actual image information. Remember, your goal isn't to print attractive histograms, but to produce good images.

Capturing and Enhancing High-Bit Data

The two methods you can use to capture or input high-bit image information are using either a scanner or digital camera that can capture true high-bit data. In all cases, you will need to set your scanner software to scan in high-bit or set your digital camera to capture either high-bit TIFF files or, better yet, camera RAW files. When I scan or shoot in high-bit, I prefer to not have the scanner or camera software interpret the file at all.

In **figure 2.83**, you see a slide scan of a wooden crucifix in a very old church in Lima, Peru. On the first scan, I set the scanner to auto and the scanner software decided where to set the white and black points. The problem with this approach is that the scanner software can't know that the lightest point is really the wooden stomach of the Christ figure, which should maintain detail and not be a specular white, which is what the Info palette readout in **figure 2.84** shows. In **figure 2.85**, I scanned the same image without any software changes and the image looks flat and uninteresting. But because I scanned it as a high-bit file, I have plenty of image information to work with.

 N o t e

Due to the size of a high-bit file and that fact that they cannot be saved as JPEGs, I have not posted any of these files on the book's web site.

figure 2.83

A high-bit scan made with the auto adjust scanner settings.

figure 2.84

The lightest point has been mapped as a pure white highlight.

figure 2.85

A high-bit scan made without adjusting any scanner settings.

To correct a high-bit scan, use this technique:

1. Select Image > Adjustments > Levels.

2. (Option + click) [Alt + click] the highlight point slider and move the slider to the left. The image will threshold (see **figure 2.86**). Observe the image and look for the first specks of white, which will reveal where the true white is of the image. In most cases, I move the highlight slider to the left, and when I see the white specs I back off a touch by moving the slider one to two points to the right again.

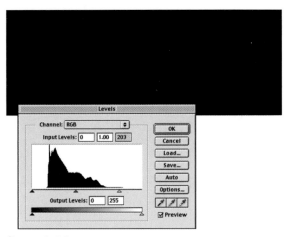

figure 2.86

Determining the true highlight point.

3. On the same Levels interface, (Option + click) [Alt + click] the shadow point slider and move the slide to the right. Once again, the image will posterize. Continue moving the slider to the right until you see specks of black in the image, as shown in **figure 2.87**. Notice that I ignore the frame of the image and concentrate on the photograph to determine where the true black point is.

4. After setting the highlight and shadow point, I used my subjective judgment and lightened the midtones a touch, as shown in **figure 2.88**. All of these corrections improved the image, while not clipping either the highlights or the shadows. As the Info palette in **figure 2.89** shows, the stomach highlights have maintained good highlight tonal information.

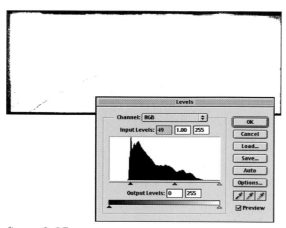

figure 2.87

Determining the true shadow point.

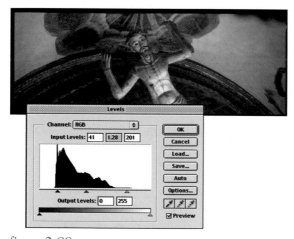

figure 2.88

Adjusting the midpoint gamma.

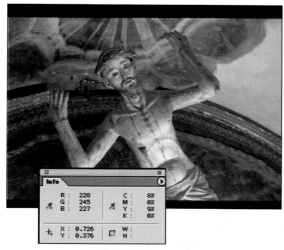

figure 2.89

Measuring the adjusted highlight values.

Other less-than-cheery aspects of working in high-bit include the facts that high-bit files are twice the size of 8-bit files, they do not support layers or Because there are no Adjustment Layers, working with high-bit files is a bit cumbersome, but the additional tonal information is well worth it. To print a high-bit image or have the ability to use layers for creative image compositing, convert it to 8-bit by selecting Image > Mode > 8-Bits/Channel.

Adjustment Layers, and numerous Photoshop tools and filters do not function in high-bit. But for many professional users, these limitations are just a bump in the road when it comes to working with the highest image quality. You can still work very creatively in high-bit by taking advantage of Photoshop history and the ability to drag selections between files.

CLOSING THOUGHTS

Even after years of working with Photoshop, it still amazes me to see how improving image tone can turn a so-so image into an absolutely wonderful one. Rely on your visual intuition to access an image and use Adjustment Layers to bring out tonal detail and information. Working with Adjustment Layers gives you the opportunity to experiment and learn from the process. You may not get the image just right the very first time you try a technique, but believe me, every time you try something new, you're learning for the next image challenge. So download the exercise files from `www.digitalretouch.org`, practice with them, and then apply the techniques to your own images. Although some of the specific values may differ, the concepts of working with Adjustment Layers, Blending Modes, and selections will hold true.

3

EXPOSURE CORRECTION

Who hasn't gone to the photo store to pick up photos, and with bated breath opened the envelope only to be disappointed by pictures that are too light, too dark, or messed up because the flash didn't go off? All these problems can be traced back to incorrect exposure. Although modern cameras have sophisticated light meters and exposure controls, strong back light or well-intentioned but incorrect camera settings can fool these modern wonders into making the wrong exposure.

Additionally, the ravages of time, displaying the photo in strong sunlight, improper storage conditions, poor chemical processing, and the transient nature of most color photographic substrates can wreak havoc on your fondest memories. When pictures fade, they don't contain any rich blacks or pure whites, and often odd color shifts are introduced.

Of course, making the appropriate exposure and protecting your photos by storing them correctly is always better than trying to apply a Photoshop fix; however, sometimes you have to rescue the pictures that fall by the wayside.

In this chapter, you'll work with grayscale and color images to

- Build up density in underexposed images
- Accentuate information in overexposed images
- Add fill-flash to open up backlit portraits
- Selectively paint light back into the picture

The worst aspect of an extreme exposure faux pas is that the original image information is missing. No amount of Photoshop finesse can rescue information that wasn't there to begin with. Exposure-challenged images might not be transformed from a croaking frog to a royal prince, but hopefully the techniques in this chapter will salvage your memories well enough for you to frame and share them with family and friends.

 N o t e

When you have the choice between scanning a print or the original film, working with the original film will most often yield better results. Even extremely over- or underexposed film contains more information than a print made from a poor film exposure. If possible, try to find the original film or ask your client whether they have it available for you to scan.

IMPROVING DARK IMAGES

Images that are underexposed are usually dark or dull without a true rich-black or clean-white. Shadows that don't have any useful information and white areas that look medium gray are also tell-tale signs that the camera meter was fooled into calculating the wrong exposure. Images that have faded over time also can be symptomatic of under-exposure, and these same techniques can be used to rescue them.

Using the Screen Blending Mode

There is nothing worse than trying to rescue a tin-type: a non-reflective photograph on a sheet of iron coated with dark enamel. Tintypes were a popular and inexpensive photographic option from 1856 through to the early part of the 20th century. **Figure 3.1** shows the original, which is almost too dark to reproduce well at all. To open up—that is, lighten—the image, I used the Screen Blending Mode on a Curves Adjustment Layer to create the results seen in **figure 3.2**.

BEFORE

figure 3.1

AFTER

figure 3.2

 **ch3_tintype.jpg**

1. Add Color Samplers to track important tonal information, as shown in **figure 3.3**. In this example, I added four Color Samplers to track the highlights on the dress, shadows on the dress, skin tones, and the studio background.

figure 3.3

Color Samplers enable you to measure and track tonal changes.

2. When you are tracking exposure changes, it is often easier to read the Info palette readout as K (black), which uses a 1–100% scale. To change the Info palette read out, click and hold the small eyedropper as shown in **figure 3.4**, and select Grayscale.

figure 3.4

Changing the Info palette read out to Grayscale is useful when tracking exposure changes.

3. Add a Curves Adjustment Layer, click OK without changing anything, and change the Blending Mode to Screen, as shown in **figure 3.5**.

figure 3.5

Using the Screen Blending Mode will lighten dark images.

Notice that even though the Curve itself has not been changed, the Info palette shows that the Screen Blending Mode is lightening the image (see **figure 3.6**).

figure 3.6

Watching the Info palette is crucial to understanding how the Blending Modes affect the image data. The first number (on the left) is the original value of the sampler, and the second number (on the right) shows the value after editing.

- Sampler 1: The hat went from 64% to 44%.

- Sampler 2: The shadow went from 95% to 92%.

- Sampler 3: The skin tone went from 74% to 44%.

- Sampler 4: The background went from 78% to 64%.

T i p

On dark, underexposed images, also try the Linear Dodge Blending Mode to increase the lightening effect and simultaneously improve image contrast.

4. To increase the lightening effect, duplicate the Curves Adjustment Layer by dragging it down onto the New Layer icon. In this example, I duplicated the Adjustment Layer twice and adjusted the opacity of the topmost layer to create the image shown in **figure 3.7**.

figure 3.7

Duplicating the Adjustment Layers will double the exposure change.

C a u t i o n

Adding excessive contrast with Blending Modes or tonal changes results in image posterization (as illustrated in **figure 3.8**) that might cause banding when printing. To avoid posterization, be careful how much pushing and pulling (lightening and darkening) of tonal values you do.

figure 3.8

Image posterization can result in banding when printing.

Transitioning a Tonal Correction

Sometimes one side of an image is much lighter or darker than the other side. You can use the Gradient tool on an Adjustment Layer layer mask to protect the good part of the image while the Adjustment Layer corrects the bad part of the image. In this example, the camera meter was fooled by the light morning sky, underexposing the lower half of the picture, as shown in **figure 3.9**. As you can see in **figure 3.10**, the final image is tonally balanced and my memories of that early morning walk have been saved.

I used a Curves Adjustment Layer with the Blending Mode set to Screen to lighten the bottom of the image; however, that blew out the sky. To isolate the Curves Adjustment Layer to the bottom portion of the image, I took advantage of an Adjustment Layer layer mask. In the places where I wanted the adjustment to affect the image, I made sure the mask was white; where I wanted to hide the adjustment, I made sure the mask was black. Because I wanted an even transition from black to white, I used the Gradient tool to create this transition. When using masks, I think of the Gradient tool as a big paintbrush that enables you to draw over the entire surface from black to white with a smooth, gray transition.

figure 3.9

figure 3.10

⊕▷⅄ **ch3_darkbottom.jpg**

1. Add a Curves Adjustment Layer and click OK. If the image is too dark (as in this case), select Screen or Linear Dodge as the Blending Mode. If the image is too light, select Multiply or Linear Burn to help darken the image.

2. If the image needs further adjustment, double-click the Adjustment Layer icon, and adjust the curve as shown in **figure 3.11**. While you make the changes, focus on the areas that need fixing. In this case, don't worry about the sky becoming much too light.

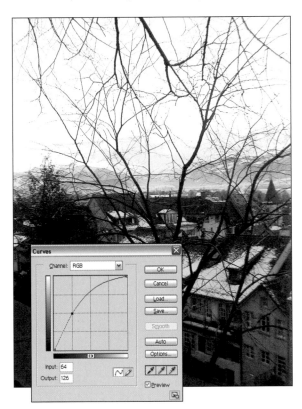

figure 3.11

Using Curves and the Screen Blending Mode will open up or lighten the underexposed areas quickly.

3. Choose the Linear Gradient tool and select the black-to-white opaque gradient from the options bar, as shown in **figure 3.12**.

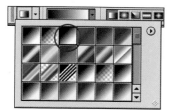

figure 3.12

Selecting the opaque black-to-white blend from the gradient library.

4. Begin the blend where you want the tonal protection to start (just above the horizon) and draw down to where the image adjustment is to your liking (see **figure 3.13**). If you don't draw the blend perfectly the first time, use the Gradient tool to redraw the gradient until the transition is to your liking. Wherever the gradient is black, the tonal correction will be hidden, and wherever you leave white, the tonal correction will be revealed.

5. To intensify the lightening effect, duplicate the Adjustment Layer by dragging it down onto the New Layer icon and adjust the layer opacity if necessary.

Painting with Adjustment Layers

Of course, not all image imperfections fall on a straight line or within one tonal area, as you saw in the previous examples. When I need to enhance irregular areas, I prefer to use Photoshop's Brush tools and a Wacom pressure-sensitive tablet to hide and show image adjustments by painting on the Adjustment Layer layer masks. In the picture of two bridesmaids (see **figure 3.14**), the main subjects are a bit too dark and the details of their hair and dresses seem lost. By lightening them, the viewer's eye is drawn to the details, as shown in **figure 3.15**.

figure 3.13

Drawing the blend on the Adjustment Layer layer mask controls where the effect is taking place.

BEFORE

© Katrin Eismann

figure 3.14

figure 3.15

🌐▷⊱ **ch03_bridesmaids.jpg**

1. Add a Curves Adjustment Layer set to Screen to lighten the image. **Figure 3.16** shows that the entire image is lightened, which washes out the image and takes tonal focus away from the primary figures.

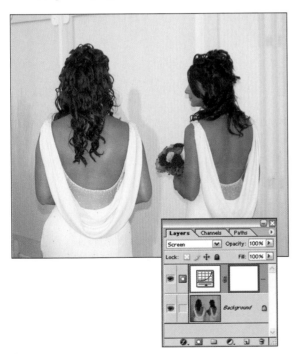

figure 3.16

The Screen Blending Mode is lightening the entire file.

2. To hide the entire tonal correction, invert the Adjustment Layer layer mask (Cmd + I) [Ctrl + I] or Select > All.

3. Select a large, soft-edged brush, set white as the foreground color, and decrease the brush opacity to 10%–35%. I prefer to work with a very low opacity so that when I brush in the change, it builds up slowly.

4. Select the Adjustment Layer and begin painting. Wherever you paint with white, the image will become lighter. Decreasing the opacity of the brush allows a gradual build up of white paint in the mask, slowly revealing the lightening effect on the woman's dresses and hair, as **figure 3.17** illustrates.

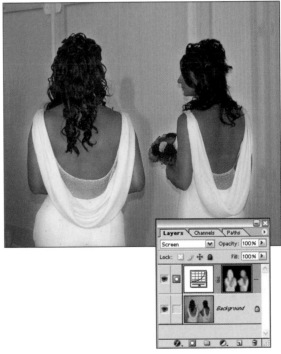

figure 3.17

Painting on the Curves Adjustment Layer layer mask allows you to carefully lighten only the areas that require it.

5. To fine-tune the lightening effect, adjust the opacity of the Adjustment Layer.

This technique gives you the ability to decide where and to what extent the tonal changes take place. The soft-edged brush will yield a soft-edged tonal transition that is difficult to detect.

DIGITAL FLASH TECHNIQUES

In terms of creating shadows and light fall-off, using an on-camera flash often can cause as many problems as they alleviate. **Figure 3.18** shows one type of flash exposure problem in which the on-camera flash wasn't strong enough to illuminate the room, and the right side of the room is darker than the left. In this instance, you'll use Photoshop to seamlessly blend the poorly lit photo with a lighter version to create the consistently exposed image you see in **figure 3.19**.

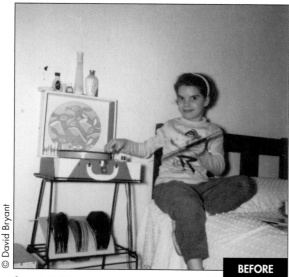

© David Bryant

BEFORE

figure 3.18

AFTER

figure 3.19

ch3_unevenflash.jpg

1. To lighten the light fall-off on the right side of the image, add a Levels Adjustment Layer, click OK, and set its Blending Mode to Screen. Invert the layer mask by selecting Image > Adjustments > Invert, which will turn off the lightening effect. The image will look as though you haven't changed anything at all, as **figure 3.20** illustrates.

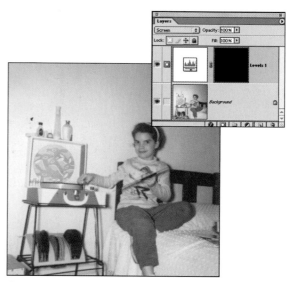

figure 3.20

Inverting the layer mask hides the change.

2. Activate the Gradient tool and make sure that the foreground color is white. On the options bar, select the Foreground to Transparent gradient (see **figure 3.21**). Working from foreground to transparent will enable you to combine multiple gradients on one layer mask to build up the effect as needed.

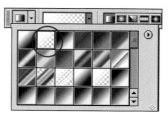

figure 3.21

Selecting the white to transparent gradient.

3. Click the Levels Adjustment Layer and, with the Gradient tool, click and drag from the outside of the image toward the inside, as shown in **figure 3.22**.

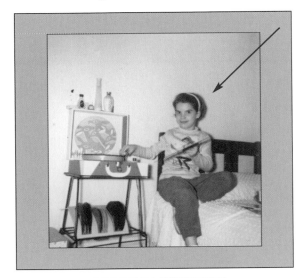

figure 3.22

Drawing in the gradient to lighten the right side of the image.

 Tip

It is easier to use the Gradient tool when working in full Screen Mode and with the image zoomed out a great deal (refer to **figure 3.22**). You can start the gradient well outside the image and subtly add the blends to lighten or darken an image.

4. Duplicate the modified layer to increase the effect, which is shown in **figure 3.23**.

figure 3.23

Duplicating the Adjustment Layer increases the lightening effect.

Adding Fill-Flash

Have you ever noticed that photographs taken in the middle of the day have really dark shadows and that when portraits are taken in front of a window, the people seem silhouetted? In these situations, the exposure problems are caused by the extreme difference between the strong light and the deep shadows, which can fool even the best camera exposure meter. When you're taking pictures, you can avoid these problems by taking your pictures in the morning or late afternoon when the sun is lower and softer or by adding light with a flash or a white fill-card. Of course, knowing those photographic tidbits after the fact doesn't help you one bit, but knowing how to add a bit of light with Photoshop is a great technique to rescue those portraits from darkness.

When working outdoors on sunny days or in high-contrast lighting situations, it is recommended to use flash or fill-flash to reduce lighting ratios and fill in the shadows. That obviously didn't happen in **figure 3.24**, and now we need to use Photoshop to open up the dark areas without changing the lighting ratio too much to achieve the effect in **figure 3.25**.

figure 3.24

figure 3.25

ch3_backlit.jpg

1. Duplicate the original image by choosing Image > Duplicate.

2. Select Image > Mode > Grayscale to convert the duplicate file to grayscale.

3. Select Filter > Blur > Gaussian Blur and use a 3- to 6-pixel Radius setting to soften the details (see **figure 3.26**). Use a lower Gaussian Blur setting for small files under 5MB and higher settings for larger files.

figure 3.26

Apply a Gaussian Blur with a 3 to 6 Radius setting.

4. Invert the tonal values with Image > Adjustments > Invert or (Cmd + I) [Ctrl + I] to create a negative image, as shown in **figure 3.27**. This negative image will be used to mask the digital fill-flash.

figure 3.27

Invert the black-and-white file to create a mask that will be light where you need more effect to take place.

5. Return to the original color image by clicking on it and choosing Select > Load Selection. Check that your black-and-white mask image is selected in the Document pull-down menu, as shown in **figure 3.28** and click OK.

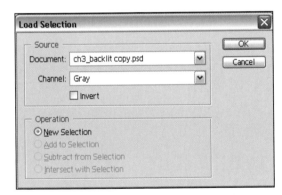

figure 3.28

Load the selection from the inverted document.

6. Select Layer > New > Layer Via Copy (Cmd + J) [Ctrl + J] to create a new layer based on the active selection.

7. Select Edit > Fill and for content, select 50% Gray. Change the Blending Mode to Color Dodge and check Preserve Transparency to tell Photoshop to ignore all clear areas of the new layer (see **figure 3.29**). Click OK.

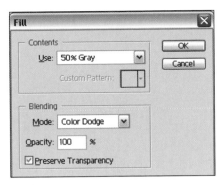

figure 3.29

Fill the active selection with 50% Gray set to Color Dodge with Preserve Transparency checked.

8. Notice how much lighter the image is now. If needed, use a large, soft-edged eraser to erase any affected areas in the sky that you don't want to be lighter, as shown in **figure 3.30**.

figure 3.30

Erase unwanted image areas that were affected with the digital fill-flash.

History and Digital Fill-Flash

As I'm sure you've noticed, there are many ways to accomplish similar effects in Photoshop. David Bryant, an avid nature photographer, developed the following method to add a subtle fill-flash to images. In nature photography, the subject of the image may be too far away to merit an effective use of flash equipment, so you can use the following technique to pop in a hint of light as needed.

1. Add a Curves Adjustment layer and adjust the dark subject to the appearance wanted, as shown in figure 3.31.

figure 3.31

Lightening the image with Curves.

2. To take a snapshot of the adjusted image, (Option + click) [Alt + click] the camera icon at bottom of the History Palette, and select Merged Layers. Name the snapshot *lighter* and click OK, as you see in figure 3.32.

3. Turn off the Curves Adjustment layer, add a new layer, and name it *lighter*. As seen in figure 3.33, your image will look as though it hasn't been changed, but the History palette reveals that you have both the original and a lighter version.

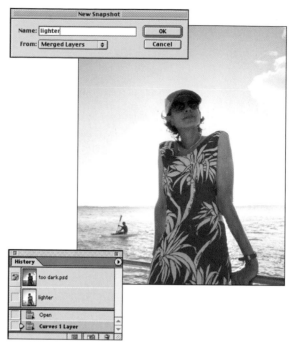

figure 3.32

Taking and naming a merged layers History Snapshot.

figure 3.33

Returning the file to its original state before painting in the lighter areas where needed.

4. With the lighter layer active, select the History Brush and click the History Set Source column to the left of the lighter snapshot, as shown and circled in figure 3.34.

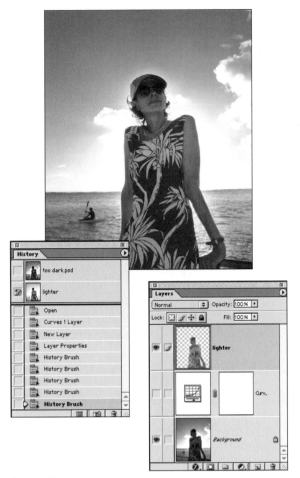

figure 3.35

Painting on the dedicated layer with the lighter History Snapshot.

6. If needed, erase any areas that have been lightened unnecessarily. When finished, adjust the opacity of the foreground layer to fine-tune the effect and select Edit > Save as to save a new version of your file without writing over the original.

The advantage of this approach is that you can precisely control over the final result and also have the ability to fine-tune the effects applied by controlling layer opacity.

figure 3.34

Setting the History Brush source.

5. Paint over the areas to be lightened, as you see in figure 3.35. If you would like the lightening effect to be stronger, set the History Brush options to the Screen Blending Mode in the options bar.

SALVAGING OVEREXPOSED IMAGES

Slide positive originals or digital camera files are images that are most likely to be overexposed. Additionally, slide films, such as Kodak Ektachrome and AgfaChrome, and many digital cameras, do not have the exposure latitude that color negative film has, which makes them more sensitive to overexposure. As with underexposure, a severely overexposed image might not give you much (if any) image information to work with. If the overexposed areas are clear, blown-out to white, or if the Info palette reads 255, 255, 255, there is no amount of Photoshop magic that can recreate image information that wasn't captured in the first place. In the following exercises, you work with very light and faded images to learn techniques to bring out subtle information and create images that are saturated and rich.

Using the Multiply Blending Mode

Photos taken on bright, sunny days are frequently prone to overexposure. And days don't get much brighter and sunnier than in the Arizona desert, as you see in the image shown in **figure 3.36**. Luckily, a quick examination using the Info palette shows we still have highlight detail, so this is a prime candidate for rescue.

Using your knowledge of what happens when an image is overexposed, along with techniques very similar to those you've already learned, you can expand the limited tonal range of this image without losing detail (see **figure 3.37**).

📎✂ **ch3_watermelon_woman.jpg**

1. Add a Curves Adjustment Layer, click OK, and set the Blending Mode to Multiply. You'll see an instant improvement in the overall density of the image.

© Elliot Lincis

figure 3.36

figure 3.37

2. If adding density with Multiply also increases an undesired color shift, you can decrease individual colors by working on individual color channels, as shown in **figure 3.38**. In this instance, I used this opportunity to fix a slight color shift with a slight adjustment of the red channel curve.

3. To intensify the effect, duplicate the Curves Adjustment Layer. Adjust the opacity if the effect is too strong. For this image, two Curves Adjustment Layers set to Multiply makes the image look muddy. To offset this, I set the Blending Mode of the topmost layer to Soft Light, as seen in **figure 3.39**. Often working with Adjustment Layer Blending Modes requires that you experiment until you find the one Blending Mode or combination of Blending Modes that are best for your image.

figure 3.38

Lowering the red channel reduces the overall red cast.

figure 3.39

Duplicating Adjustment Layers and combining Blending Modes can be an effective image correction method.

Correcting Overexposed Images from Digital Cameras

Digital cameras don't offer nearly the exposure latitude of traditional film—meaning that if the light is very bright and contrasty or if you overexpose the image, the file will be too light and lack highlight detail. Often the midtone and shadow information will be washed out and gray. The image in **figure 3.40** is overexposed by only about half a stop, but for critical portrait work that can already be too much to achieve quality results. **Figure 3.41** shows the Info palette read out of the woman's skin tones that reveal the red channel is already at 255 and carries no usable information. After adding density to the file, the image is richer (see **figure 3.42**). I learned the following technique from Lee Varis and am very impressed with how easy yet effective it is.

ch03_overexpose.jpg

figure 3.41

The Info palette reveals that the red channel is over-exposed.

To improve the delicate highlight exposure of the red channel:

1. Inspect the three channels to see which one yields the best image tonality. As shown in **figure 3.43**, the green channel has the smoothest grayscale rendition.

© Phil Pool Photography

BEFORE

figure 3.40

AFTER

figure 3.42

Red

Green

Blue

figure 3.43

Look at the three channels to find the best one.

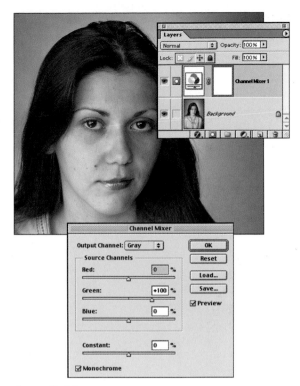

figure 3.44

Adding the green channel image information.

2. Add a Channel Mixer Adjustment Layer, check Monochrome, and set the Red and Blue values to zero and the Green to 100%, as seen in figure 3.44.

3. After accepting the Channel Mixer, the image will be in black and white. The final step is to change the layer Blending Mode to Luminosity, which adds the green tonality to the file and corrects the exposure without changing image color, as shown in figure 3.45.

figure 3.45

Changing the Blending Mode to Luminosity improves image exposure without changing image color.

Reducing Specular Highlights

In this example, the charming portrait of a little girl is softly lit but the highlights on her arm are too "hot" and very distracting, as seen in **figure 3.46**. By toning down the specular highlights on her arm, the final image in **figure 3.47** keeps you focused on her face and eyes. The best thing about using Photoshop to cut down on distracting image elements is that you can experiment with a variety of solutions, as shown in **figure 3.48**, where I reduced the highlight by 50%, which maintained the integrity of photographer Sal Sessa's portrait lighting.

BEFORE

figure 3.46

AFTER

figure 3.47

figure 3.48

A 50% highlight reduction quiets the specular highlight but keeps the photographer's portrait lighting.

To reduce or remove over-exposed highlights on the girl's arm requires a combination of the Clone Stamp tool and layer Blending Modes.

1. Add a new layer and change its Blending Mode to Darken. Activate the Clone Stamp tool and click "Use All Layers" in the options bar. Carefully clone good skin information over the highlight as shown in **figure 3.49**.

figure 3.49

Cloning on a Darken layer to build up highlight reduction.

2. As **figure 3.50** shows, I used four separate layers to carefully build up the image density. To keep the layers organized, I linked the four highlight layers and selected New Set From Linked, as shown in **figure 3.51**.

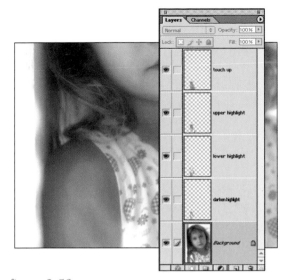

figure 3.50

Building up density on numerous layers gives you greater control.

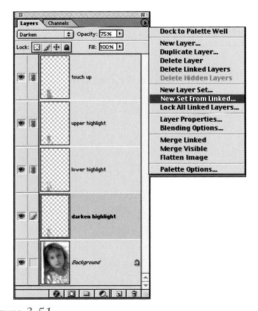

figure 3.51

Linking the layers to create a layer set.

3. To experiment with how much highlight to show or hide, add a new layer on top of the layer stack. Hold down (Option) [Alt] and select Layer > Merge Visible to merge all the visible layers up, as shown in **figure 3.52**. To successfully merge all layers up, it is very important to keep the (Option) [Alt] key pressed until Photoshop has completed the Merge Visible.

figure 3.52

Merging all visible layers onto a new layer.

4. Finally, I turned off the visibility of the layer set and, by changing the layer opacity, could decide exactly how much highlight to show or to hide, as shown in **figure 3.53**.

figure 3.53

Varying the strength of the highlight reduction with layer opacity.

Balancing Exposure and Fading

One of the toughest challenges any retoucher faces is balancing inconsistent exposure and/or fading in multiple areas. The original image in **figure 3.54** is faded to different degrees from all edges. The corrected rendition in **figure 3.55** still needs some restoration work, but at least the exposure is consistent.

figure 3.54

figure 3.55

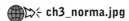 ch3_norma.jpg

To correct the multiple exposure and fading artifacts, you'll use masked Levels Adjustment Layers, as you did in the last example, and introduce the power of an Overlay-neutral color layer to selectively balance tonal exposure.

1. Add a Levels Adjustment Layer and move the midtone slider to the left to lighten the image (see **figure 3.56**). Because this is an Adjustment Layer, you can fine-tune it later by adjusting the layer opacity.

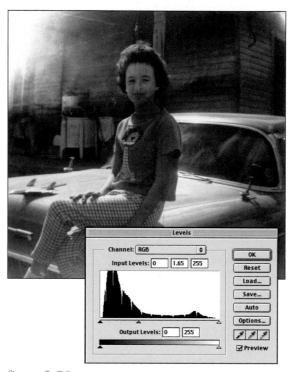

figure 3.56

Use a Levels Adjustment Layer to lighten the image.

2. Name the layer *lower* and use a large, soft-edged black brush on the layer mask to hide the image correction where it is not needed. In this case, the upper part of the image is already lighter and doesn't need additional lightening. Painting with black on the image adjustment layer mask hides the lightening effect from areas that do not need it, as shown in **figure 3.57**. Often I'll start with a linear gradient and then use a soft brush to touch up the transition areas. Paint with black to hide and white to show the tonal correction.

© Matt Matheine

figure 3.57

Masking out the top part of the image protects it from unneeded lightening.

figure 3.58

Individual Adjustment Layers enable you to balance image exposures.

3. Duplicate the "lower" Levels Adjustment Layer (Cmd + J) [Ctrl + J], name it *upper*, and invert its layer mask by pressing (Cmd + I) [Ctrl + I]. Move the midtone slider to the right until the exposures balances out. You can go back and adjust the midtone slider on the lower layer if need be. **Figure 3.58** shows the image corrected and masked with two Levels Adjustment Layer.

4. Make a new Levels Adjustment Layer, name it *center*, and move the midtone slider to the left to lighten the image. Reset the color picker to default black and white by tapping D, and make sure that black is the foreground color. Working in full screen mode, mask the edges using the Gradient tool set to Foreground-to-Transparent, which allows you to pull multiple gradients on one layer mask (**figure 3.59**), as you did in the previous exercise.

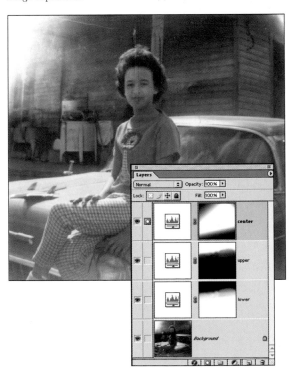

figure 3.59

Building up and controlling tonal corrections with multiple Adjustment Layers.

5. To refine the exposure even further, add a new layer by choosing Layer > New Layer. Name the layer *paint areas* and Select Overlay in the Blending Mode option. Check the box Fill with Overlay-Neutral Color (50% gray).

6. On this 50% Gray Overlay layer, painting with a brush that uses a tone darker than 50% gray will darken (burn in) the image, and painting with a lighter than 50% tone will lighten (dodge) the image. Set a soft-edged brush to 10% opacity, black, and start painting in areas that need a hint of darkening. Toggle to white by pressing X, and paint in areas that need lightening as shown in figure 3.60.

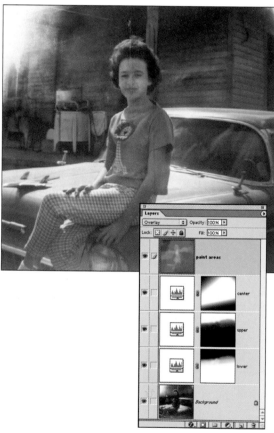

figure 3.60

On a 50% gray layer set to Overlay Blending Mode, painting with black will darken the image and painting with white will selectively lighten image areas.

PAINTING WITH LIGHT

Good photographers are very sensitive to the light, and I don't mean they get sunburned quickly. Rather, they understand how the sun rakes over a landscape in the early morning or evening and brings out hidden textures and colors; they know how they can work with light to create a flattering portrait. Photoshop isn't omnipotent (yet), but with a bit of selective lightening and darkening you can make a dull, lifeless photograph pop off the page. If you've ever worked in a traditional darkroom, these techniques will seem similar to the dodging and burning techniques used to emphasize the atmosphere of the photograph.

The original image (see figure 3.61) doesn't have any drastic exposure problems, but it lacks the dramatic mood that the solo tree and stormy sky should convey. By using Photoshop to accentuate the darks and lights, the viewer's attention is focused on the tree, as shown in figure 3.62.

figure 3.61

figure 3.62

ch3_lonetree.jpg

1. Load the image luminosity by (Cmd + Option + ~) [Ctrl + Alt + ~].

2. Select Layer > New > Layer via Copy (Cmd + J) [Ctrl + J] to create a new layer based on the selection.

3. Change the new layer's Blending Mode to Overlay.

4. Duplicate this layer once or twice to strengthen the image contrast and saturation, as shown in **figure 3.63**.

Tip

You also can load image luminosity by (Cmd + clicking) [Ctrl + clicking] the composite channel icon in the Channels palette.

figure 3.63

Apply the Overlay Blending Mode to the new layers.

5. Add a new layer, fill it with a 50% gray, and change its Blending Mode to Overlay.

6. To paint in the lighter rays of light, use a large, white, soft-edged brush at 2% to 3% opacity, and paint on the gray Overlay layer, as shown in **figure 3.64**.

figure 3.64

Use a white, soft-edged brush at 2% to 3% opacity on a Neutral Overlay Layer to create a new light.

CLOSING THOUGHTS

All in all, it is always better to start with a well-exposed picture; however, for those times when the light meter is fooled, the batteries run out, or the ravages of time wreak havoc on a beloved photo, turn to these Photoshop techniques to do the image justice.

4

WORKING WITH COLOR

We are very sensitive to color, and our eyes are tremendous tools to see and compare color. The emotional and subliminal importance of color in our world cannot be denied. For retouchers, being sensitive to color values can make the difference between a so-so print and a print that looks as vibrant as the memories it represents.

The importance of color challenges us to work with our visual memory in combination with the best that Photoshop has to offer: Adjustment Layers, the Info palette, the Histogram dialog box, painting and selection tools, and Blending Modes. In this chapter, you work with color images to learn

- Additive and subtractive color correction with image variations and color balance
- Global color correction with Levels and Curves
- Selective and interchannel color correction
- Correcting color temperature problems

Many of the tools and techniques used to improve tone, contrast, and exposure discussed in Chapters 2, "Improving Tone and Contrast," and 3, "Exposure Correction," serve as the foundation for working with color. I highly recommend that you review those two chapters before diving into the wonderful world of color.

COLOR ESSENTIALS

There are two types of color in the world: additive and subtractive. In the additive world, a light source is needed to create color. When the primary colors (red, green, and blue) are combined, they create white, as shown in figure 4.1. You monitor is an example of additive light.

In the subtractive world, color is determined by the absorption of light. When the secondary colors—cyan, magenta, and yellow—are combined, they create black-brown, as shown in figure 4.2. Printing ink on paper is an example of subtractive color. In creating inks for print, impurities in the pigments result in a muddy black-brown when cyan, magenta, and yellow are combined. To achieve rich shadows and pure blacks, black is added to the printing process, which also cuts down on the amount of the more expensive color inks used.

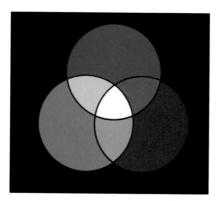

figure 4.1

The additive color space is formed by the red, green, and blue primary colors.

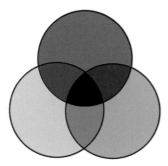

figure 4.2

The subtractive color space is formed by the cyan, yellow, and magenta primary colors.

Combining additive primaries yields the subtractive primaries, and combining the subtractive primaries creates the additive primaries. For the retoucher, understanding this opposite relationship can be very useful when identifying and correcting color problems. For example, if an image is too blue, you have two ways to approach the problem: either increase yellow (which is the opposite of blue to neutralize blue) or decrease the blue in the image. Both yield the same result: an image with less blue.

In digital imaging, the four most prevalent color modes are RGB, CMYK, Lab, and HSB:

- RGB is the additive color space that monitors, scanners, digital cameras, and color slide film originals work or exist in. The advantages to color correcting and retouching in RGB include these: smaller file sizes; equal values of red, green, and blue will always result in a neutral color; and a larger RGB color space allows the file to be converted into multiple gamuts and repurposed for multiple final output destinations.

- CMYK (cyan, magenta, yellow, and black) is the subtractive color mode. Many people (especially people with prepress or printing experience) prefer doing color correction and retouching in CMYK because they are more comfortable with CMYK color values, and editing colors that are in the same gamut as your printer can help avoid unhappy surprises after the ink hits the paper.

- Lab is a three-channel color mode in which the black and white L (luminosity) channel information has been separated from the color information. The "a" channel carries red to green, and the "b" channel carries blue to yellow information, and it can range from +128 to −128. Lab is a device-independent color space used by color management software and by Photoshop when converting RGB files to CMYK. Color correcting in Lab is a delicate task, because the slightest move on the "a" or "b" channels can result in a very strong color shift. On the other hand, Lab is a useful color mode when you are adjusting exposure or cleaning up color artifacts from digital camera files, as discussed in Chapter 5, "Dust, Mold, and Texture Removal."

- HSB stands for hue, saturation, and brightness. Hue refers to the color, brightness refers to the amount of light in the color, and saturation determines the amount of color. You can take advantage of HSB to emphasize or de-emphasize color in portrait retouching, as shown in Chapter 10, "Glamour and Fashion Retouching."

Each color mode has numerous pros and cons, all of which have been described in detail in *Real World Photoshop* by David Blatner and Bruce Fraser (Peachpit, 2002), *Professional Photoshop* by Dan Margulis (Wiley, 2002), and *Photoshop Color Correction* by Michael Kieran (Peachpit, 2002). Rather than reworking information that is well explained by these digital maestros, I propose we learn how to identify and correct colorcasts in antique and contemporary photographs.

Are All Color Casts Evil?

There are only two types of color casts in the world: those that accentuate the image and those that detract from the image. Positive color casts include the golden tones of the early morning or the cool blue cast on a late winter afternoon (see figure 4.3), the warm color created by candlelight, and the color tones created when the photographer filters the lens or light to create or accentuate the color atmosphere. Undesired color casts occur if the photographer used the wrong color film to take a picture, the picture has faded over time, light has leaked into the camera, a scanner introduces a color cast, or an undesired color is being reflected into a photograph (as the blue carpet is doing to the fur of the white cat in figure 4.4). I'm sure you've seen pictures taken in a stadium or in an office in which the color temperature of the light doesn't match the color balance of the film used. The orange, red, or green color casts introduced by using the wrong color film or not compensating for the light temperature with photographic filters are both what I would categorize as undesired. Another example of an undesired color cast occurs when sunlight is filtered through green tree leaves and the people in the picture look slightly Martian-like.

© Alamy Photo

figure 4.3

Taken on a late winter afternoon, the blue light striking the buildings in New York adds to the mood of the image.

© Diane Tremblay

figure 4.4

This is an example of an undesired color cast. The blue carpet the cat is laying is adding a blue tinge to the cat's white fur.

IDENTIFYING A COLOR CAST

The color correction process always starts by identifying the color cast—you have to know what the problem is before you can apply a solution. Color casts, also referred to as a *shade* or *tinge*, are easier to identify in lighter image areas, such as a white shirt or wall or in neutral areas. For example, a gray sidewalk would be a good place to look for a color cast. When evaluating an image for color, find a neutral reference, something that should be white, near white, or gray. If it looks—for discussion's sake— slightly blue, then you know that the image has a blue cast. Interestingly enough, clearing up the color cast in the lighter and neutral areas usually takes care of most of the required color correction work throughout the entire image.

The tools used to identify a color cast are your visual memory, the Info palette, the individual image channels, and practice. Color casts that are similar, such as blue and cyan or magenta and red, take a bit of practice to identify correctly. If you have a color cast in your highlights, nine times out of ten you'll have a color cast in the entire image. Just because color casts are harder to see in dark areas doesn't mean that they're not there. Once you have identified the color cast, think globally and take care of the general color cast problem first. Thankfully, correcting the big problem usually takes care of many of the smaller problems along the way.

UNDERSTANDING COLOR CORRECTION WITH IMAGE VARIATIONS

If all this talk about identifying color casts is making your head spin, don't worry. Photoshop Variations (Image > Adjustments > Variations) is a very useful tool if you're just starting out or need a refresher on color correction. Variations is similar to the color ring-around chart that photographic printers have been using for years to see which way to move color when making a color print. The color correction part of Variations shows you six pictures, each representing one of the primary colors (red, green, blue, cyan, magenta, and yellow) opposite its counterpart (red to cyan, green to magenta, and blue to yellow), as shown in **figure 4.5**. For example, if you have an image with a blue color cast, clicking the yellow image would add yellow and remove the blue.

Notice how easy it is to see the color change in the more neutral areas, such as the water and the building, while the saturated red of my jacket barely changes at all. This illustrates how easy it is to see color casts in neutral and light areas and how near to impossible it is to see color shifts in saturated areas.

Next to the OK and Cancel buttons are radio buttons that you click to control which image area to affect: Shadows, Midtones, Highlights, or Saturation. When using Variations to do color correction, I recommend that you start with the midtones and then refine the highlights. The only problem with Variations is that it is not an Adjustment Layer, so your color correction is applied directly to the image pixels. To ensure that you don't alter original image data, always work either on a duplicate file or duplicate the Background layer.

The original image shown in **figure 4.6** was taken indoors in fluorescent light with a digital camera that was set to daylight color balance, turning the image yellow-green. With a few clicks in Variations, the image is neutral and much more pleasing (see **figure 4.7**).

🌐⏵⏴ **ch4_greenjohn.jpg**

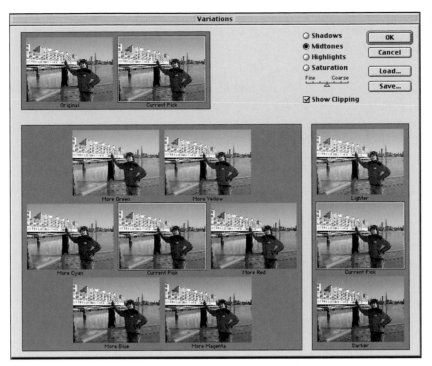

figure 4.5

The Variations dialog box is a useful tool to identify color casts and offers you many options for color correction.

figure 4.6

figure 4.7

1. Use the Eyedropper tool and the Info palette to measure an area in the image that should be neutral. Because you haven't seen this room, how can you know what the real color is? Use your visual memory of a similar scene and you can guess that the wall in the background could be white or at least a very light neutral color. **Figure 4.8** shows the readout of 156 Red, 183 Green, 130 Blue.

figure 4.8

Start by sampling an area you believe should be neutral and examining the color readout in the Info palette.

In relationship to the other colors, the much higher green readout in this example is a dead giveaway of a strong green color cast, and the low blue readout tells you that this image also has a yellow color cast. Properly adjusted, all three colors will be within one or two points of one another.

2. Duplicate the Background layer. This will protect the original pixels while you experiment with Variations to do the color correction.

3. Select Image > Adjustments > Variations and click the Midtones radio button. To see how Variations applies the opposite color principle, move the strength slider under the Saturation radio button to the right as seen in **figure 4.9**.

4. To work subtly, move the strength slider toward Fine to reduce the strength of each change, as shown in **figure 4.10**. Click More Blue to reduce the yellow, and then click More Magenta to reduce the green component. To strengthen any changes, just click the same color image again. Variations updates the center image to reflect the current change.

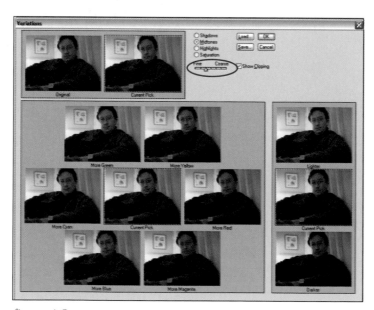

figure 4.9

Moving the slider controls the strength of the Variations change.

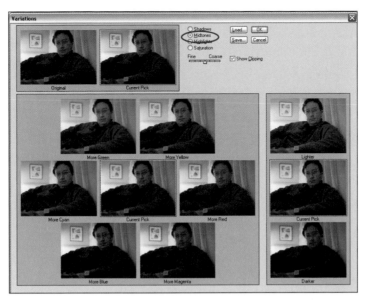

figure 4.10

Start your Variations color correction with the midtones.

5. Adding the blue and magenta into the mid-tones might make the image darker. You can offset this by clicking the Lighter image on the right side of the interface.

6. Finally, click the Highlight radio button and click More Magenta once or twice to take out the last vestige of the green color cast.

7. Click OK and compare the before and after images using (Cmd + Z) [Ctrl + Z] to undo and redo the Variations. Or toggle the visibility of the duplicated Background layer on and off to reveal the original Background layer.

8. You can also check the results with the Info palette as shown in **figure 4.11**, where the RGB readout is now 158, 162, 162, which is an acceptable neutral for a snapshot like this one.

 T i p

When using Variations, you can undo all changes by clicking in the upper-left corner of the original image.

figure 4.11

Check the neutral image areas with the Eyedropper and Info palette to double-check that the color cast has been removed.

Ron Hirsch, a retired engineer and reader of the first edition of this book, was kind and generous to send me an empirical analysis of Image Variations versus Photoshop Color Balance which explains how Image Variations results can be achieved with Color Balance. You can find this analysis as a PDF in the chapter 4 section of www.digitalretouch.org.

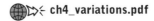 ↺⤴ **ch4_variations.pdf**

MIMICKING THE COLOR DARKROOM WITH COLOR BALANCE

If you've ever done any photographic color printing, using Photoshop's Color Balance Adjustment Layers will seem familiar to you. Like Variations, it also works on the principle of increasing or decreasing opposite colors to color balance an image.

Figure 4.12 shows a class photo that was taken in the middle of the summer on a very bright day. To soften the light, the group was positioned under a tree. The combination of shooting at high noon (when the light has a high color temperature with a high blue component) and the light coming through the leaves added a blue-green color cast to the image. This made the people's skin tones too cool. Figure 4.13 shows the same image after I applied a Color Balance Adjustment Layer. People's skin tones are now less green and more red, and white shirts are actually white. Also notice that the grass in the picture isn't as green anymore. Because the subject of the image is the people and not the grass, it's okay to let the unimportant image areas (the grass) be less attractive. Concentrate on the essential, which, in this case, is the people's skin tone.

figure 4.13

🌐➔ **ch4_group.jpg**

1. Check the image with the Eyedropper tool and the Info palette. Notice that the white shirts have a high blue value and the skin tones are also too green and blue (see figure 4.14). The white shirts show more blue because white with detail (white that is not overexposed) has a higher reflectance and will show the color cast much more readily.

figure 4.14

Checking the image with the Eyedropper and Info palette reveals the green and blue color cast.

© Katrin Eismann

figure 4.12

2. Add a Color Balance Adjustment layer.

3. Always start the color-correction process with the most important image areas. In this case, the group's skin tones are more important than the shirts. Select Midtones for the Tone Balance and increase magenta (to decrease green in the image) by moving the Magenta-Green slider to the left (see figure 4.15). A green color cast can be similar to a cyan color cast, so I added 5 points of red to warm up the skin tones a touch.

figure 4.15

Work on the image midtones to remove the green color cast.

 N o t e

Red and magenta color casts can look very similar, as can blue and cyan, and green and yellow, and working on the similar color of the color cast can help clear up color problems. In this example, adding magenta reduced the green and the addition of red removed any traces of cyan.

4. Select the Highlights Tone Balance radio button, increase the red by 10 points, and decrease the blue with a 30-point move toward the yellow, as seen in figure 4.16.

figure 4.16

Work on the image highlights to remove the blue color cast.

GLOBAL COLOR CORRECTION

As you know by now, Photoshop often gives you three or more ways of reaching the same end result. Some people don't like this and believe that their way is the only way. Puh-leeze! Color correction is an art form that relies on your perception, experience, and interpretation of the image. With the following exercises, we'll use Levels and Curves to rescue some pretty sad photos from color cast fates worse than death.

Using Auto Color Correction

New in Photoshop 7 is a much-improved Auto Color Correction function—one that you can control to achieve some remarkable results. I am usually the first one to shy away from anything with the word "auto" or "magic" in its name. The new Auto Color Correction offers a number of controls with which you can get into the color balance ballpark quickly and easily—especially when working with digital camera files. Once you understand how

Auto Color Correction works, it can save you a lot of time. Note that I am not referring to the Auto Levels, Auto Contrast, or Auto Color menu commands in the Image > Adjustments menu. I don't recommend those commands at all because you have no control over the values Photoshop uses to calculate the changes, and worst of all—you are not working with an Image Adjustment layer.

Both the Levels and Curves dialog boxes have an Auto button. Clicking Auto will perform the default corrections, regardless of where you access it. Because the interface is smaller with Levels, I use this one because I can see more of the image and get identical results. Clicking Options brings up the Auto Color Correction Options interface (see **figure 4.17**). It is here that you can cycle through the types of corrections or influence which values Auto Color references.

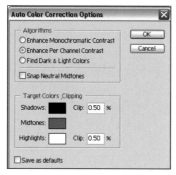

figure 4.17

The Auto Color Correction options can be set from either the Levels or the Curves dialog box.

The Auto Color Correction Options Interface has six settings that enable you to control how the color is affected:

- Enhance Monochromatic Contrast: Photoshop clips all color channels at once, using identical values for each, making shadows darker and light areas brighter. This is the same as Image > Adjustments > Auto Contrast, or moving the shadow and highlight slider in Levels to where image information begins on the RGB or CYMK composite histogram.

- Enhance Per Channel Contrast: Photoshop will adjust each channel separately. This is identical to moving the shadow and highlight sliders of the individual image channels to where the image information starts. This is how Image > Adjustments > Auto Levels works.

- Find Dark & Light Colors: Photoshop uses the lightest and darkest pixels in an image for the Shadow and Highlight values. This is the same as Image > Adjustments > Auto Color and may or may not introduce unwanted color casts.

- Snap Neutral Midtones: With this selected, Photoshop looks for a nearly neutral color in your image and then forces it to gray. Image > Adjustments > Auto Color uses this option.

- Target Colors Clipping: Enter values here to tell Photoshop the percentage of tones to ignore. For example, entering 0.02% for both Shadows and Highlights will skip the brightest and darkest 0.02% before starting calculations. The default 0.5% value is too high. If you want calculations to be based on non-neutral colors, clicking a color swatch will open the Color Picker, where you can choose any color as the Shadow, Midtone, or Highlight target.

- Save as Defaults: Clicking this tells Photoshop that these are the settings you want to use anytime you click the Auto button in Levels or Curves. Note: If you select this option, the Clipping value you enter will also be the new defaults for the Auto Levels, Auto Contrast, and Auto Color menu commands.

The Beauty Is in the Auto Details

Now that Adobe has added the ability to control the Auto Color Correction, I find myself adding a Levels or Curves Adjustment Layer and clicking through the options to see what is going to happen. Many times the results are very good—if I pay attention to the details.

To get the best results from Auto Color, start by checking Find Dark and Light Colors and Snap Neutral Midtones and making sure that Save as

Defaults is checked. Don't worry if this ruins your image for now. By setting these as defaults, you're ensuring that Photoshop is starting with Auto Color when you click Auto in either Levels or Curves. Click OK. If making this change ruined your image, just choose Edit > Undo and the change to the image will be reversed, but the settings will be remembered.

To continue controlling how Auto Color works, reopen the interface to adjust the Target Colors Clipping values, which are both too high at .50% and will result in blocked up shadows and blown out highlights. Start by reducing the shadow value to 0 and using the up arrow on your keyboard to go up .01% at a time. Keep an eye on the image shadow and highlights; values lower than the default will create pleasant, open shadows with information and printable highlights that aren't pure paper white.

The midtone default of a perfectly neutral gray may or may not be the best choice for your images. In fact, the perfect neutral may be visually too cold. You can adjust the midtone, and best of all, as with the previous changed settings, the change is interactive.

In the image in **figure 4.18**, the model car is a bit flat and due to the tungsten light, the overall image is yellow. Adjusting the midtone solves the problem.

figure 4.18

The neutral gray midtone default may not be the best choice.

© Katrin Eismann

⊕⊳⊰ ch4_bluecar.jpg

1. Add a Levels Adjustment Layer and click Options, which in this case brings up the default settings described previously.

2. To reduce the yellow cast, I clicked the midtone color swatch in the RGB values, left the red and green alone at 128, and raised the blue values by 20 points (see **figure 4.19**).

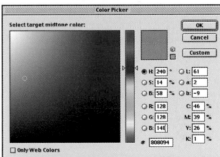

figure 4.19

Adjusting the midtone by raising the blue value.

3. You can achieve the same result by simply dragging the color picker circle within the color picker. Keep an eye on the image to see the effect. In this case, the yellow was minimized and as a bonus, the blue car became even bluer.

Crop Before Clicking Auto

Consider cropping your image before using Auto Color Correction. David Bryant sent me the example in figure 4.20, where he tried Auto Color Correction but was not happy with any of the results. It wasn't until he noticed and cropped out the narrow white border on the bottom and right edge of the print that the Auto Color Correction worked, as in figure 4.21.

The portrait in figure 4.22 shows an unattractive color shift that is only too typical of color prints from the 1970s and 80s. Using our knowledge of Auto Color Correction, we can fix many of the overall color problems, as shown in figure 4.23.

BEFORE

figure 4.20

AFTER

figure 4.21

BEFORE

figure 4.22

AFTER

figure 4.23

 ⊕▷⸚ **ch4_teenager.jpg**

1. Crop the image to remove the white border. As **figure 4.24** shows, you can rotate the Crop tool to straighten out the image while cropping. To rotate your crop, move the mouse about a quarter-inch to the outside of the corner handle. The mouse will change into a curved arrow that you can use to rotate the crop bounding box.

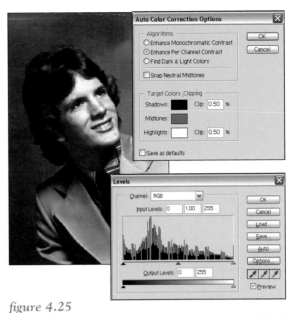

figure 4.25

Add a Levels Adjustment Layer and Click Options.

figure 4.24

Cropping and rotating the image before using Auto Color Correction.

2. Add a Levels or Curves Adjustment Layer. In this example, I used Levels, because the dialog box is smaller and lets me see more of the image. Click Options to access the Auto Color Correction settings. You should see a change in your image as soon as Auto Color Correction Options pops up, and it's not a good change, as **figure 4.25** sadly illustrates. The image is now much too contrasty and coldly blue.

3. Click through the three options. With this image, Enhance Channel Contrast with Snap Neutral Midtones is the most effective. Because the default Clipping values are too high, I changed them to 0.20%, which reduced the highlights on his lapel and maintained image detail (see **figure 4.26**).

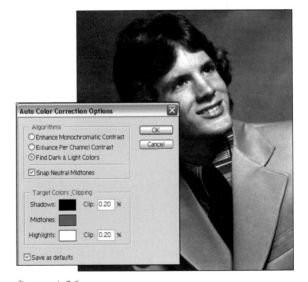

figure 4.26

Changing the Option settings from the defaults can make a big difference.

4. Click OK to accept the Options settings and click OK on the Levels dialog box to commit the changes. Compare the image before and after Auto Color Correction by turning the Adjustment Layer visibility off and on.

All in all, explaining how to use Auto Color takes longer than actually making the changes to achieve good and quick results.

Color Correction with Levels Eyedroppers

Working with the Levels or Curves eyedroppers to define the one, two, or three neutral areas of white, gray, or black will often remove a bothersome color cast. **Figure 4.27** shows a scene photographed with a Nikon D100 digital camera in the late afternoon in Helsinki, Finland. You'd never know it from the photograph, but the building exterior is actually snow white. With a few clicks in Levels, you can restore the gleaming white facade, as seen in **figure 4.28**. Please note: The color cast in this example is not typical of the Nikon cameras, rather it was my fault for taking the picture with the wrong camera settings while rushing around before sunset.

© Katrin Eismann

figure 4.27

figure 4.28

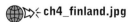 ch4_finland.jpg

N o t e

Before using the Levels or Curves eyedroppers, define the white and black target colors as described in Chapter 2 "Improving Tone and Contrast." For printing to an inkjet printer, use the HSB scale and set the white target color to 96% brightness, or RGB 245, 245, 245, and click OK. Double-click the black eyedropper and set the shadow target color to 5% on the HSB scale, or RGB 12, 12, 12.

1. The first step is to identify the color cast. If you're working with a well-calibrated monitor and have a good sense for color, you'll see that the building is too yellow. If you're not sure about color or your monitor, use the Info palette. Set your Eyedropper to Sample 3 by 3 Average on the options bar, and look for something you know should or could be neutral. This image has large expanses of white, but every image will be different. When you position the Eyedropper over a neutral color, the Info palette will reveal the color cast (see **figure 4.29**). In this case, the very low blue value of 83 signifies that the image is very weak in blue, which translates to strong in yellow, so the image has a yellow color cast.

figure 4.29

The values in the Info palette help you identify the color cast.

2. I added a Levels Adjustment Layer and selected the white eyedropper. I clicked the lightest part of the building to define a new white point. Clicking with the eyedropper not only redefines the pixels clicked to white; it also neutralizes them. In the Info palette, I noted that the values of red, green, and blue are equal, proving that I removed the color cast, as shown in **figure 4.30**. You should experiment to find the best neutral points. Try as many areas as you like. Each click of the eyedropper will re-examine and adjust the image all over again.

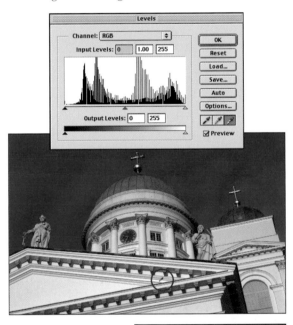

figure 4.30

Using the Levels white eyedropper to define a new white point improves overall color and contrast.

 T i p

(Option + drag) [Alt + drag] the Highlight slider to the left, as you see in **figure 4.31**. Photoshop will reveal where the true highlight is. In this image, I ignored the lightest areas in the specular highlights of the golden crosses and concentrated on the building as circled. This technique works for the shadow point as well.

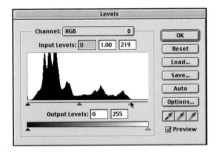

figure 4.31

Finding the highlight point of an image.

3. Next select the midtone eyedropper and click the shady side of the building, as shown in **figure 4.32**. If you think about it, a white building in the shade should be gray, so this is a good way to find a neutral midpoint.

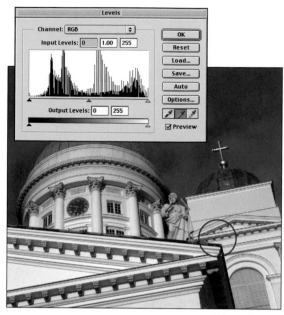

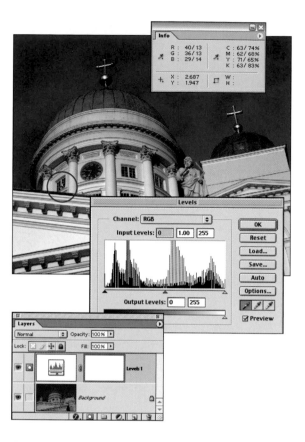

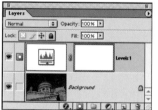

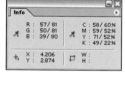

figure 4.32

Using the Levels gray eyedropper to define a neutral midpoint removes even more of the color cast.

figure 4.33

Using the black eyedropper on a black point improves image density. Notice that it makes the sky come to life!

4. On many images, correcting for the white point and midtone may be enough. However, on this image, I also selected the black eyedropper and used the darkest of the little windows to set the new black point (see figure 4.33).

5. After defining the white and black points, take a second look at the image. If the image looks too dark or too light, use the midtone slider to lighten (by moving the midtone slider to the left) or darken (by moving the slider to the right).

Multiple Color Corrections with Levels

Often, pictures taken at the same time will share the same problems. Whether it was bad lighting, bad processing, bad storage, or simply bad luck, you can save time and effort by fixing one, then applying that same adjustment to the rest.

The images in **figure 4.34** were all taken at the same event, and all suffer from the same unfortunate lighting. By using a Levels adjustment layer on one, then sharing that same adjustment layer with the others, I was able to fix all four, as seen in **figure 4.35**, without four times the work.

⊕⟩⟨ ch04_costumeparty.jpg

BEFORE

AFTER

figure 4.34

figure 4.35

1. First we need to adjust one of the images using the Auto Color Correction technique addressed previously. Add a Levels Adjustment Layer and click Auto. As **figure 4.36** shows, the initial Auto Color setting is rather good, but we can still improve the image with one more click.

2. We have an ideal neutral reference source to work with—the white wall in the background. Notice how the right side is still slightly green? By clicking the wall with the gray Levels eyedropper, the last hint of the colorcast is removed as seen in **figure 4.37**.

figure 4.36

Using only Auto Color.

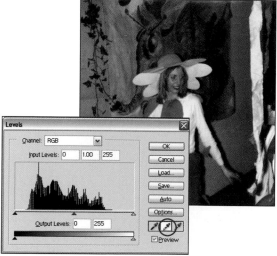

figure 4.37

Correcting the color by clicking on the white wall with the midtone eyedropper.

3. Click OK to accept the image correction.

4. Without closing your corrected image, open another of the problem images and drag the adjustment layer from the corrected image onto the second image, as in **figure 4.38**. This applies the same correction to the new image.

figure 4.38

Dragging the adjustment layer to a new image.

Subtle Color and Exposure Improvement with Curves

Not all images have overwhelming or obvious color casts. In fact, some images require a delicate touch to remove the color cast and adjust exposure. In this example, the photograph is off just a bit—meaning that it is only slightly too dark and red (see **figure 4.39**) In this example, I set new black, white, and gray points and improved the exposure with a Curves Adjustment Layer, and then fine-tuned the overall saturation with a Hue/Saturation Adjustment Layer. These changes, shown in **figure 4.40**, enable you to appreciate the beauty of the young woman.

figure 4.39

figure 4.40

⊕⍰⊳▷⫶ **ch4_flowergirl.jpg**

1. Add a Curves Adjustment Layer. Use the white eyedropper to set the wall just above her flower to white, the black eyedropper to set the shadow beneath her chin to black, and the gray eyedropper to set the wall in the upper left as neutral gray (see **figure 4.41**).

figure 4.41

Setting new white, black, and gray points using the Curves eyedropper.

2. Boost the shadows and midtones by dragging the center of the curve upward to lighten the image and add the sparkle of a well-exposed photograph (see **figure 4.42**). Be careful to monitor the highlights on the girl's skin and flower in the Info palette so they are not forced to pure white.

figure 4.42

Lighten the image with Curves.

3. Not all portraits require the following step, but in this instance the teenager's tanned arms are over saturated and visually distracting. To reduce the saturation, I added a Hue/Saturation Adjustment Layer and decreased the overall saturation by –25, as seen in **figure 4.43**.

Using the gradient tool set to default black and white, I drew a gradient on the Hue/Saturation layer mask to shield the face from the desaturation, as shown in **figure 4.44**.

figure 4.43

Decreasing the saturation reduces the heavy orange cast.

figure 4.44

Taking advantage of the layer mask to control where the change takes place.

Using Curves with Luminosity

In most cases, using the target eyedroppers in Levels or Curves is an excellent method for removing color casts and adjust image contrast. But as with all good things, sometimes they do add unwanted density or saturation. To avoid the unwanted punch, combine the power of a Levels or Curves Adjustment Layer with the Luminosity Blending Mode, as shown in **figures 4.45** and **4.46**.

figure 4.47

Using eyedroppers and a Curves adjustment makes the image too saturated.

2. Changing the Blending Mode of the Curves Adjustment Layer to Luminosity as seen in **figure 4.48** offsets the unwanted saturation while maintaining the neutral tonal values. Toggle the Blending Mode from Luminosity to Normal to appreciate the difference.

© Katrin Eismann

BEFORE

figure 4.45

AFTER

figure 4.46

⊕⇨ **ch4_flowerpot.jpg**

1. I used the Curves black, gray, and white eyedroppers on the areas indicated in **figure 4.47** and opened up the exposure with one Curves adjustment. This added too much false saturation to the clay pot.

figure 4.48

Changing the Adjustment Layer Blending Mode to Luminosity lessens the false saturation.

THE NUMBERS DON'T LIE

You're tired, had a fight with the dog, the kids played with the monitor dials, and you're just not sure what the original image really looked like. Many factors, including your mood, age, gender, and the second drink last night, can influence your color vision. So what are you supposed to do if the files are piling up and you have to get them done before going home tonight? When in doubt, do your color correction by the numbers to balance images with a mathematician's precision.

Working by the numbers entails monitoring the values in the shadows, midtones, highlights, and skin tones while you adjust individual color channels with Levels or Curves. When the highlight, midtone, and shadow RGB values are equal, your color cast problems will disappear. Working with skin tones (also called *flesh tones*) takes a bit more interpretation because people's skin varies with age, race, and sun exposure (this is addressed in a later section, titled "Balancing Skin Tones with Curves").

T i p

Here are some specifics for color correcting by the numbers with RGB files:

- To balance highlights: Use the highest value in the Info palette as the target and match the lower values to the higher.

- To balance midtones: Use the middle value as the target (as read in the Info palette) and match the higher and lower values to the middle one.

- To balance shadows: Use the lowest value as the target (as read in the Info palette) and match the higher values to the lower.

Balancing Neutral Tones with Levels

Color correction by the numbers always begins with you identifying reference points. Look for a highlight, a neutral midtone, and a shadow point to reference. In the following example, I used the cat's forehead for the highlight reference point, a shadow on the railing as the midtone reference,

and the shadows under the railing as a dark reference point. In the example in **figure 4.49**, the carpet is making kitty blue. After a color correction, she looks very contented, as shown in **figure 4.50**.

figure 4.49

figure 4.50

⊕ᐅᐸ **ch4_bluecat.jpg**

1. Add Color Samplers to the highlight (forehead), the shadow (darkest shadow under the railing) midtone (shadow on the top railing) as reference areas, as shown in **figure 4.51**.

2. Add a Levels Adjustment Layer. To eliminate the color cast in the highlights, the three RGB values should all be made equal by matching the two lower values to the highest value. In this example, the 187 readout of the Red channel is the highest value and will be the target number to match.

figure 4.51

Adding the Color Sampler reference points. The readout of the #1 Color Sampler is measuring and monitoring the image highlights. The lower green and blue values reveal the color cast.

3. In the Levels dialog box, I selected the channel with the lowest highlight value, the blue channel, and lowered the highlight value (the field farthest to the right) by tapping the down-arrow key until it matched the target of 187 in the Info Palette readout (see **figure 4.52**). This does not change the Input level in the Levels dialog box to 187, but rather adjusts the Input Level until the number for the blue channel in the Info palette reads 187.

figure 4.52

Increase the blue channel highlight value to balance the highlights.

4. I then selected the green channel, placed the mouse cursor in the highlight field, and tapped the down arrow until the green value in the Info palette was 187, as shown in **figure 4.53**. Again, be sure to look at the numbers in the Info palette and match the two lower values to the highest value.

figure 4.53

Increase the green highlight value to balance the highlights.

5. When balancing shadows (marked by Color Sampler #2), use the lowest number as your target. In this example, the red values are the lowest, and I reduced the green and blue values a touch to match the target value of 4. Select the green channel and click in the Input Levels shadows box, and use the arrow keys to raise the green shadow to match the target of 4. Repeat on the blue channel to match the target of 4.

6. To balance the neutral areas, I worked with the midtone target values (on the top railing) by changing the midtone value (marked by Color Sampler #3) to match the median value of 114. In this example, I matched the red and blue channels to the 114 value of the green channel. Click in the Input Levels midtones box, and adjust the value by tapping the arrow keys.

7. Finally, I opened up the midtones by moving the composite (RGB) midtone slider to the left just a bit, as shown in figure 4.54.

figure 4.54

Open up the midtones by moving the midtone RGB slider to the left.

After adjusting the highlights and then moving on to the midtones or shadows, you may notice that the highlight values change again. This may happen because Photoshop is referencing the color settings in the Color Preferences and is adjusting the highlight to reflect your color settings. If the highlights are within 1–2 points of one another, the print will be neutral. When I use this technique, I lay more value on the highlights versus the shadows, and I keep an eye on the highlights more fastidiously.

You may be wondering why I just didn't use a Levels or Curves adjustment layer and click the cat's forehead with the white eyedropper. But doing that would have forced the cat's fur to a very light white and I would have lost a lot of the white fur detail, as you see in figure 4.55.

figure 4.55

Using the Levels white target eyedropper on areas that need to maintain tonal detail may force the area to paper base white, which is undesirable.

Balancing Skin Tones with Curves

Most of the recognized color values for reproducing skin tones are based on prepress experience and are therefore expressed in CMYK values. The schematic in figure 4.56 shows that at one end of the spectrum the skin of a light baby has equal amounts of yellow and magenta without any cyan or black. Moving to the other end, as people mature, the amount of yellow increases in relationship to the magenta. The tanner or darker they are, the higher the amount of cyan ink is. The far end of the spectrum represents people of African descent with the additional black ink needed to accurately represent darker skin.

Here are some specifics for color correcting by the numbers on skin tones in CMYK files:

- In light-skinned babies and young people, yellow and magenta are equal.
- In adults, yellow is up one-fifth to one-third greater than magenta.
- Cyan is around one-fifth to one-third lower than magenta value and makes people look tanner and darker.

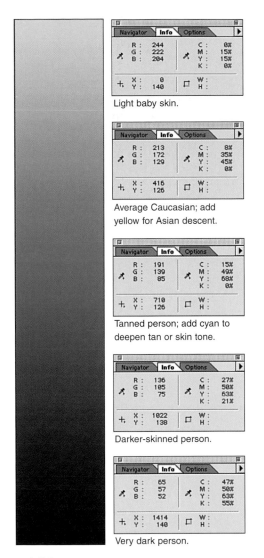

Light baby skin.

Average Caucasian; add yellow for Asian descent.

Tanned person; add cyan to deepen tan or skin tone.

Darker-skinned person.

Very dark person.

figure 4.56

CMYK *representation of skin tones is shown here.*

- Only people with very dark skin should have noticeable amounts of black ink in their skin tones.

- Find the cyan value; magenta should be double that of cyan, and yellow should be around one-fifth to one-third higher than magenta (20c 40m 50y).

As Dan Margulis explained in the online ColorTheory discussion group, "Persons of Hispanic or Asian ancestries tend to share approximately the same range, which is roughly the same as the dark half of the Caucasian population. Persons in these ethnic groups always have significantly more yellow than magenta, normally 10 to 15 points. Cyan plus black tends to be one-quarter to one-third of the magenta value, occasionally higher in the case of unusually dark or very tan skin."

"The ethnicity loosely known as black or African-American has a much wider range of possibilities than any other. Cyan is usually at least one-third of the magenta value but there is no upper limit and there may also be significant black ink. In the case of someone with light ("coffee-colored") skin, the yellow is significantly higher than the magenta. However, unlike other ethnicities, as the skintone gets darker, the variation between magenta and yellow decreases, so that in the case of a very dark-skinned person, the values would be almost equal."

Visit www.retouchpro.com to download Bruce Beard's skin and hair color reference charts, as shown in figure 4.57.

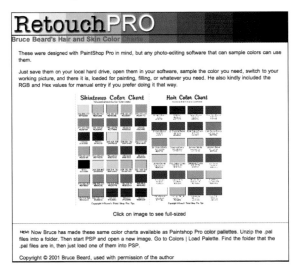

Figure 4.57

Download Bruce Beard's skin and hair color charts.

Color correction in RGB is dependent on the Photoshop color space in which you are working. If you use the wrong working space, the numbers may look awful even though they should be correct. I personally have had fewer problems with skin tones when using ColorMatch RGB because it has a narrower color gamut and is less saturated.

When color correcting skin tones in RGB, keep the following in mind:

- Red is the opposite of cyan, and it will be the highest color component.

- Green is the opposite of magenta, and it will be one-fifth to one-quarter lower than red.

- Blue is the opposite of yellow, and it will be the lowest value—anywhere from one-third to one-half the value of the red values.

- The lighter-skinned the person is, the closer to equal these RGB values will be, with red being slightly higher.

- The darker-skinned the person is, the lower the blue values will be.

 T i p

These tips will help you when working with portrait color correction and retouching:

- When correcting in RGB, set the Info palette's second readout to CMYK and watch the relationships between the two color modes.

- To get an overall feel for the skin tones of a person, measure an average medium value on the person's face. Avoid dark shadows and extreme highlights.

- A woman's make-up can distort the readout. Try to avoid areas that have a lot of make-up, such as cheeks, lips, and eyes.

- Collect patches of various skin tones (see figure 4.58). Select a color-corrected patch of skin, run the Gaussian Blur on it to destroy any vestige of film grain, copy it, and create a file with various skin tone swatches. Refer to these skin colors when color correcting and during advanced portrait retouching sessions.

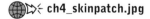 **ch4_skinpatch.jpg**

figure 4.58

A collection of blurred skin samples can be used as a reference for color correction.

In figure 4.59, the original picture suffers from a color problem, but I'm not even sure what the problem is. In fact, there are many times when I can't seem to identify the problem, which is exactly when I rely on the Info palette and the color correction by the numbers technique to create a pleasing image (see figure 4.60).

figure 4.59

figure 4.60

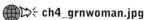 **ch4_grnwoman.jpg**

1. Start by clicking the Eyedropper in the tool-bar, drag down to the Color Sampler tool, and add three Color Samplers to the image: one on the lightest part of the sweater, and two on the skin (one on the cheek and one on the neck), as shown in **figure 4.61**. The reason for the one on the neck is that there is rarely make-up there.

figure 4.61

Thoughtful placement of Color Samplers is an essential first step for any critical color correction.

2. Next, add a Curves Adjustment Layer and click Color Sampler #1 with the white eye-dropper. This defines a neutral value and sets the highlight to the correct printing density, as shown in **figure 4.62**.

figure 4.62

Clicking the whitest highlight that still contains detail with the white eyedropper.

3. I looked at Color Samples #2 and #3 on the Info palette and saw that there was too much yellow and not enough magenta in the skin-tones. To target the exact skin values you want to correct, activate the curve that needs adjusting. In this case, I started with the yel-low curve, moved the mouse into the image, and (Cmd + clicked) [Ctrl + clicked] the area in the image to add a handle onto the curve, as shown in **figure 4.63**.

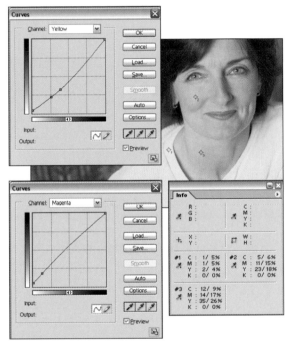

figure 4.63

Using the individual yellow and magenta curves to correct the skintones.

4. By pulling the yellow curve down, I reduced the yellow, and on the magenta curves, I increased magenta to remove the green color cast and make the woman look healthier.

Tip

While in the Curves dialog box, (Cmd + click) [Ctrl + click] the area that you want to change to add a handle to the curve that you can manipu-late with the mouse or the arrow keys.

Pressing Ctrl + Tab on both platforms will move from point to point on the curve.

5. Finally I lightened the overall exposure using the composite (CMYK) channel, as shown in **figure 4.64**.

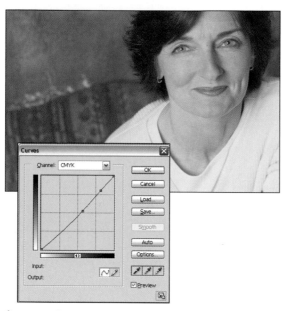

figure 4.64

A *final tweak of the exposure using the composite channel.*

Combining CMYK and RGB

Scanners and digital cameras capture image data in RGB; therefore, many of your images will be in RGB. As mentioned, many of the known skin-color values are in CMYK. Color correction in CMYK offers you the additional control of being able to change the black plate and, in the case of skin tones, the cyan plate, which, if it is too high, can make a person look pasty. I am not recommending converting an RGB file to CMYK, making the color corrections, and then converting back to RGB. Unnecessary mode changes should be avoided to reduce rounding errors and file decimation. But there is a way to color correct a portrait in CMYK that results in an RGB file without image degradation. The portrait in **figure 4.65** is the original image captured with a Nikon D1x as an RGB file, and **figure 4.66** is an RGB file that was corrected in CMYK without converting the original file to CMYK.

figure 4.65

figure 4.66

In this example, the skin tones have too much yellow, as the Info palette readout reveals in **figure 4.67**. The yellow is 50% higher than the magenta.

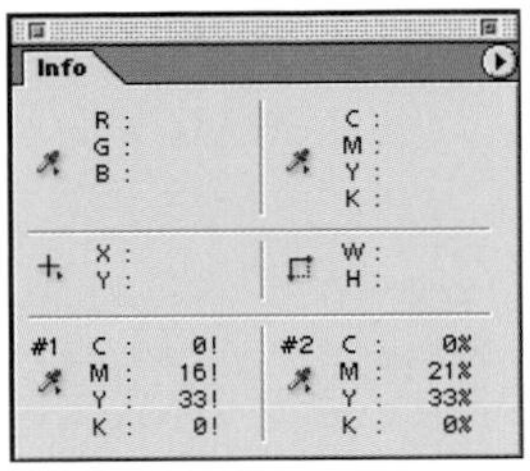

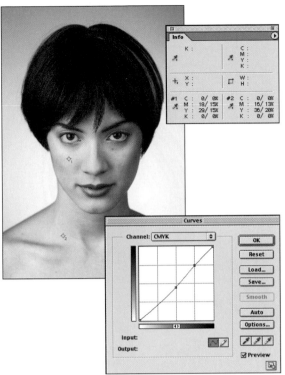

figure 4.67

The Info palette shows the skin tones are too yellow.

1. Select Image > Duplicate, and then Image > Mode > CMYK. Working on this duplicate file, I dropped down to the yellow curve and added a handle by (Cmd + clicking) [Ctrl + clicking] the woman's cheek. I moved this handle down to reduce the yellow (see figure 4.68).

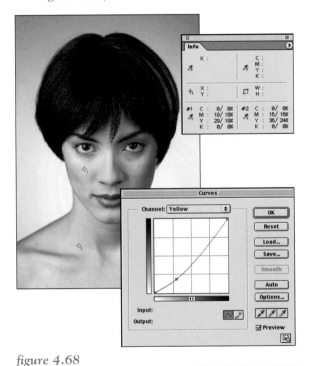

figure 4.68

Reducing yellow with Curves.

2. I returned to the composite CMYK curve to lighten the exposure slightly, as seen in figure 4.69. Because you can't drag Adjustment Layers between files that don't have the same color mode, you need to use the sneaky method of flattening the CMYK file, selecting all, and then selecting Edit > Copy.

figure 4.69

Lightening the exposure with Curves.

3. Activate the original RGB file and select Edit > Paste, which will paste the color-corrected file back into the RGB file and you will have two very similar files—one in RGB (on the left in figure 4.70) and one that was corrected in CMYK (on the right).

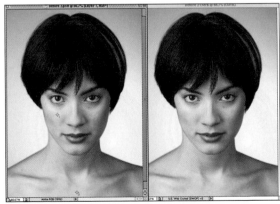

figure 4.70

Viewing RGB and CMYK versions side by side.

4. To maintain the original luminosity values of the RGB file, change the pasted layer's Blending Mode to Color, as **figure 4.71** shows. The end result is a color-corrected file in RGB that you can continue working with.

figure 4.72

A portrait in Adobe RGB 1998 working color space.

figure 4.71

Changing the corrected layer's Blending Mode to Color to maintain image tonality.

Assigning False Color Profiles

When working in RGB with printing in mind, the two most common Color working spaces are ColorMatch and Adobe RGB 1998. Adobe RGB has a larger color gamut, which I find useful for creative artwork and for producing photographic output, such as the Kodak Durst Lambda and Fujix prints. ColorMatch has a narrower gamut that better reflects offset printing, such as the book you're reading right now.

You can influence how Photoshop describes and portrays color by assigning color profiles of the Photoshop working spaces. The next time you open an image—especially a color portrait—and the person looks too saturated or red (like the one in **figure 4.72**), try this technique to reduce the saturation and red-to-magenta color shifts.

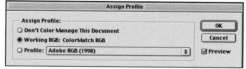

figure 4.73

Assigning the ColorMatch profile to reduce image saturation.

⊕⊳⊱ ch4_profile.jpg

Select Image > Mode > Assign Profile, as shown in **figure 4.73**, and select ColorMatch. The image's color gamut is quickly brought within the smaller color gamut of ColorMatch and the over saturated—almost sunburnt look—disappears.

SELECTIVE COLOR CORRECTION

Until now, you've worked on global color correction, but images can have different problems in different areas. Sometimes one part of the image will be fine and another area is way off color. Differing color casts can occur due to poor storage conditions, mixed lighting when the photo was originally taken, or misprocessing. Always start with the global color correction, and then select the problem areas that remain and apply local color correction.

Targeting the Problem Color

In figure 4.74, the color cast is rather subtle, but the lower blue readout in the Info palette reveals that the neutral tone of the studio background does have a yellow cast. Another way to see color casts is to look at the individual grayscale channels. Because the studio background is supposed to be neutral gray, all three color channels should have the same black density. As you can see in figure 4.75, the red and green channels are almost balanced with 66% and 68% density, but the blue channel is only at 54%. Wherever the channel is lighter, more light is allowed through, creating a color cast.

Red channel, 66

Green channel, 68

Blue channel, 54

figure 4.75

Checking the balance of individual channels.

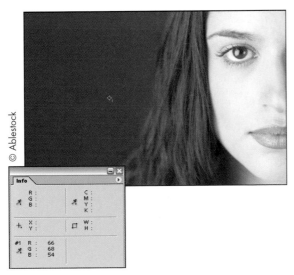

© Ablestock

figure 4.74

The Info palette reveals a subtle yellow color cast.

At first I thought this would be a simple file to color correct; just add either a Curves or Levels Adjustment Layer, use the gray balance Eyedropper tool to click the neutral background to remove the color cast, and I'd be done. But after neutralizing the backdrop, I noticed that the young woman was still much too yellow (see **figure 4.76**), and the challenge remained to select only the yellow to achieve a balanced image, as shown in **figure 4.77**.

figure 4.76

The skin tones are too yellow.

figure 4.77

The final balanced image.

📀▷𝄓 **ch4_yellowport.jpg**

1. I added a Curves Adjustment Layer and clicked the studio backdrop with the gray eyedropper to neutralize the overall color cast. As you can see in **figure 4.78**, the young woman's skin is still too yellow.

figure 4.78

Even after neutralizing the backdrop by clicking with the gray eyedropper, her skin tones are still too yellow.

2. The yellow problem isn't on the Adjustment Layer, but rather on the Background layer. Always work on the layer that contains the problem, which in this case is the yellow cast remaining in the Background layer. Activate the Background layer.

3. To select just the yellow components of the image, I chose Select > Color Range and selected Yellows from the drop-down menu, as shown in **figure 4.79**. The Color Range interface shows how Photoshop is making a selection mask that we can use in combination with any type of Adjustment Layer.

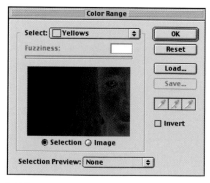

figure 4.79

With the Background layer active, select the yellows with Color Range.

4. Photoshop may pop up a warning box that says that no pixels were selected more than 50%. You can ignore this warning, because the selection will still be active. Photoshop just won't display the dancing ants!

5. I added a Curves Adjustment Layer (see figure 4.80). In the Layers palette, a mask is automatically created from the Color Range selection. Wherever the mask is black, no color correction will take place, and wherever it is white or lighter, more color correction will occur.

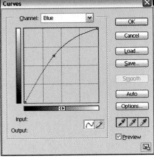

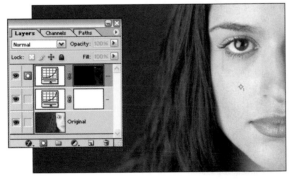

figure 4.80

Adding a Curves Adjustment Layer automatically creates a layer mask based on the selection.

6. I switched to the blue curve (because blue is the opposite of yellow) and dragged it upward to remove the yellow color cast. Then I adjusted the green curve. Although these curve adjustments may look extreme, the mask makes the effect much more subtle, as seen in figure 4.81.

7. Finally, to intensify the effect, I changed the Blending Mode to Multiply. Please note—you may not need to change the layer Blending Mode in all cases.

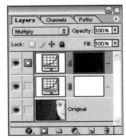

figure 4.81

I adjusted the blue and green curves to remove yellow, and then changed the Blending Mode to Multiply.

ALLEVIATING EXTREME COLOR PROBLEMS

Color-correction issues can range from subtle to extreme, and sometimes correcting very bad images may seem like a daunting task. In the following section, you tackle some of the worst color problems quickly and relatively painlessly.

Sometimes an image is so dark or discolored that you're just not sure what to fix first. Should you tackle the density issue or the heavy color cast first? There is not a single solution that always applies, but in many cases images that are both very dark and color contaminated can benefit from the following treatment to remove heavy color casts caused by age, smoke damage, or underexposed images taken in mixed lighting. The photograph in **figure 4.82** was taken in 1912. The nine decades that followed made the print darken down and absorb contaminants from the cardboard it was mounted on. **Figure 4.83** shows the same image with the undesirable color cast and dark exposure removed.

© Colin Dearing

BEFORE

figure 4.82

AFTER

figure 4.83

🌐⤳✂ **ch4_soccerteam.jpg**

1. Open the problem image and add a Levels Adjustment Layer.

2. Activate the red channel (Cmd + 1) [Ctrl + 1] and move the shadow and highlight levels sliders to where the majority of the information begins, as shown in **figure 4.84**.

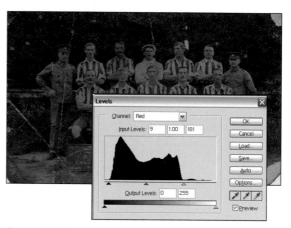

figure 4.84

Moving the red channel shadow and highlight sliders.

3. Select the green channel (Cmd + 2) [Ctrl + 2], and move the shadow and highlight levels sliders to where the majority of the information begins, as shown in **figure 4.85**. Repeat the process on the blue channel (Cmd + 3) [Ctrl + 3] Levels histogram.

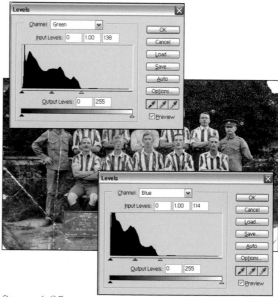

figure 4.85

Adjusting the green and blue channel histograms.

4. If the image requires lightening or darkening, return to the composite histogram (Cmd + ~) [Ctrl + ~] and adjust the midtone slider (to the left to lighten the image, or to the right to darken), as shown in **figure 4.86**.

figure 4.86

Darkening the image by moving the midtone slider to the right.

Extreme Color Correction with Levels

I sincerely hope you never have to work with an image that is as bad as the one in **figure 4.87**. The original film was poorly stored and processed, resulting in a very dark image with a dominant green cast. In a case like this, the goal is to take the pathetic and create the acceptable, as shown in **figure 4.88**.

As discussed, identifying the color cast is always the first step in the color correction process. In this case, your eyes would have to be closed not to see the green problem, but take a moment to really look at the image. What is this a picture of? It's a woman standing by a wall. Look again—read the image more closely—and look for clues that will help you make the best color decisions. The straw hat and open midriff hint that it's a picture of a woman on a summer day. With that clue, you can imagine that the dress could have been white. Keeping this scenario in mind will guide your color correction. Use your visual memory and color perception to develop a scenario to guide your color correction.

figure 4.87

figure 4.88

ch4_greenwoman.jpg

1. Add a Levels Adjustment Layer. The strong color contamination and tonal problems push the histogram severely to the left (see figure 4.89).

figure 4.89

The Levels histogram is strongly biased to the left—a dead giveaway for a dark or underexposed image.

2. Look for a point in her dress that could be pure white. See how the sun is coming down from the upper left and hitting the edge of her skirt that is in the breeze? Click that with the Levels white eyedropper to remove the color cast, as shown in **figure 4.90**.

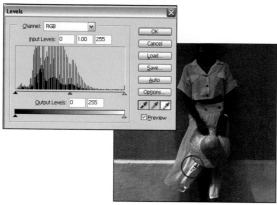

figure 4.90

Clicking with the white eyedropper eliminates the color cast.

3. If need be, open up the midtones of the image by sliding the gray midtone triangle carefully to the left (see **figure 4.91**). In this example, don't worry that her face is still too dark; that is a selective problem and shouldn't be treated while working on the global problem.

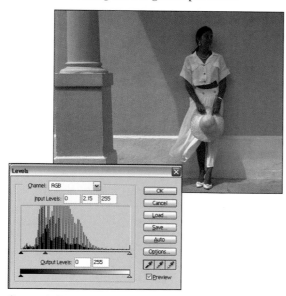

figure 4.91

Moving the midtone slider to the left lightens the image.

 T i p

You can zoom and pan while the Levels and Curves windows are open by using the following command keys:

- Pan in the image: Hold down the spacebar to access the Hand tool.

- Zoom in: Press (Cmd + Space + click) [Ctrl + Space + click]. (Cmd + "+") [Ctrl "+"].

- Zoom out: Press (Cmd + Option + Space + click)[Ctrl + Alt + Space + click]. (Cmd + "-") [Ctrl "-"].

 T i p

Sometimes it's just easier to start over. When you are working with Adjustment Layers, if you don't like where the color correction is going, you can get back to the original image by pressing (Option) [Alt] to change the Cancel button to Reset. Click and the image will revert to its original settings.

CORRECTING COLOR TEMPERATURE PROBLEMS

As I mentioned earlier, color casts can happen when you use the wrong color temperature film for the lighting situation at hand. For example, using daylight film indoors can lead to green or orange pictures. Our eyes don't see color temperature while taking the photograph, because our brain balances light to white no matter how cool or warm the light really is, but these color casts show up on film.

In the following example, I was photographing in a museum in England. I had only daylight film and the museum was illuminated with fluorescent lighting fixtures—a lethally green combination, as **figure 4.92** shows. With a few Photoshop steps, I was able to change the color temperature of the file from fluorescent green to neutral daylight, as you see in **figure 4.93**. A useful correction method is to compensate for the undesired color temperature of the light by filtering the image with the opposite color.

figure 4.92

figure 4.93

 ch4_grnknight.jpg

Note

It is always better to use either the right color temperature film for the task at hand or to filter the lens or your lights to balance the color temperature. As I've said many times before, if the picture is taken correctly, there will be less work to do on the computer, and a smaller chance of unnatural results. However, this often requires professional equipment, including a color meter, color correction filters, and gels that you might not have on hand.

1. Use the Eyedropper tool to sample an area that is midtone to highlight and contains the offending color cast (see figure 4.94).

2. Add a new layer to the image and fill it with the sampled color using Edit > Fill > Foreground Color.

3. Change the layer's Blending Mode to Color.

4. Invert the color by selecting Image > Adjustments > Invert or (Cmd + I) [Ctrl + I] to change the selected offending color into its opposite.

figure 4.94

Select the offending color with the Eyedropper tool.

5. Lower the opacity of the layer. My experience has taught me that 50% is effective, as shown in figure 4.95.

6. In some cases, you might need to boost the contrast with Curves, as shown in figure 4.96.

figure 4.95

Lower the opacity of the fill layer.

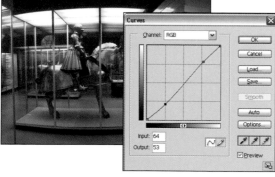

figure 4.96

Fine-tune the image contrast with Curves.

An alternative to this method builds on it while adding richness to the image. Follow steps 1 through 4 and continue by double-clicking the Color layer to access the advanced Blending Options shown in figure 4.97. Uncheck red and blue, leaving only green. After clicking OK, you can duplicate this layer and adjust the opacity to intensify the correction (see figure 4.98).

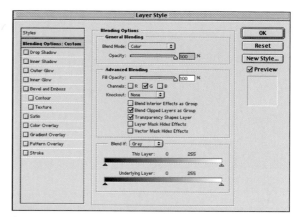

figure 4.97

Uncheck red and blue in the advanced Blending Options.

figure 4.98

Duplicate the layer and the adjust opacity to intensify the correction.

Correcting Mixed Color Temperature

There are many times when you have to take pictures in mixed lighting situations—such as an office with fluorescent ceiling lights while the windows are letting in daylight or, as shown in figure 4.99, a room where the majority of the space is lit with tungsten light but the uppermost ceiling floods are fluorescent. Photographs with mixed lighting are confusing to our eyes, as our eyes naturally neutralize color temperature without us being aware of it. To correct for the mixed lighting, Mark Beckelman worked selectively to create the image in figure 4.100.

figure 4.99

figure 4.101

Selecting the color-contaminated area.

figure 4.100

figure 4.102

Creating a color filter to offset the blue light.

1. After scanning in the 4×5-inch color negative and doing initial global exposure correction, Mark needed to correct the blue of the faux skylights.

2. He started by sampling the blue of area with the Eyedropper tool. Then he selected the area with the Pen tool and converted the path to a selection, as shown in figure 4.101.

3. After adding a new layer, Mark filled the active selection with the blue and then inverted the color by selecting Image > Adjustments > Invert. After reducing the opacity to 50% and changing the Blending Mode to Color, he had filtered the blue color contamination out of the photograph, as shown in figure 4.102.

4. Being the careful professional that he is, Mark opted to reduce the slight green tinge in the tablecloths by first carefully selecting them, as shown in figure 4.103. Upon adding a Levels Adjustment Layer, he reduced just the green midtones of the selected areas by modifying the green channel values in the Levels Adjustment layer (see figure 4.104).

figure 4.103

Selecting just the tablecloths.

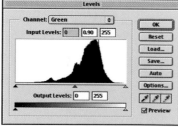

figure 4.104

Fine-tuning by removing just the green midtones in the selected area.

Thinking Ahead with a Macbeth Target

When you are photographing in mixed lighting conditions, it can be difficult to identify a neutral area in the image. But with a bit of planning ahead and the ability to drag Adjustment Layers, you can color balance even the trickiest images with astounding ease.

Figure 4.105 shows a photo I took in a crafts boutique. The two most apparent aspects to the image are the awful orange color cast caused by the tungsten lights on the candle display and the Macbeth ColorChecker in the image. The Macbeth target is a known reference in printing and photography, and it is produced to careful specifications. You can purchase them as letter size or in a smaller 4×5-inch size in professional camera stores or at www.calumetphoto.com. For color balancing, the white to gray to black row of squares is of great use.

© Katrin Eismann

figure 4.105

Photo with and without the Macbeth ColorChecker.

⊕⊳⊱ **ch4_macbeth1.jpg**

⊕⊳⊱ **ch4_macbeth2.jpg**

1. Compose and light the subject.

2. Place the Macbeth ColorChecker into the picture and take a picture with the same exposure you'll use for the rest of the shoot.

3. Remove the Macbeth ColorChecker from the set and shoot the photo as you normally would.

4. Bring both images into Photoshop and add a Levels or Curves Adjustment Layer to the image with the color checker. With the gray eyedropper, click the third gray square, as circled in **figure 4.106**, and use the white eyedropper to click the white square. In some cases, I also use the black eyedropper on the black square, but it isn't always necessary.

5. With the Move tool, drag the Levels Adjustment Layer from the first image to the second image. This applies the target color-corrected adjustment to the image (see **figure 4.107**). Best of all, you won't need to guess at what may or may not be neutral in the image.

figure 4.107

Applying the neutral adjustment layer to the "real" image.

If you don't have a Macbeth ColorChecker, you can experiment with this technique with a Kodak step wedge or another known reference card that has a white, neutral gray, and black area.

INTERCHANNEL COLOR CORRECTION

Photoshop offers many different perspectives for retouching. For example, my photographic training allows me to work out imaging solutions from a photographic and darkroom perspective, whereas people with a lot of prepress and printing experience will approach Photoshop from a different point of view. As I was working on this book, I had the pleasure of having my Photoshop eyes opened by Chris Tarantino, who comes to Photoshop with 20 years of dot-etching and high-end prepress experience.

When Chris looks at a CMYK file, the first thing he looks at is the flesh tones. As Chris explains, "When the flesh looks good, the viewer will be attracted to the product." His color correction process always starts by evaluating the individual color channels for tone, gradation, and transitions that he can take advantage of to shape the color of an image. Rather than working with Adjustment Layers, Chris does all his color correction through the Apply Image command. The Apply Image command allows you to mix varying amounts of different channels with each other with precise control.

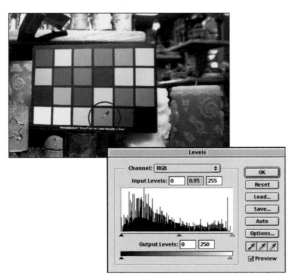

figure 4.106

Clicking the gray and white squares to neutralize the color cast caused by the mixed lighting in the store.

In the following example, Chris color corrected the photograph of the model for a very demanding high-quality import catalog. As you can see in **figure 4.108**, the model's skin tones are too ruddy and, due to lack of tonal separation, the clothing is disappearing into the background. After applying inter-channel color correction, the model's face is clear, and the sweater has been color corrected to match the merchandise, as shown in **figure 4.109**. Chris creates selection masks for each image element.

Chris always starts with the skin tones, and upon inspecting the four channels (shown in **figure 4.110**), he saw that the magenta channel was too dark, blocked up, and lacking in detail. However, the cyan channel had a full range of gray throughout that he could use to add tone and detail to the magenta plate.

figure 4.108

figure 4.109

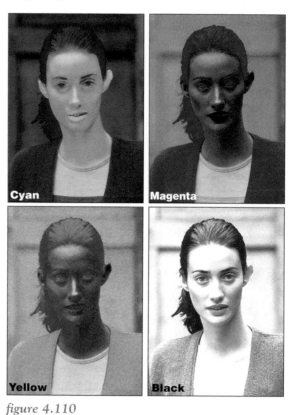

figure 4.110

Chris starts by looking for detail, gradation, and information in each of the individual color channels.

Chris selected Image > Apply Image and, as shown in **figure 4.111**, he blended 25% of the cyan channel into the magenta channel. Interestingly enough, he used the magenta channel to mask itself out by checking Mask and Invert. Wherever the magenta channel had been dark, it would now be light, and the cyan grayscale information could be added to provide tonal detail for her face.

By using the better channel to replace the weaker one, Chris can simultaneously apply color correction and build up tonal and detail information, as you see in figure 4.112.

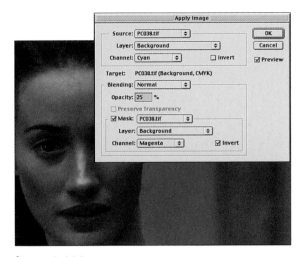

figure 4.111

Chris uses the Apply Image command to add good cyan grayscale information to the weaker magenta plate.

figure 4.112

After improving both the magenta and yellow color plates, the model's skin is much clearer.

CLOSING THOUGHTS

The importance of good color—pleasing color—cannot be underestimated. Trying out the techniques in this chapter on your own images will teach you more than any book. So open up some images and learn to really see color, both to remove it and to accentuate it—it's all-important.

III

Essential Restoration, Repairing,
and Rebuilding Techniques

5

**DUST, MOLD, AND
TEXTURE REMOVAL**   **137**

6

DAMAGE CONTROL AND REPAIR   **165**

7

**REBUILDING, REARRANGING,
AND RE-CREATING PORTRAITS**   **183**

8

**REFINING AND POLISHING
THE IMAGE**   **223**

5

DUST, MOLD, AND TEXTURE REMOVAL

Cleanliness is next to godliness, and without start-ing a religious debate, I am sure you agree with me that the bane of all retouchers is dust, mold, moiré patterns, print texture, and film grain. Removing these problems can be a time-consuming, eye-straining, arm-numbing endeavor that can really take the fun out of digital retouching. In this chapter, you face the worst problems and learn the best techniques for rescuing your images from the evils that lurk in historical negatives, glass plates, prints, contemporary film, and digital images.

The problems tackled in this chapter include

- Removing dust, mold, and scratches
- Minimizing moiré patterns and paper texture
- Reducing digital camera color artifacts

These are the tools used to conquer these dusty and dirty challenges:

- Layers and Blending Modes
- The Clone Stamp tool
- The Healing Brush and Patch tool
- Photoshop filters

So roll up your mousing sleeve, and let's get to work.

Depending on the severity of the problem, you can use numerous Photoshop techniques, many interchangeably or in combination, to clean up dust and mold. My favorite technique is to avoid the problem in the first place by cleaning the negative, print, or scanner before making the scan. By carefully brushing or blowing loose dust off a negative or print, you're removing the source of the problem. Never rub film, prints, or scanner platens very hard because you can scratch and permanently damage them.

Because there isn't one perfect method to remove dust specks or to reduce mold damage, this chapter includes a variety of methods to tackle these problems. Dust problems are most often seen as very small specks of dark or light pixels, and mold damage looks mottled, patterned, or discolored and affects larger areas. By experimenting with or combining methods, you'll develop techniques to take care of your image's worst problems.

DUSTBUSTING 101

An important concept to recognize is that there is no dust in a digital file. The dust was on or in the original. In the digital file, all you really have is lighter or darker pixels in contrast to darker or lighter backgrounds. Taking advantage of this concept can speed up your dustbusting sessions.

The Float and Move Technique

Use the float and move technique on unimportant image areas such as skies or backgrounds to quickly disguise dust on large surfaces. Duplicating a troublesome area with a slight offset and applying a Lighten Blending Mode (to remove dark spots and Darken Blending Mode to remove light specks) is a quick and easy way to remove many flaws. I first heard about this technique from Stephen Johnson (www.sjphoto.com) as he was retouching numerous glass plate negatives for his wonderful book, *The Great Central Valley* (University of California, 1998).

Figure 5.1 and **figure 5.2** show before and after detail of the identical area that was cleaned up with the float and move technique. Notice how the dust

and mold has been minimized in the right wall. Because I didn't float and move any important image areas such as the woman's face, they still have dust and damage that will require individual attention later in the retouching process.

© Eismann family archive

BEFORE

figure 5.1

AFTER

figure 5.2

T i p

To make your dustbusting time as short as possible, squelch the temptation to tediously remove dust spots with the Clone Stamp or the Healing Brush tool. The idea is to spend the least amount of time on unimportant image areas and save your time and visual concentration for the important parts of the image. To remove the dust efficiently, use quick and easy methods on the unimportant image areas—in this case, the walls—which will save you time and energy to carefully remove the dust on the important areas: the woman's face and clothing.

⊕▷⌖ **ch5_erika.jpg**

1. Select the Lasso tool and set the Feather to 1 to 3 pixels. The amount of feather depends on your file size. A 10MB file needs a larger feather than a 1MB file.

2. Make a selection around the dusty areas, as shown in **figure 5.3**.

figure 5.3

Roughly selecting the dusty area helps hide any obvious edges on the wall after retouching.

3. Transfer this selection onto a new layer by selecting Layer > New > Layer via Copy (Cmd + J)[Ctrl + J].

4. Press V to select the Move tool and use the keyboard arrow keys to nudge the new layer down two pixels and two pixels to the right.

5. Change the moved layer's Blending Mode to Lighten to hide the dark spots (see figure 5.4).

figure 5.4

After moving the new layer, change the Blending Mode to Lighten to hide dust.

6. Activate the background layer and select the wall on the left side, as shown in **figure 5.5**.

figure 5.5

Selecting the left wall.

7. Select Layer > New > Layer via Copy (Cmd + J) [Ctrl + J]. Press V to select the Move tool and use the arrow keys to nudge the new layer down two pixels and two pixels to the right. Change the moved layer's Blending Mode to Lighten to hide the dark spots (see **figure 5.6**).

8. To use the Clone Stamp tool to remove the last dust specks, add a new layer at the top and name it *Dust Removal*.

figure 5.6

After moving the new layer, change the Blending Mode to Lighten to quickly hide the dust.

9. Set the Clone Stamp options to work in Normal mode at 100% Opacity and—most importantly—on the options bar, click Use All Layers. This tells the Clone Stamp tool to sample down through all visible layers.

10. Working on the dedicated Dust Removal layer, use the Clone Stamp tool as you usually would: (Option + click) [Alt + click] to sample good image areas and then clone over the dust, as shown in figure 5.7. In figure 5.8, I've turned off all layers except for the Dust Removal layer for you to see what it looks like.

11. To use the Healing Brush to clean up the final dust specs, add a new layer to the top of the layer stack. Then (Option) [Alt] Layer > Merge Visible and use a small hard Healing Brush to clean up the dust details. For detailed information on the Healing Brush, please see "To Clone or to Heal?" later in this chapter.

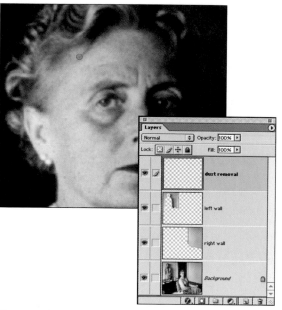

figure 5.7

Zoom in to see and carefully remove the dust on important image areas.

figure 5.8

The isolated Dust Removal layer.

 T i p

Matching the size of the brush to the size of the dust speck to be removed ensures that you don't overcorrect the image surrounding the dust speck. Use the keyboard shortcuts to control the size of the brushes:

- Left bracket ([) decreases brush size.
- Right bracket (]) increases brush size.

ERADICATING MOLD, MILDEW, AND FUNGUS

The best way to avoid mold, fungus, and mildew problems is to store your photographs in a humidity-controlled environment with a relative humidity of 65% or less. According to Henry Wilhelm's book, *The Permanence and Care of Color Photographs* (Preservation, 1993), the problem lies in the fact that "gelatin, the major component of the emulsion of films and prints, is unfortunately an excellent nutrient for fungi." To make matters worse, insects are attracted to fungus, and they're more than happy to munch on your valuable photographs, too.

To Clone or to Heal?

The Healing Brush in Photoshop 7 is a fantastic tool to remove dust, mold, and damage, and to do high-end portrait retouching. As with any finely tuned piece of equipment, the more you know about the Healing Brush, the better you will be able to control it to perform invisible image restoration and retouching.

Sadly, many users seem to think that the Healing Brush is simply a souped-up Clone Stamp tool when nothing could be further from the truth. In fact, the only true similarity between the Healing Brush and Clone Stamp tool is that both tools enable you to sample from one image area by (Option + clicking) [Alt + clicking] then painting to cover up image damage or blemishes.

- When the Healing Brush samples, it analyses separately the texture, color, and luminosity attributes of the source area. When you paint, it merges the texture from the sample area into the color and luminosity of the destination area. The Clone Stamp literally duplicates the clone source and paints it over the original information.

- To create a seamless merge between the retouched areas and the image, the Healing Brush adds a 10–12 pixel spread to the brush.

Due to this built-in spread, it is highly recommended that you use a hard-edged brush with the Healing Brush. The Clone Stamp tool is more effective with a larger (in relationship to the problem you're trying to fix) and softer brush.

- The Healing Brush can work only on layers with actual pixel information—that is, the background layer or layers with pixel data. This means that you cannot use one of my favorite Clone tool techniques for adding an empty layer: checking Use All Layers in the options bar and cloning onto the empty layer. To work around this detail, work on a merged layer, as shown in the "Removing Fungus" section in this chapter.

- With the Healing Brush, using short brush strokes of 1 to 1 1/2 inches and releasing the mouse allows the healing algorithm time to calculate and will result in better healing than making long sweeping strokes.

- When you are using the Clone Stamp, resample image areas often to avoid the "clone of the clone" patterned look. When using the Healing Brush, it is extremely helpful to *avoid* this habit of continually resampling source area. Sampling good texture area once and painting often works *much* better. For best results, unlearn the Clone Stamp technique of sampling often. Yes, I know that this is difficult at first, but keep your left hand away from the Option or Alt key, and you'll be a better healer for it.

- When working near image edges, Select > All to keep the Healing Brush from averaging in white from outside the image.

- When working along an edge in an image with the Healing Brush, just like the Clone stamp, it is very important to sample and brush parallel to the edge you are repairing.

Is the Clone Stamp Dead?

The Clone Stamp is still a useful tool—granted, you will be using it a lot less often than you did with Photoshop 6, but it is still a good tool for repairing or retouching fine details and rebuilding large areas of missing image information. The upper-left corner of figure 5.9 is missing. I used the Clone Stamp initially to build up the missing image area and then used the Healing Brush to fine-tune the repair, as shown in figure 5.10. Because the Healing Brush can't heal onto an area that has no image information, it is often useful to clone image information over empty areas and then use the Healing Brush to fine-tune the clone.

1. I duplicated the background layer and used a large soft Clone Stamp tool to roughly cover up the missing image information, as shown in figure 5.11.

2. I used the Healing Brush to heal the cloned area to conceal any telltale patterns and to add the original texture into the newly created image area (figure 5.12).

figure 5.11

The roughly rebuilt corner.

© Colin Dearing

figure 5.9

figure 5.12

The Healing Brush blends in the texture of the paper, making the repair virtually invisible.

figure 5.10

The Clone Stamp tool also is excellent at cleaning up high contrast image areas. Due to the Healing Brush's inherent nature of spreading the healing effect by 10 to 12 pixels, image areas that have a high tonal difference tend to get blurry and smeary, as you can see in figure 5.13. To avoid the Healing Brush blurriness, you can either use a selection to control where the Healing Brush works (see figure 5.14) or use the tried-and-true Clone Stamp to repair image areas adjacent to image areas with great tonal differences.

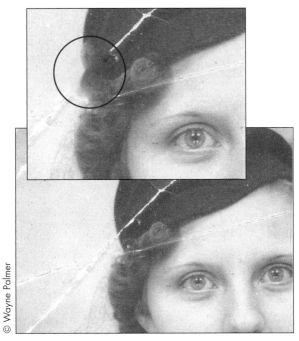

© Wayne Palmer

figure 5.13

The first image shows the unretouched damage, and the second shows how the Healing Brush can blur high-contrast areas.

figure 5.14

Use a selection to control the Healing Brush's coverage.

Removing Fungus

At the first sign of a fungus attack, gently clean the film with a cotton swab and Kodak Film Cleaner. Then scan in the film and use the Clone Stamp and Healing Brush tools to rid the world of this evil. On the other hand, removing mold from a print should be done only by a professional photo conservator because the mold or fungus can grow deeply into the paper fibers. Do not try to wash, clean, or treat original prints unless you can live with the consequences that anything you do to the original print might actually damage the paper more than the mold already has. Figure 5.15 and figure 5.16 show a before and after in which I removed the mold with the Healing Brush. Because this image has many different types of textures (in the basketball, the little girl's skin, and the grass in the background), it is an ideal candidate for the Healing Brush.

© Eismann family archive

BEFORE

figure 5.15

AFTER

figure 5.16

 ch5_mold.jpg

1. Duplicate the Background layer and name it *Mold Removal* (see **figure 5.17**). Ensure that the Healing Brush options are set to Normal.

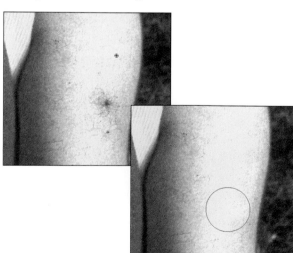

figure 5.17

Work on a duplicate layer with the Healing Brush in Normal mode.

2. Zoom in on the mold on the girl's arm, as shown in **figure 5.18**. Working on the dedicated Mold Removal layer, (Option + click) [Alt + click] to sample a good image texture area and paint over the mold. Use short brush strokes and remember to work within similarly toned areas. Don't try to heal across the girl's arm into the grass.

figure 5.18

Sample from a similarly textured area and use short strokes.

3. With the arm done, move onto the basketball and start by sampling good basketball texture. Heal over the mold and notice how well the Healing Brush maintains the essential basketball texture while removing the mold (see **figure 5.19**).

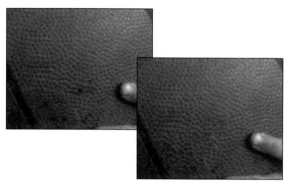

figure 5.19

Notice that the Healing Brush maintains the texture of the basketball.

Healing with Pattern

The Healing Brush also can heal from pattern, which enables you to move through an image quickly without having to pay attention to the area from which you are sampling. This feature is especially efficient when there is a well-defined image texture or grain structure to use.

In **figure 5.20**, you see a charming yet extremely damaged photo. The restoration artist, Fabrizio Fiorbianco from Naples, Italy, did a fantastic job of taking out all the white spots while maintaining the image's integrity (see **figure 5.21**). Prior to Photoshop 7, if I saw an image like this on my monitor, I'd be canceling any social engagements I had planned for that weekend. But with the Healing Brush, and more importantly, with the option to heal from pattern, you can work through a file much more quickly.

🌐⤳ **ch5_speckles.jpg**

BEFORE

figure 5.20

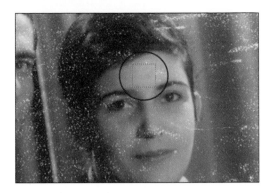

figure 5.22

This small, cleaned up area will be used to improve the entire image.

AFTER

figure 5.21

1. The first step in healing from a pattern is to create an image-specific pattern to use. Find an area of the image that has representative texture and take a few minutes to clean it with the Healing Brush.

2. With the Marquee tool set to 0 feather, select the clean area (see **figure 5.22**). Select Filter > Pattern Maker. The Pattern Maker works by taking a selected area and processing it into a pattern that can be tiled.

3. Click Generate and ignore the fact that your image is covered with the selected texture. Pay attention to the Tile in the lower-right corner; this is the generated pattern you will use to heal. The goal is to create a pattern that shows as few visible artifacts or lines as possible (see **figure 5.23**). Any time you tile an image, you run the risk of repeating artifacts. With larger tiles, it takes fewer tiles to cover a given area, which lessens the degree of repetition. In this example, my original sample was 128 by 128 pixels, so I doubled that to 256 by 256 pixels. Pattern Maker applies smoothing to help blend the tile edges. I increased the smoothness setting to 2 for a more seamless pattern.

4. If need be, click Generate Again, and Pattern Maker will keep recalculating patterns. If you like a previous pattern more, you can cycle through previously generated pattern tiles by clicking the small left and right triangles, marked in **figure 5.24**.

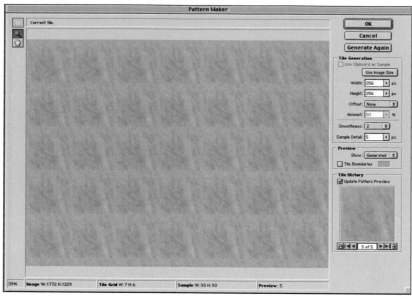

figure 5.24

Cycle through pattern tiles by clicking the left and right triangles.

figure 5.23

Clicking Generate creates new random patterns based on your settings.

5. After deciding which pattern you like, the next two steps are extremely important. Click the small Save icon under the generated tile to save the pattern and name it.

6. Then click Cancel to exit the Pattern Maker dialog box without ruining your image.

7. Select > Deselect and activate the Healing Brush, click Pattern on the options bar, and select the images pattern from the pattern library, as shown in figure 5.25.

figure 5.25

Select your pattern from the pattern library.

8. Now paint over the white spots with short brush strokes, and Photoshop will use the image's pattern to heal the damage, as shown in figure 5.26.

figure 5.26

With the Healing Brush set to Pattern, paint with short brush strokes.

Fabrizio very smartly avoided high-contrast image areas with the Healing Brush and restored them with the Clone Stamp tool. This avoids the Healing Brush blurriness that going over tonally different areas may add to an image.

Working with the Patch Tool

The Patch tool, nested with the Healing Brush in the toolbar, lets you repair a selected area with pixels from another area or with a defined pattern. Like the Healing Brush tool, the Patch tool matches the texture with the luminosity and color of the sampled pixels to the source pixels. Similar to the Healing Brush, the Patch tool works best with small initial selections. In figure 5.27, you see one of the most damaged contemporary images I've ever had to repair. The original medium format slide original had been discarded on a New York street and I found it in a puddle between piles of trash. It took me approximately eight hours to repair the entire file (see figure 5.28).

figure 5.27

figure 5.28

🌐 ▷< **ch5_sweater.jpg**

After using the float and move technique (described earlier in this chapter) to minimize the worst of the damage on the unimportant background areas, I had to get down to work and repair the numerous gouges and tears and replace missing image information. I used the Healing Brush on her face, but I used the Patch tool on the larger areas in the background and her sweater to fix the worst of the image's damage quickly and easily.

The most important decision to make before using the Patch tool is whether to patch from source, destination, or pattern. You make this choice in the options bar when the Patch tool is active.

- Source: Requires that you select the damaged image information (see **figure 5.29**) and, with the Patch tool, move the selection to a good image area (see **figure 5.30**). When you release the mouse, the originally selected area will be healed, as shown in **figure 5.31**. To continue working, either choose Select > Deselect (Cmd + D) [Ctrl + D], or simply select a new area to be patched—all of which will drop the selection around the newly patched area, as seen in **figure 5.32**.

figure 5.30

Move the selection to a good image area.

figure 5.31

Release the mouse, and the Patch tool heals the original selected area.

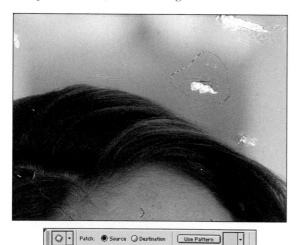

figure 5.29

Roughly select the damaged image area.

figure 5.32

Deselect the selection to complete the process.

- Destination: Select good image information (as shown in **figure 5.33**) and use the Patch tool to move the selection over the damaged image area (see **figure 5.34**). Before you release the mouse, you can align the good image information with the pattern of the area to be patched.

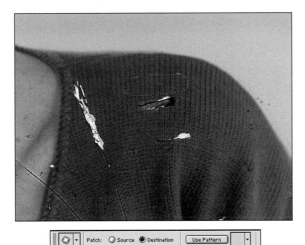

figure 5.33

Selecting good image information with the Patch tool.

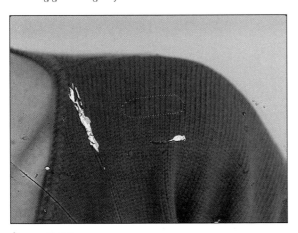

figure 5.34

Drag the good image information over the damaged image areas.

- Pattern: The Patch tool also can heal with a pattern. After generating an image-specific pattern with the Pattern Maker as you did when using the Healing Brush, make a selection (see **figure 5.35**), activate the Patch tool, and click the Use Pattern button in the

options bar. Patching with a pattern can be a timesaver on large, unimportant image areas such as backdrops or skies, as shown in **figure 5.36**.

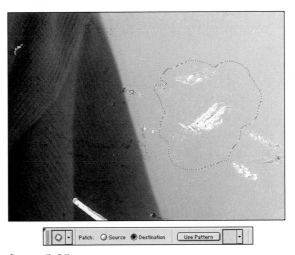

figure 5.35

Select the damaged image area.

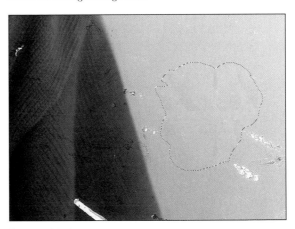

figure 5.36

Patching with pattern is ideal for large and less important image areas.

To match more complex patterns, use the float and patch technique that I learned from Russell Brown at Adobe. This little-documented method enables you to float a temporary patch and transform it into position to match even the most challenging patterns.

1. Select good image information, as shown in **figure 5.37**, and set the Patch tool to destination.

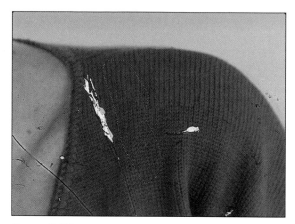

figure 5.37

Selecting good image information.

2. With the Patch tool active, (Cmd + Option + click) [Ctrl + Alt + click] inside the selection to create a floating patch.

3. Keep the modifier keys depressed and move the selection into position.

4. Still keeping the modifier keys depressed, press (Cmd + T) [Ctrl + T] to open the Free Transform bounding box (see **figure 5.38**); then release.

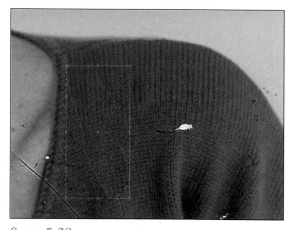

figure 5.38

After floating and moving the patch, activate Free Transform.

5. Use Free Transform to rotate, scale, or otherwise modify the patch to fit the area, as shown in **figure 5.39**. Click Enter to accept the transformation.

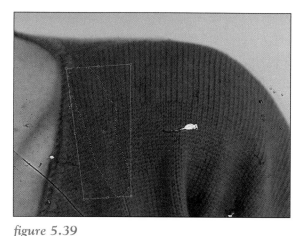

figure 5.39

Narrowing the bottom of the patch allows the sweater ribbing to blend.

6. Now make sure that the Patch tool is active and move the mouse into the active selection. Reposition the patch by one pixel to reactivate the healing engine and tap the Enter key again to tell Photoshop to heal with the transformed information. The last move with the Patch tool can be as slight as a single pixel move, but you have to do it to reawaken the healing engine and achieve the results shown in **figure 5.40**.

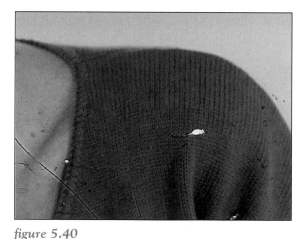

figure 5.40

After reactivating the healing engine, the large gash is practically invisible.

Before using the Patch tool, take a moment to evaluate the image damage to decide which of the three options to use. My personal approach is to use Source when the damaged area is oddly shaped, use

Destination when you need to match an image texture or structure, and use Pattern to lay down a fast fix that you can refine with the Healing Brush if need be. Working with the Patch tool is often even easier and faster than working with the Healing Brush. See Chapter 9, "Portrait Retouching," for a quick technique to hide skin blemishes with the Patch tool.

REDUCING PRINT TEXTURE AND MOIRÉ ARTIFACTS

Removing textures, patterns, offset moiré, and digital camera artifacts have caused many a digital retoucher to lose both sleep and hair. By using a combination of creative input techniques, Photoshop filters, layers, and layer masks, you can achieve very good results as long as you are able to compromise. A retouched image that started with a strong paper texture will never look as smooth or crisp as an original from a negative or from an untextured print. In the early to mid twentieth century, photographic supply companies offered dozens of black-and-white papers. Many of these were textured, which looked interesting at the time, but are a nightmare to scan and retouch today.

There are a number of approaches to reducing print texture, including these:

- Concentrate on the important image areas and let the unimportant image areas be blurred.

- Minimize the texture in the scanning phase by either overscanning the image as described in the following section or by using the descreen function in the scanning software to minimize the print texture.

- Use a camera or digital camera to make a copy of the negative or file. By using either very soft light or polarized light, you can influence how much of the pattern is visible.

Reducing Print Texture and Reflections Before Retouching

Experiment with reducing print texture in the input stage with the following techniques. Please note that I used the word *experiment*—each print brings

specific challenges in terms of texture, size, warping, how reflective the surface is, and other damage that needs to be de-emphasized. The time you use to experiment, make mistakes, and learn how to do copy work or scan a textured print will be well worth it in saved retouching hours.

- Over scan the image by 300 to 400% and step the file down via Image > Image Size in 2 to 4 increments. The close-up in **figure 5.41** reveals a stipple paper texture throughout the entire image. Stepping the image down by three steps makes it a bit softer but, more importantly, the texture has been softened out of existence (see **figure 5.42**).

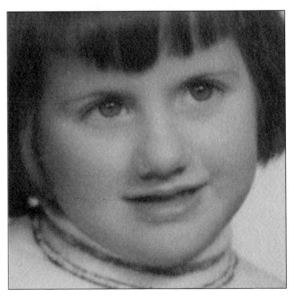

figure 5.41

The original image with a close-up that reveals distracting image texture.

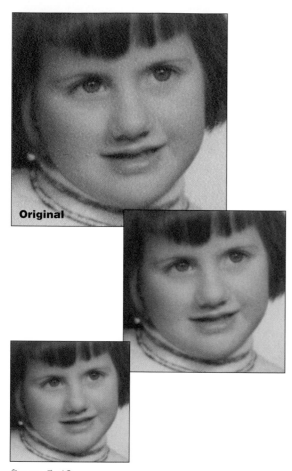

Original

figure 5.42

Stepping the file down in three steps via Image Size reduces the bothersome texture.

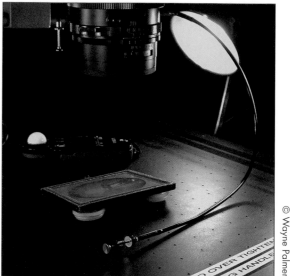

© Wayne Palmer

figure 5.43

Tilting the original can reduce reflections.

- When working with copy negatives, three techniques make it easier to reduce texture and reflections: Make a copy negative or have a copy negative made of the print that you'll then scan in. When doing this copy work, use polarizing filters on the lights and the camera lens and look through the camera viewfinder as you turn the filter to see the effect as the lighter areas of the texture darken and lighten. As you can see in **figure 5.43**, tilting the original slightly is helpful in reducing reflections on glass or in the dark silvery areas of an image.

- As Wayne Palmer, of Palmer Multimedia Imaging, explains, "A case can be made for a digital-copy negative versus scanning or using film. I have had very good results shooting an image with a Canon EOS 10D and Speedlite 550EX flash and then retouching the digital file. To light the print with soft diffuse light and avoid reflections, I rotate the flash head up so that light is bouncing off a large white surface at about a 45° angle to the image. This method doesn't work with images under glass, in which case I would use my conventional lights, medium format film, and copy stand."

- Scan in images with a flatbed scanner—but scan the print two to three times and rotate the print between scans. Experiment with angles and use the scan in which the light that bounces off of the print makes the texture least visible. This also works very well for images that have silvering and damage problems, as shown in **figure 5.44**. As you can see on the left, the tear across the boy's face is very apparent while the area by his feet show very little silvering. On the right side, the silvering by the feet is very bad, but the crack across the boy's face is invisible. **Figure 5.45** shows you how I scanned them—one was scanned in the proper orientation and then, without changing scanner settings, all I did was lift the print, rotate it by 90 degrees, and rescan it. By taking the good pieces from the image with the crack and copy pasting them onto the print without the crack, I re-created a whole image, as you see in **figure 5.46**.

figure 5.45

Scan once, and then turn the print and rescan without changing settings.

figure 5.44

Scanning on an angle can lessen apparent print defects.

figure 5.46

The final image after combining the best pieces from each scan.

- Use the descreen function in the scanner software to reduce the texture. You'll need to experiment with the best descreen settings for your prints and your scanner software. **Figure 5.47** shows a small print from 1980 that was scanned without the descreen function of the scanner software. **Figure 5.48** shows the same print scanned in with the filter settings, and **figure 5.49** shows that it is very important not to scan textured prints with the scanner sharpening turned on.

figure 5.47

Scanned with descreen on.

figure 5.48

Scanned with no scanner filtration.

figure 5.49

Never use scanner sharpening for textured images.

Reducing Paper Texture

The secret to minimizing paper texture without getting too many gray hairs is to compromise—let the unimportant image areas blur out and concentrate your efforts on the important image areas. The following technique uses a combination of blurred and masked layers with spotting retouch layers to achieve the final results. Because each image is unique and such a large variety of paper textures is available, there are no quick fixes or easy answers to this problem. **Figure 5.50** shows a crop of the original scan and **figure 5.51** is the retouched version.

🌐⯈⭕ **ch5_texture.jpg**

1. Duplicate the original layer and apply a Gaussian Blur with a high radius setting to blur the image so that the texture disappears, as seen in **figure 5.52**.

2. Add a layer mask and use a large, soft black brush set to 50% to 75% opacity to paint back the important image areas. In **figure 5.53**, I have painted back the little girl's face and sweater while leaving the unimportant background blurred.

figure 5.50

figure 5.51

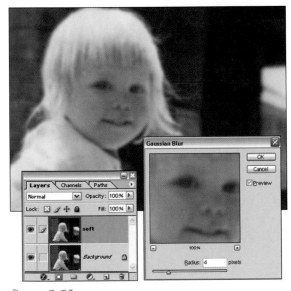

figure 5.52

Blurring the texture.

figure 5.53

Painting on the mask with black to hide the blur effect on the little girl's face.

3. Find the visual balance between blurred and the original image by painting with a low-opacity white soft brush on the dark areas of the layer mask. In this example, I used a 20% white brush on the layer mask to paint back some of the softness onto the little girl's skin, as seen in **figure 5.54**. If you go too far, press X on the keyboard to switch the brush color back to black and paint back over the area. Toggle the visibility of the blurred layer off and on to reveal any important image detail that needs to show through or any textured area that needs masking. Paint on the layer mask using black to reveal or white to conceal. Pay special attention to high-contrast edges.

figure 5.54

The softness of the child's skin can be brushed back in by painting with white on the layer mask.

4. Increasing the contrast in the little girl's eyes, mouth, and hair will draw the viewer's eye away from the unimportant image areas. As shown in **figure 5.55**, I increased the image contrast with a Levels Adjustment Layer.

figure 5.55

Bring the viewer's attention to the child's face by selectively increasing the image contrast. Start by applying a global contrast adjustment.

5. Fill the Levels Adjustment Layer layer mask with black and use a small, soft, white brush on the Levels mask to trace over the eye contours, mouth, and a few hair strands. This paints in the added contrast, as shown in **figure 5.56**.

figure 5.56

Painting on the layer mask adds the contrast on the facial features of the little girl.

6. To finish the image, use the Healing Brush tool on a merged layer to clean up remaining image damage.

Removing Print Patterns

You may have to deal with numerous types of paper patterns, including linen, stipple, honey-comb, and speckle—and depending on how obvious they are, you can try the following technique to reduce or remove them by using a combination of the Dust & Scratches filter coupled with the power of the Healing Brush. I couldn't see speckles on the actual print, but after I scanned it, the problem was all too obvious, as shown in **figure 5.57**. To create the results shown in **figure 5.58**, follow these steps:

BEFORE

figure 5.57

AFTER

figure 5.58

⊕▷⊱ **ch5_print_specks.jpg**

1. Duplicate the background layer and select
   Filter > Noise > Dust & Scratches. Increase
   the radius until the speckles disappear. Then
   raise the threshold to bring back as much
   image detail as possible. In this example, I
   used the settings shown in **figure 5.59**. The
   Dust & Scratches filter will, of course, also
   reduce important image information such as
   eyes and lips—but we'll take care of that in
   a few steps.

figure 5.60

Selecting the less important image areas.

4. Activate the Patch tool and select the pattern
   created for this image, as shown in **figure
   5.61**. Then click the Use Pattern button in
   the options bar.

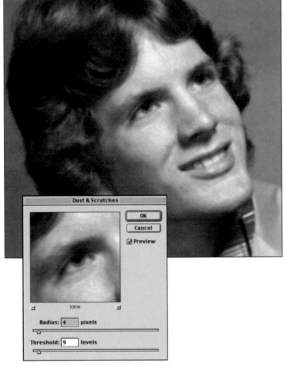

figure 5.59

*On a duplicate layer, adjust the Dust & Scratches radius and
threshold level.*

figure 5.61

Selecting the pattern.

2. After running the filter, select Edit > Define
   Pattern and name the pattern. Next, it is
   imperative that you select Edit > Undo to
   undo the Dust & Scratches filter.

3. Use the Lasso tool with a 5-pixel feather to
   select the most important image areas (such as
   the eyes and lips) and then Select > Inverse.
   This selects all less important image areas, as
   shown in **figure 5.60**.

Depending on the image size and amount of RAM
you have, patching with a pattern may take a few
minutes. To fine-tune the important image areas
such as the teenager's eyes and mouth, activate the
Healing Brush and click Use Pattern. It is essential
that you check the Use Aligned button as circled in
figure 5.62, and with a small, hard-edged brush,
heal away the remaining specks. In some instances,
you may need to use the Clone Stamp tool to refine
delicate details.

BEFORE

figure 5.63

figure 5.62

Healing from pattern to clean up the details.

AFTER

figure 5.64

Reducing Offset Moiré

Sooner or later, a client will come to you with only a printed image clipped from a magazine or brochure for you to work with. After scanning it, you may find that the entire image is covered with moiré rosette patterns caused by four-color separation offset printing (see **figure 5.63**). The following retouching technique, developed by the late Carl Volk, works well for removing moiré problems. In this process, you are throwing the image out of focus a little, and then trying to sharpen the contrasty areas without sharpening the dot pattern. **Figure 5.64** shows the detail of the improved image after this resizing and blurring process.

Before you start trying to repair the damage, ask the client politely if she might have a photographic original. If not, swallow hard and follow these recommendations to minimize the horrid moiré effect.

Also, be aware that the best time to fix moiré is during the scanning. Most scanners have descreen routines that work at least as good as, and probably better than, anything you can do later in Photoshop.

    N o t e

I am not condoning scanning images from magazines, books, or stock catalogs because that would be breaking U.S. copyright law. Rather, I am recognizing that at some point, you or a client may have only a magazine or brochure image of her factory (for example) for you to use. Or in the worst-case scenario, the original negative or film has been lost or damaged and the only image available is a prescreened one.

1. Scan the printed piece at three to four times higher resolution than you will need for your final print.

2. Start with the following values, which you might need to adjust for your own moiré problem images. Apply a .5-pixel Gaussian Blur to the Red channel, .7 pixels to the Green, and 1 pixel to the Blue.

Use keyboard shortcuts to quickly access the individual channels in your image. Use (Cmd + 1) [Ctrl + 1] for Red, (Cmd + 2) [Ctrl + 2] for Green, and (Cmd + 3) [Ctrl + 3] for Blue. (Cmd + ~) [Ctrl + ~] will return you to the composite image. When one of the separated channels is active, pressing ~ will keep the color channel active but enable you to preview the full-color image in the Photoshop window.

3. To resample the file down 25%, select Image > Image Size. Change the Width unit of measurement to percent and enter 75. (The other values will change automatically when Constrain Proportions is checked, as it should be.) Be sure to check Resample Image.

4. Repeat the Gaussian Blur procedure on each channel with approximately 25% lower Gaussian Blur amounts. The .7 amount can be dropped down to .5 and the .5 to .3. The 25% lower values are used because the image size has been reduced by 25%.

5. If the moiré pattern is still visible, resample the image down 25% again.

6. After the image starts looking better and you are approaching your final resolution and size, choose Filter > Sharpen > Unsharp Mask. For a file that is 300dpi (or close), use these settings: Amount, 100; Radius, 1.7; Threshold, 12 to 16. After using the Unsharp Mask filter to offset the softness added with the Gaussian Blur and image resizing, the image details should look acceptably sharp. As described in Chapter 8, "Refining and Polishing the Image," you should use the Unsharp Mask filter carefully because you don't want to create ugly, white-halo artifacts around image edges.

7. Resample the image down to final size. After resizing the image, you might need to run the Unsharp Mask filter again to create a pleasingly crisp image. Use a smaller Radius setting on this final pass of the Unsharp Mask filter.

As you can imagine, going through all these steps is a last resort technique to remove moiré. It would be best to start from the original film.

Reducing Digital Camera Noise and Moiré

Digital camera technology is based on a variety of other technologies, including scanning, three-shot, and one-shot cameras.

The one-shot cameras work just like your film camera, except that a CCD (Charged Coupled Device) or CMOS chip (complementary metal-oxide semiconductor) with a color mosaic filter replaces the film. The CCD structure, in combination with the filter, can cause color artifacts that look like little twinkles of colored lights or rainbow-like moiré patterns. They might be visible in areas of high-frequency, fine-detail information, such as eyelashes, flyaway hair strands, specular highlights, small branches of trees, or woven fabrics, as shown in **figure 5.65**.

figure 5.65

Digital moiré occurs in high-frequency image areas, such as those between these thin palm fronds.

Even if you don't use a digital camera, you might pick up moiré patterns when scanning images with fine fabrics. You can use the following techniques to take care of those problems.

Blurring and Sharpening in Lab Color Mode

Moiré and color artifacts show up as problems in the color channels. By separating the color information from the black-and-white image information, you can fix what's broken—the color artifacts—without affecting what's not: the tonal information.

T i p

When using any of these techniques to remove moiré or color artifacts, make sure that you view your image at 100% monitor view to see accurately what is occurring.

⊕⏵⊱ **ch5_moire_crop.jpg**

1. Select Image > Duplicate and then Image > Mode > Lab Color to convert the duplicated RGB file to Lab.

2. Make the "a" channel active and then press ~ to see the full-color image. Run the Gaussian Blur filter with a high-enough radius to soften the artifacts. Don't try to eradicate all artifacts at once because you will be repeating the Gaussian Blur filter on the "b" channel in the following step (see **figure 5.66**).

figure 5.66

Blurring the "a" channel to lessen the color artifacts.

3. Select the "b" channel and run the Gaussian Blur filter. Use a higher radius than you used on the "a" channel because the "b" channel usually has more color artifact problems. Please note: I have often also used the Dust & Scratches filter rather than the Gaussian Blur filter on the "a" and "b" channels with excellent results.

4. Select the Lightness channel and choose Filter > Sharpen > Unsharp Mask to sharpen the black-and-white information, as shown in **figure 5.67**.

figure 5.67

Sharpening the Lightness channel to sharpen the black-and-white image information.

N o t e

It would be unwise to use these values as the right values for all image problems. The Gaussian Blur and Unsharp Mask settings shown here offer good starting points. You might need to increase or reduce values to fine-tune the artifact removal in your images.

5. Make the composite channel active and inspect the image for stray color artifacts. Use the Sponge tool set to Desaturate to brush away any artifacts that the global approach might have missed.

6. Using this Lab blur and sharpen technique can sometimes desaturate the entire image, making it look flat and faded. To offset this undesired side effect, use a Hue/Saturation Adjustment Layer to boost the saturation, as seen in figure 5.68.

figure 5.68

Boosting overall saturation.

 Note

In addition to the Gaussian Blur filter, experiment with the Median and Dust & Scratches filters to blur the color artifacts.

This technique might sound like a lot of steps but, thankfully, the entire procedure and settings are actionable. By making a Photoshop Action, you can batch process an entire folder of digital camera images in a fraction of the time it would take to do this step-by-step. Go to www.digitalretouch.org and download the Action moiré_removal.atn. Another practice file, ch5_costume.jpg, is also on the site.

 ch5_ moiré_removal.atn

ch5_costume.jpg

Tip

If you work with a lot of digital camera files, it makes sense to make a modest investment in Quantum Mechanic Lite or Pro (www.camerabits.com) to do all the previously described work for you and do it better. Both Quantum Mechanic Lite and Quantum Mechanic Pro are designed to remove color noise and artifacts. They work very well with Kodak's cameras and high-end cameras that don't do similar filtering in their host software.

Avoiding Moiré Patterns When Shooting Digital Pictures

If you notice moiré problems while you're taking pictures with digital cameras, you can lessen them with the following tips:

- Move the camera a few inches closer to or farther away from the subject to change the relationship between the grid of the CCD color filter and the high-frequency information that is causing the problem.

- Open the aperture to use a larger *f*-stop. This decreases the depth of field, which means that less of the subject matter is in focus. The out-of-focus parts have lower spatial frequency content and hence fewer aliasing artifacts. The in-focus areas might still reveal some artifacting.

- Some people recommend defocusing the camera a smidgen and then over-sharpening the file in Photoshop. I'm not a huge fan of that approach, but I offer it as a technique you can experiment with if you like.

MAINTAINING IMAGE STRUCTURE

Photographer John Warner was asked to photograph the lawn of a croquet field, which had been aerated to promote lawn growth. The problem was that John needed to photograph the playing surface for a promotional brochure before the grass had a chance to recover, as shown in **figure 5.69**, so he used Photoshop to repair the lawn faster than Mother Nature could have (see **figure 5.70**).

🌐⤳ **ch5_lawncare.jpg**

1. John duplicated the Background layer and named the layer Lawn Care.

© John Warner Photography

BEFORE

figure 5.69

AFTER

figure 5.70

2. He selected Filter > Noise > Dust & Scratches and raised the Radius setting until the white spots were obliterated, as seen in **figure 5.71**.

figure 5.71

Adjust the radius of the Dust & Scratches filter to remove the flaws in the duplicated layer.

3. He increased the Threshold setting to bring back the texture or film grain of the image, as seen in **figure 5.72**, and clicked OK.

4. Of course, that made the cottages complete mush. To bring the cottages back into focus, John added a layer mask by clicking the Add Layer Mask icon on the Layers palette.

figure 5.72

Increasing the threshold of the Dust & Scratches filter to maintain image texture.

5. John activated the Lawn Care layer mask by clicking it. Then he used the Gradient tool to draw a black-to-white blend on the layer mask to block the Lawn Care layer from affecting the cottages and upper part of the croquet field, as shown in **figure 5.73**. Wherever the mask is black, the underlying layer will be revealed—or in this context, wherever the mask is black, the original, crisp cottages are visible.

figure 5.73

A gradient layer mask will hide areas that you don't want affected.

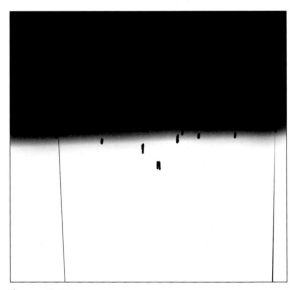

figure 5.74

Painting on the layer mask to restore important image details.

6. Upon careful examination, John noticed that the wickets and sideline demarcation had also been obliterated. To bring them back into focus, John temporarily reduced the opacity of the Lawn Care layer so he could see the wickets, clicked the Lawn Care layer mask, and used a small black brush to paint over the wickets (see **figure 5.74**), which revealed the original sharp image information. To see what the mask alone looks like, (Option) [Alt] click the layer mask, as you see in **figure 5.75**.

figure 5.75

Viewing the layer mask.

7. When finished, he restored the Lawn Care layer opacity to 100%, as shown in **figure 5.76**.

The Dust & Scratches technique is a fabulous time-saver. You'll find that it's worth the few moments it takes to adjust the Dust & Scratches filter radius setting to balance the removal of dust, damage, or unwanted marks with the threshold to maintain image texture.

CLOSING THOUGHTS

In most cases, removing dust and mold while maintaining image structure is all that is needed to bring an image back to life. In the worst-case scenario where time, damage, and missing pieces are plaguing your images, you'll need to use the emergency room techniques discussed in Chapters 6, "Damage Control and Repair," and 7, "Rebuilding, Rearranging, and Re-creating Portraits."

figure 5.76

The final image.

6

DAMAGE CONTROL AND REPAIR

The torture we put our old photographs through—storing them in damp basements, carrying them in wallets, folding, tearing, cutting, scribbling on them, and pasting them into albums—all leave the telltale marks, cracks, rips, tears, and misshapen corners. So if this is so bad for photographs, why do we put them through the gauntlet of abuse? Because we value, treasure, and cherish them. We like carrying pictures of loved ones in our wallets or purses; we take pleasure in making the family photo album or collage; and sadly, we often don't realize that the basement isn't the best place to store a valuable print.

So rather than relegating the damaged photos to a dark, forgotten, basement corner, let's get them out, scan them in, and learn to

- Eliminate scratches
- Remove wires and clutter
- Repair tears, rips, and cracks
- Make stains and discoloration disappear

The tools and techniques used to conquer these challenges include

- The Clone Stamp tool
- The Healing Brush and Patch tools
- Paths, layers, and layer masks
- Selections and adjustment layers

ELIMINATING SCRATCHES

One of the most pedestrian and irritating things you will need to retouch are scratches caused by dirty film processors, coarse handling, or specks of dust on the scanner or digital camera CCD (charged coupled device). But take heart; with the following techniques, you'll make those scratches disappear with ease and panache.

Combining the Clone Stamp and the Healing Brush

Old photos and negatives are often plagued with numerous irregular scratches, but you can hide them quickly and easily. **Figure 6.1** shows an original print that curled over time and cracked when it was stored incorrectly and weight was placed on it. **Figure 6.2** shows the repaired file. The Healing Brush is an ideal choice for removing thin cracks like those shown in the right side of **figure 6.1**. When you need to remove larger rips or tears (like those on the left side of the figure), combine the Clone Stamp tool and the Healing Brush to create a dynamic duo of crime fighting—I mean scratch removal.

🌐 ⊅꞉ **ch6_scratch.jpg**

1. To protect the Background layer, duplicate it and name it *scratch removal*.

2. For the thin cracks on the right, select the Healing Brush with a hard brush that is just large enough to cover the scratch. In most cases, when using the Healing Brush, I prefer to leave Aligned unchecked so that the Healing Brush samples from the same texture over and over again. When you are removing straight scratches, the Healing Brush is more effective with Aligned checked (see figure 6.3).

3. Move the mouse 1 to 2 brush widths to the left or right of the scratch and (Option + click)[Alt + click] to set the Healing source. For healing an area with an obvious directional pattern like this one, you can try to anticipate the point from which the data will be pulled by sampling slightly above or below where you first apply the brush.

figure 6.1

figure 6.2

figure 6.3

Setting up the scratch removal layer and the Healing Brush parameters.

4. To spare yourself the trouble of having to draw along the entire scratch, Shift + click the Healing Brush at the top of the scratch.

5. Release the mouse button and move the brush about an inch down the scratch, and Shift + click again. The Healing Brush will heal in a perfectly straight line (see **figure 6.4**).

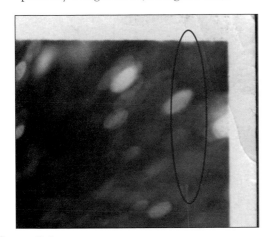

figure 6.4

After Shift + clicking along the scratch.

6. Continue Shift + clicking your way along the thin scratch on the right.

 T i p

To rebuild the larger, thicker tears or damage, use the Clone Stamp or Patch tool to create initial image information and then follow up with a few passes of the Healing Brush. This is a quick way to cover up large tears or missing image information caused by torn away print emulsions or damaged corners.

7. To repair the larger cracks on the left side of the image, activate the Clone Stamp tool and (Option + click) [Alt + click] to sample good image information cover roughly the white tear and simultaneously lay down texture information that the Healing Brush will use, as shown in **figure 6.5**. Additionally, by covering up the white tear, you have a better chance of avoiding the Healing Brush blurriness that can appear when you are healing over wide tonal differences.

figure 6.5

The tear after roughly using the Clone Stamp tool and after cleaning up with the Healing Brush.

8. Activate the Healing Brush and paint over any telltale cloned areas.

 T i p

When you are restoring close to high-contrast image areas with the Healing Brush, use a selection both to control where the Healing Brush works and to reduce the chance of creating blurry areas (see **figure 6.6**).

figure 6.6

Using a selection to control where the Healing Brush works.

Removing damage and scratches is akin to pulling back the veil of time. Fabrizio Fiorbianco did an astonishing job of removing the tears and rips while maintaining the charm of the original image, as you can see in **figures 6.7** and **6.8**. Fabrizio restored this image in Photoshop 6 and relied on careful use of the Clone Stamp tool. As the last section showed, you can achieve similarly brilliant results with careful use of the Clone Stamp tool and the Healing Brush.

© Fabrizio Fiorbianco

figure 6.7

figure 6.8

REMOVING UNWANTED ELEMENTS

Wires, cables, and clutter serve only to distract the viewer from what is really important in the picture. You can use this technique when preparing real estate photos. By taking out the distracting telephone wires and electric cables, the homes come to the visual foreground and look much more attractive (translation: more sellable).

Dismantling Wires or Cables

To remove telephone wires, cables, or smooth, long, thin scratches, start by tracing the problem with the Pen tool, and then stroke the path with the Clone Stamp or Healing Brush. In the example in **figure 6.9**, the wires and shadow detract from the picture of the bell tower in the Algarve in Portugal, and without the wires, the image looks much cleaner (see **figure 6.10**).

🌐▷〈 **ch6_wires.jpg**

© Katrin Eismann

figure 6.9   *figure 6.10*

1. Select the Pen tool and click the Paths icon on the options bar (circled in **figure 6.11**). Draw one path along the wire and name it, and draw a second path over the shadow. Each Photoshop file can have thousands of paths, and it is a good idea to name them as they are created.

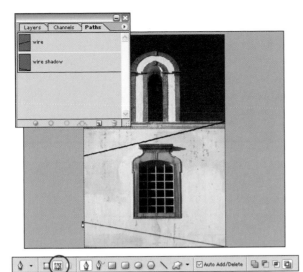

figure 6.11

Creating paths with the Pen tool along the wire and shadow.

2. Add a new layer, select the Clone Stamp tool, click Use All Layers, and set the brush to be a bit larger than the wire shadow. Move the mouse 1 to 2 brush widths from the wire shadow and (Option + click) [Alt + click] to define the clone source.

3. Select Stroke Path from the Paths palette menu (see **figure 6.12**). Select the Clone Stamp from the pull-down menu and click OK.

figure 6.12

Accessing the Stroke Path command.

4. Repeat with the path you made for each wire. If the alignment of the Clone Tool fix does not line up with the original image, simply erase the misaligned area and reclone over the area. To hide shorter sections of wire, I prefer to use the Shift + click method I described in the first scratch-removal example in this chapter.

5. If needed, add a new layer and (Option) [Alt] Layer > Merge Visible and fine-tune the repair with the Healing Brush.

Tip

If the Clone Stamp tool is active, you can just tap the Enter key (not the Return key on the Apple keyboard) by the numeric keypad, and Photoshop will stroke the active path with the Clone Stamp.

Hiding Clutter and Distractions

In the excitement of taking a picture, we often forget to look at the entire scene. We might not notice distracting clutter, bits of garbage on the sidewalk, or as seen in **figure 6.13**, the palm tree coming out of the woman's head that looks like a fantastic primal headdress. By removing the clutter and distractions, you can focus the viewer's attention on the picture and clean up the living room without getting out the vacuum (see **figure 6.14**).

figure 6.13

figure 6.14

You can't physically take something out of a digital image without leaving a white hole, but you can cover up distractions. You also could take the subject out of the image and put her on a new background (addressed in Chapter 7, "Rebuilding, Rearranging, and Re-creating Portraits"). In the following example, the palm tree coming out of the woman's head truly distracts from the picture; with just a few minutes of work and a tighter crop, you can produce a much better image.

🌐▷⳾ **ch6_palmtree.jpg**

1. On a duplicate layer, use the Lasso tool to make a generous selection around the clutter to be removed. If the area is large or irregularly shaped (like the palm tree), start with a smaller area (see **figure 6.15**).

figure 6.15

Roughly selecting an area to be covered.

2. Press Q to enter Quick Mask mode and run the Gaussian Blur filter to soften the edge of the mask (see **figure 6.16**). This is identical to applying a feather to a selection, but the advantage is that you can see the effect that the blur, i.e. the feathering, is having on the selection edge.

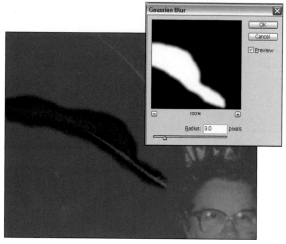

figure 6.16

Blurring the Quick Mask is identical to feathering the selection, except that you have an accurate preview of the effect.

3. Press Q again to exit Quick Mask mode and activate the selection.

4. With any selection tool, move the selection to an area that has uncluttered, good information, as shown in **figure 6.17**.

5. Create a new layer via copy with (Cmd + J) [Ctrl + J]. Use the Move tool to drag the good information over the bad. The result is shown in **figure 6.18**.

6. Continue the process with the remaining leaves and make sure to cover up any obvious edges, repeating patterns, or tone differences with the Clone Stamp tool set to Use All Layers.

7. Add a new layer (Option) [Alt] Layer > Merge Visible and go over the entire image at high magnification with the Clone Stamp and Healing Brush.

8. The final step is to crop the image if needed. In this example, the dark window above the women's heads doesn't add to the image and takes away visual focus. By cropping the image as you saw in **figure 6.14**, you can bring the image together much more strongly.

figure 6.17

Move the selection over to an area with good information.

figure 6.18

After floating the replacement area and moving it over the palm frond, you might need to do a bit of cleanup with the Clone Stamp tool to fine-tune the results.

REPAIRING TEARS, RIPS, AND CRACKS

Over the years, the photographs we cherish tend to get folded, cracked, torn, and damaged. If you're lucky, you'll at least have all the pieces to reconstruct the image. If you're not so lucky, you'll have to make up image information to reconstruct the missing pieces. In the following examples, the image was torn into pieces, which Wayne Palmer scanned on a flatbed scanner and then recombined in Photoshop to create the final image shown in figure 6.20.

As you can see in figure 6.19, the original print has been torn into five pieces. At first this looked like a daunting job, but after scanning the pieces on a flatbed scanner (Wayne used a piece of foam core to gently hold the pieces in place), the challenge morphed into a puzzle that required piecing the parts together and removing the ragged edges to make the image come to life, as you can see in figure 6.20.

figure 6.19

figure 6.20

ch6_rip.jpg

T i p

When scanning large print pieces or prints that are larger than your flatbed scanner platen, do not change the print orientation by rotating pieces. That will vary the reflectance of the paper texture between the pieces, making them difficult to merge.

1. Using the Lasso tool without feather, roughly select the first piece, as shown in figure 6.21.

figure 6.21

Roughly select a piece of the image with the Lasso tool.

2. Select the Magic Wand and (Option + click) [Alt + click] the white areas within the selection to subtract the large white areas of the scanner lid (see figure 6.22). Don't worry about removing the ripped paper edges from the selection; they may contain valuable image details.

3. (Cmd + J) [Ctrl + J] or Layer > New > Layer via Copy to place the selected print piece onto its own layer. I highly recommend naming the layers, as shown in figure 6.23.

4. You can make new layers only out of selections with pixel image information. Select the Background layer and repeat steps 1 and 2 for each piece of the image.

figure 6.22

Subtracting excess image information from the selection.

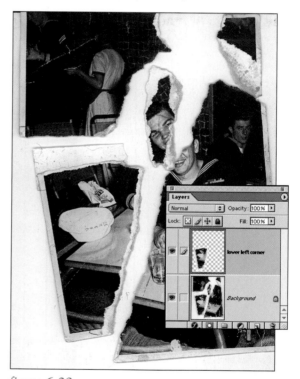

figure 6.23

After copying a section to its own layer, it is best to name it.

5. Because the Background layer is still intact, it could be confusing to see it while you are moving the individual pieces around. To block it from view but maintain the image data,

click the Background layer and add a new layer. Fill this with white to conceal the original Background layer.

6. When you have all the pieces on their own layers, the next step is to straighten them out. Select View > Show > Grid to use the grid and guides as a visual aid for alignment. Use Edit > Free Transform to position and rotate each piece roughly into place, as shown in figure 6.24.

figure 6.25

Setting Auto Select Layer and Show Bounding Box will allow you to easily grab and move pieces with the Move tool.

figure 6.24

Use Edit > Free Transform to position and rotate each piece roughly into place.

7. With the Move tool set to Auto Select Layer and Show Bounding Box, grab the lower-left corner piece and move it toward the large right piece (see figure 6.25). These two pieces come together well, but the ripped edge of the right corner print is covering up good image information of the left corner.

8. To control how the pieces come together, you could erase the ripped paper edge, but that approach is risky because it can be difficult to control, and by erasing, you are deleting pixels—something which always makes me very nervous. To control what is visible without actually removing it, use a layer mask on the piece of the image that is blocking good image information. In this case, the ripped edge of the large right piece is covering image information of the left piece.

9. Add a layer mask and use a small, hard-edged black brush to paint over the ripped edge. It will look as though you are erasing, but you're not, as you can see in figure 6.26. The black brush on the layer mask is concealing the image information, not deleting it.

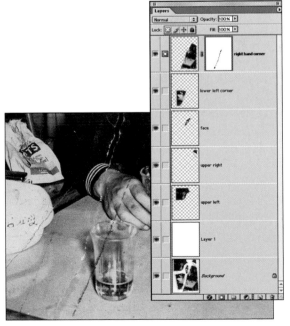

figure 6.26

Adding a layer mask and painting on it with a black brush hides the ripped edges without actually deleting them.

10. Continue moving pieces together and adding layer masks wherever the torn paper is blocking good image information, as seen in figure 6.27.

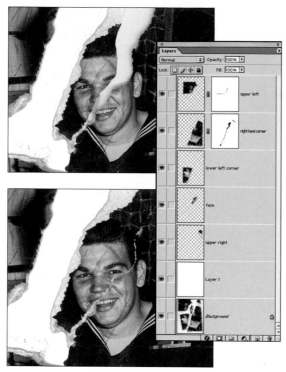

figure 6.27

Continuing to match pieces together while hiding torn areas with layer masks.

11. Once the pieces are together, add a new layer to the top of the layer stack and (Option) [Alt] Layer > Merge Visible to flatten all of the layers into one, as you see in figure 6.28.

12. Use a combination of Cloning and Healing as described previously to repair the remaining cracks and to build up image data.

All in all, when the pieces initially came out of the original envelope, the job looked like a hopeless cause. By thinking of the pieces as a puzzle, Wayne was able to piece them together seamlessly to create the final image, which the client loved.

figure 6.28

Refine the rotation on a merged layer with the Clone and Healing tools.

REMOVING STAINS AND DISCOLORATION

The only dirt that you should remove from the physical print original is the type that you can brush or blow off easily. A professionally trained conservator should be the only one to treat stains that are embedded in the film or print emulsion. There are many types of stains and discoloration that can befall an image, ranging from overall yellowing to density changes caused by sun, fire, or water damage to child-inflicted scribbling with pens, markers, or crayons. To hide these injustices, you take advantage of channel information to rebuild the image with layers, cloning, and healing; and sometimes you even borrow image information from parts of the image that aren't stained.

Removing the Stain of Age

Photographs change over time. Especially older photographs, which may not have been processed to archival standards, have a tendency to yellow as the paper oxidizes and reacts with the cardboard it is mounted on or the box it is stored in. We can't stop time, but we *can* stop the staining. In **figure 6.29**, you see the original portrait of Ellie Kennard's great grandmother in Newfoundland, Canada. **Figure 6.30** shows the image with the staining removed and with a slight sepia tone.

© Ellie Kennard

BEFORE

figure 6.29

AFTER

figure 6.30

The first thing you need to recognize when working with old images from the 19th and early 20th century is that they were not in color and did not have a heavy yellow or sepia tone. They were originally black-and-white images, meaning that the color you see in the yellowed print is not important and it makes sense to pull the best black-and-white image from the file before doing any restoration work. The easiest and least effective method to change a color image to black and white is to use the Image > Mode > Grayscale feature in Photoshop. I highly recommend that you do not use this; I explain why in Chapter 8, "Refining and Polishing the Image." In the meantime, trust me and work along.

ch6_stain.jpg

1. Before converting a file to grayscale, always inspect the image channels either by clicking the words *red*, *green*, and *blue* in the channels palette or by using the command keys (Command) [Ctrl] 1, 2, and 3 to see the difference of the three channels (see **figure 6.31**). By inspecting the channels, you can see which ones have image information that you either want to preserve or ignore. You can see that the red and green are faint but still have useful information and that the blue channel is the most robust; but, alas, it also reveals the most image damage.

Composite RGB

Red channel

Green channel

Blue channel

figure 6.31

Inspecting the individual color channels reveals many differences in detail and apparent damage.

2. Taking this knowledge into account, add a Channel Mixer Adjustment Layer and click Monochrome in the lower-left corner. By adjusting the sliders to add some of the red and green and a lot of the blue (see **figure 6.32**), you can create a black-and-white image that has good tonality and detail without including all of the damage that the blue channel is carrying.

figure 6.32

Adjusting the Channel Mixer sliders to use only the best information from each channel.

3. Next you need to be very realistic and decide which parts of the image are not important. In other words, it doesn't make any sense to spend time repairing the sky when it is practically pure white due to the lack of blue response in the photographic emulsions available in the 19ᵗʰ century. Ellie selected the sky area by drawing around the figures with the Lasso tool.

4. Ellie sampled a light gray from the image, added a new layer, and filled the selection by selecting Edit > Fill > Use Foreground Color set to normal.

5. Then Ellie added a hint of monochrome noise to the sky (see **figure 6.33**). The noise adds visual texture and minimizes the sterile computer look.

6. Ellie then (Cmd + clicked) [Ctrl + clicked] the sky layer to load the layer transparency and, with the sky gray as a foreground and white as a background color, she selected Filter > Render > Clouds, as shown in **figure 6.34**. If the computer clouds are too artificial, select Edit > Fade Clouds immediately after running the filter and reduce the opacity.

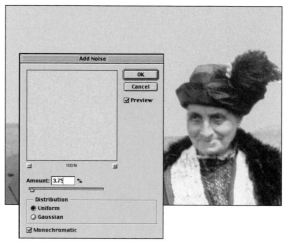

figure 6.33

Adding monochrome noise after filling the area with light gray.

figure 6.34

After using Filter > Render > Clouds on the active area.

7. To control the brightness of the sky without affecting the rest of the image, Ellie added a Levels adjustment layer that was grouped with the sky layer. She chose Layer > New Adjustment Layer and checked the Group With Previous (see **figure 6.35**). She reduced the brightness of the sky by lowering the Output Levels highlight value to 235.

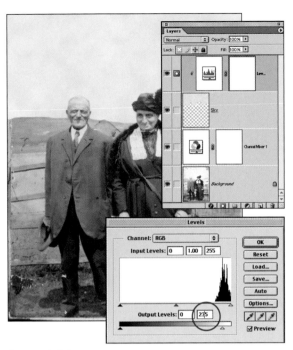

figure 6.35

Using a grouped Levels adjustment layer to selectively control the brightness of the sky.

figure 6.36

After setting the blend mode to Multiply and adjusting the opacity.

8. The next step is very interesting. Ellie wanted to add a bit of density to the people's faces. She started by selecting her great grandmother's head and then selected Edit > Copy Merged, which copies all visible and selected image information.

9. With the original head selection still active, Ellie choose Edit > Paste Into, which pastes the head exactly back into position. Then Ellie changed the Blending Mode of the separate head layer to Multiply and adjusted the opacity to 40%. This is a fantastic method for building up the density of specific image areas, as demonstrated in **figure 6.36**.

10. To balance the photograph, Ellie added additional canvas and cloned in some extra earth to the lower part of the image. Ellie then cleaned up the remaining image damage with the Clone Stamp and Healing Brush as described previously to remove the last vestiges of image damage.

11. The finishing touch Ellie added was to infuse the image with a slight sepia tone that suggests the age of the photograph without dominating it. Photoshop comes with two excellent actions to add sepia. To load them, click the fly-out menu of the Action palette and select Image Effects. Click the Sepia Toning (layer) action and click the Play button on the bottom of the Layers palette.

12. The sepia action adds a Hue/Saturation Adjustment layer, on which Ellie adjusted opacity to create the final image shown in **figure 6.37**.

All in all, this may seem like a lot of work for one photo. But if you consider that this is the only image Ellie has of her great-grandmother, the few steps it takes to create a good black-and-white image, rebuild the sky, and remove damage is minor in relationship to the enriched heritage of her family history.

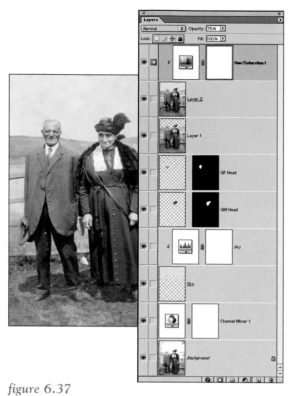

figure 6.37

The final image after adjusting the sepia layer opacity.

figure 6.38

BEFORE

© Art Johnson

figure 6.39

AFTER

⊕▷⊱ **ch6_toddler.jpg**

Balancing Stains

Art Johnson of Memories In Minutes Inc., emailed me the before and after images you see in **figures 6.38** and **6.39**. We have no idea what happened to the original print—perhaps the stains are photographic chemicals that are darkening over time, or they may be a coffee spill. Either way, the dark splotches have to go. If you face similar image problems, before you grab the Healing Brush, take a moment to identify the true source of the problem. In the case of density stains, you need to adjust the tone of the dark stains to match the majority of the image.

1. Upon inspecting the image channels, Art saw that the red channel was practically pristine and that the blue channel was terribly damaged, as shown in **figure 6.40**. This prompted him to add a Channel Mixer adjustment layer and add the red channel and subtract blue channel information to create a black-and-white image (see **figure 6.41**). By adjusting the balance of red and blue, Art balanced out the tonal differences very well.

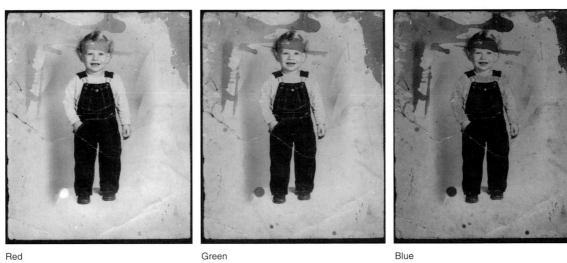

Red   Green   Blue

figure 6.40

Inspect the three image channels before using the Channel Mixer to convert to black and white.

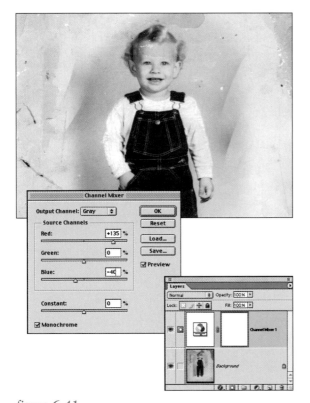

figure 6.41

Using a Channel Mixer to eliminate the green and blue channels.

2. In this image, the background is very damaged, but it also isn't important. Art decided to separate the toddler from the background to create a new studio background for the child. He roughly selected the toddler with a 5-pixel feather Lasso and chose Edit > Copy Merged and then Edit > Paste to lift and place the child onto its own layer and leave the damaged background behind, as the Layers palette in **figure 6.42** shows.

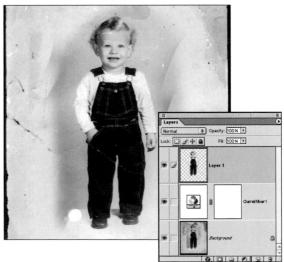

figure 6.42

Selecting only the child and placing her on her own layer.

3. After activating the background layer, Art used the Motion Blur filter (Filter > Blur > Motion Blur) on the original background (see **figure 6.43**) to deftly remove a lot of damage with a modicum of effort.

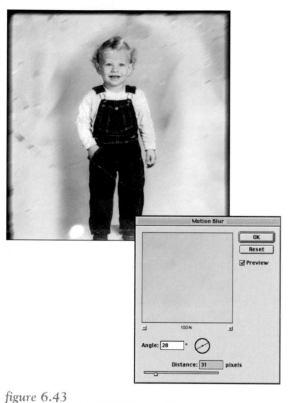

figure 6.43

Using the Motion Blur filter on the background.

4. Art added a new layer on the very top of the layer stack and chose (Cmd + Option + Shift + E) [Ctrl + Alt + Shift + E] to merge all visible layers up. He named it *clean up* and used the Clone Stamp tool and the Healing Brush to remove the remaining cracks and specks on the clean up layer.

5. To add the final painterly touch to the studio backdrop, Art added a new layer and selected a spatter brush from the brush palette, as shown in **figure 6.44**. By adjusting the Brush Tip Shape, Shape Dynamics, Scattering, and Texture, Art created a roughened brush that he used to add a hint of texture to the background.

In conclusion, when you face stains of varying density, balance the tone, and most stains will blend into the image. Although the Healing Brush and the Clone Stamp tool are fantastic tools, it is often easier and more effective to balance the tone rather than trying to cover tonal differences with the Clone Stamp or Healing Brush.

figure 6.44

Adding a painterly touch by painting on a new layer with a roughened brush.

Erasing Pen Scribbles

The combination of old photos and blue ballpoint pens are an irresistible combination for young children. Bob Walden was asked to restore the image in **figure 6.45**, which seemed like a daunting task until he inspected the three channels shown in **figure 6.46**. As soon as he understood that the pen damage was visible in the red and green channels but not in the blue channel (see **figure 6.47**), he was able to create the image without adding too many gray hairs or wasting a lot of time.

BEFORE

figure **6.45**

AFTER

figure **6.46**

ch6_scribble.jpg

RGB   Red channel

Green channel   Blue channel

figure **6.47**

Looking at individual color channels shows that the pen scribble isn't visible on the blue channel.

1. To separate the blue channel from the red and green channels, Bob activated the blue channel, as you see in **figure 6.48**. He then selected Image > Mode > Grayscale. Photoshop will discard the other two channels, leaving the blue channel as a grayscale image.

figure **6.48**

Activating only the blue channel and discarding the other channels.

2. With the pen scribbles out of the way, the restoration process is much less complex. After repairing the largest scratches and tears, Robert used a combination of painting and cloning to remove the woman in the background and the phantom foot visible in the lower-left side of the image.

3. As you can see in **figure 6.49**, the tear goes directly over the little girl's face on the right, and she is missing a nose. Robert borrowed the nose from the girl on the left by selecting it with a Lasso with a one-pixel feather.

4. He then selected Edit > Copy and Edit > Paste and moved the new nose into position on the little girl's face.

figure 6.50

Copying just the head to a new layer and then scaling it.

figure 6.49

Before and after pasting in a replacement nose, obtained by copying from the other girl.

5. Robert felt that the girl's head on the right was a bit too small, so he selected it and copy pasted it onto a new layer and used Edit > Free Transform to scale it up by 5%, as shown in **figure 6.50**.

6. The final cleanup was accomplished with the Clone Stamp and Healing Brush to create the final image shown in **figure 6.51**.

All in all, repairing damage such as stains, discoloration, and energetic scribbling may seem like an exhausting endeavor—but by analyzing where the damage is and isn't, you can save yourself a lot of time and mouse clicks.

figure 6.51

The final image after cleanup.

CLOSING THOUGHTS

Although repairing tears or removing clutter sounds like a mundane endeavor, I hope that the techniques shown in this chapter have given you some creative approaches to ridding the world of scratches, wires, and clutter. Most importantly, always keep in mind how valuable the photo is that you're working on—the people, the memories, the captured moment might be the only reminder you or your client has of something or someone near and dear to them. By removing those scratches and damage, you're giving them back their memories as clear as the day the picture was taken.

REBUILDING, REARRANGING, AND RE-CREATING PORTRAITS

The worst images you will need to repair are the ones that are so damaged by mold, fire, water, and abuse that entire portions of the image are either missing or damaged beyond recognition. In these disaster cases, asking the client for the original negative or a better print is futile because there are none. The secret to replacing, rebuilding, and repairing the beyond-hope images is to beg, borrow, and steal image information from either whatever is left of the original image or to find suitable substitutes to re-create missing backgrounds and body parts.

Although this all may sound like a digital rendition of Stephen Sondheim's *Sweeney Todd*, in which the barbershop was really a butcher shop, rebuilding pictures isn't as gruesome as it seems. So get ready to sharpen your digital scalpel and learn to

- Re-create backgrounds
- Build a background collection
- Rebuild a portrait
- Rearrange a portrait
- Reconstruct color

The tools and techniques we'll use include these:

- Creating and positioning new backgrounds
- Working with Layer Effects and Styles, Adjustment Layers, and Clipping Groups
- Healing Brush and Patch tools
- Channel swapping and color sampling

N o t e

Many of the techniques used to remove dust and scratches as explained in Chapters 5, "Dust, Mold, and Texture Removal," and 6, "Damage Control and Repair," will serve as the foundation for repairing the almost hopeless examples used in this chapter. Keep in mind that I've opted to concentrate on explaining the new techniques not addressed up to this point.

RE-CREATING BACKGROUNDS

Re-creating or rebuilding backgrounds can be as straightforward as lifting a person off the original image and placing her onto a blank background or as involved as finding suitable replacement background images to create a brand new environment. Backgrounds can come from a variety of sources, including other photographs; CD image stock; digital files you've created in Photoshop, Painter, or Deep Paint; and even cloth, textures, or objects you've scanned in with a flatbed scanner. After downloading the tutorial images from www.digitalretouch.org, you'll be able to practice many of the techniques described here.

When you are replacing or re-creating backgrounds, you can choose from four primary working options:

- Clone the existing background over the damaged area.
- Lift the object or person off the original picture and place it onto a new background.
- Paste the new background into the working file, underneath the subject of the photo.
- Rearrange people or objects to minimize distracting backgrounds.

Your first option of cloning or healing the existing background over damaged areas is self-explanatory, and as long as you work on an empty layer with the Clone Stamp tool or on a duplicate layer with the Healing Brush, you can't get into trouble. The additional approaches are explained in the following sections, giving you a great deal of creative flexibility.

Concentrating on the Essential

The power and finesse of the Healing Brush and Clone Stamp tools is both a blessing and a curse. The ability to invisibly repair and replace damaged image information seems magical. Yet the magic's Siren call can lead you to waste time and effort on image areas that are better cropped away or replaced entirely.

In the example in figure 7.1, the center of the original photograph is in relatively good condition, but the background shows a variety of scratches, stains, and rust-like spots. The restoration done by Laurie Thompson in figure 7.2 is clear, compelling, and intelligently done. Rather than wasting a lot of time and effort cleaning up the image background, Laurie separated the couple from the damaged background and created a digital studio backdrop as described here.

 ch7_damaged.jpg

After duplicating the original scan, Laurie started the restoration by selecting the couple. Of course, there are many ways to make a selection in Photoshop—in this case, Laurie used the Quick Mask technique.

1. To enter Quick Mask, press Q. Although your image won't look different, there are a number of signifiers that let you know that you're in Quick Mask mode, such as the darkened Quick Mask button in the toolbar and the newly created Quick Mask channel in the Channels palette.

figure 7.1

figure 7.2

2. Using a hard-edged black brush, Laurie painted over the couple. Because she is in Quick Mask mode, it looks as though she is painting with a translucent red brush, which signifies where she is painting on the mask (see **figure 7.3**).

figure 7.3

Quick Mask mode shows painted (masked) areas in red.

3. It is often easier to see whether all the essential image areas have been masked by turning off the view column of the RGB channels, as shown in **figure 7.4**. Laurie cleaned up the last vestiges of white on the mask by quickly painting over them with a black brush.

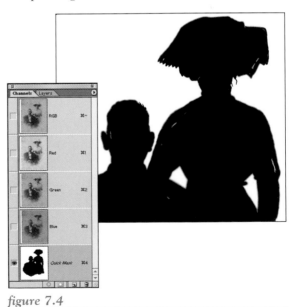

figure 7.4

Turning off all but the Quick Mask channel to clean up the mask.

4. Tapping Q changes the temporary Quick Mask into an active selection, as shown in **figure 7.5**. Notice that the background is selected—use Select > Inverse Selection to invert the selection so that the couple is selected.

figure 7.5

Leaving Quick Mask mode changes the temporary mask into an active selection of the background.

5. Choose Layer > New > Layer Via Copy to place the couple onto their own layer (see **figure 7.6**). More importantly, the couple has been lifted off the damaged background. Rename the layer by double-clicking the layer name and typing a meaningful name.

6. To create the digital backdrop, press D to reset the Color Picker to the default colors and use the Eyedropper tool to sample the original image color from an undamaged image area.

7. Add a new layer, drag it below the couple layer, and activate the Gradient tool.

8. Select the first gradient from the Gradient Presets, which is always foreground to background color or, as seen in this example, the sampled image color to white. Click the radial Gradient button on the Options palette, as circled in **figure 7.7**. Working in full-screen

mode (press F), start the gradient in the center of the image and drag outside the image. By working in full-screen mode, and ending the gradient outside the image you create a fade with a majority of color inside the image, as seen in **figure 7.7**.

figure 7.6

Copying the selection to a new layer.

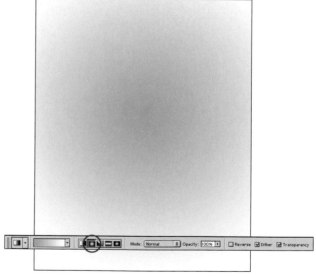

figure 7.7

Drawing a foreground-color-to-white radial gradient on a new layer.

9. This synthetic gradient will not look realistic as a background for the antique image—it is too smooth and pristine. Laurie started by adding noise (Filter > Noise > Add Noise) with Monochromatic checked to add a bit of texture to the background, as seen in figure 7.8.

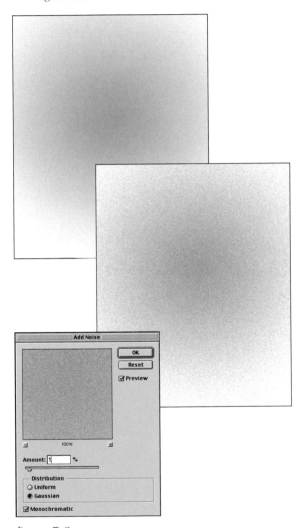

figure 7.8

Blurring the noise slightly reduces the obvious results of adding noise.

10. To avoid the too obvious Photoshop filter look, Laurie then blurred the background with Gaussian Blur to create the textured background (see figure 7.9).

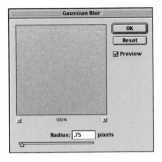

figure 7.9

Making the new background look more realistic by adding noise.

11. To remove any telltale image edges, rather than using the Eraser tool, Laurie added a layer mask to the couple layer and painted with a small black brush to conceal any distracting edges, as shown in figure 7.10.

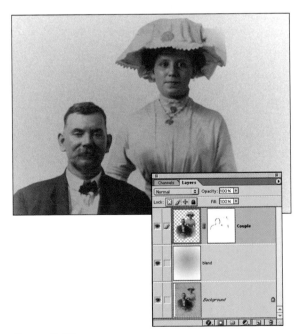

figure 7.10

Painting on a layer mask to clean up image edges and transitions.

12. To add visual separation between the couple and the background, Laurie added a Levels Adjustment layer, as seen in **figure 7.11**, to lighten the background a bit. The added distinction between the figures and the background gives the couple a better visual presence.

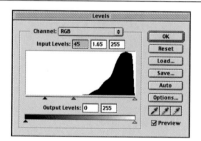

15. She added a Solid Color Adjustment Layer and selected white as the fill color. By adjusting the opacity of the color fill layer (see **figure 7.12**), Laurie was able to add a subtle transition that softens the image edges beautifully.

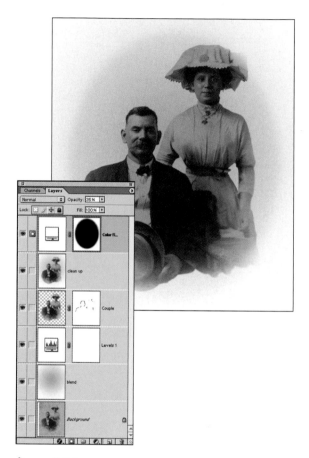

figure 7.11

Lightening the backdrop with a Levels Adjustment layer.

13. After adding a new layer on top of the layer stack, Laurie held (Option) [Alt] and selected Layer > Merge Visible to flatten the working layers up onto the new layer. She refined the image details such as scratches and edge artifacts with the Healing Brush.

14. As a final touch, she vignetted the image by selecting the image with the Elliptical Marquee tool with a 25-pixel feather and then inversed the selection.

figure 7.12

Adding a Solid Color Adjustment layer automatically adds a layer mask based on the elliptical selection.

By not wasting your time, energy, and effort to repair damaged backgrounds or non-essential image information, you are saving your patience, concentration, and time for the most important image areas. **Figures 7.13** (before) and **7.14** (after) show two more excellent examples of image rebuilding done by Sean Melnick.

© Sean Melnick

BEFORE

figure 7.13

AFTER

figure 7.14

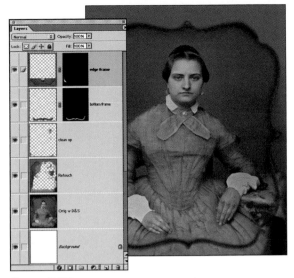

figure 7.15

Sean combined many different scans into one file, masking all but the best information from each layer.

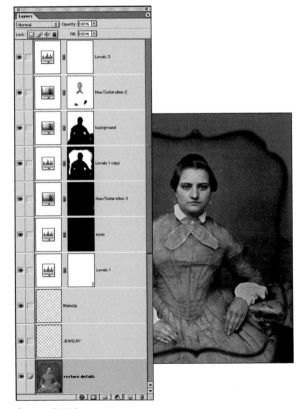

figure 7.16

After correcting and rebuilding each layer, Sean repainted the colors on a merged layer.

1. As Sean Melnick explained the process to me, "First several scans were taken of the images, some with different papers and materials over them to prevent reflections from the mirror-like surface of the tintypes from obliterating important image information."

2. After a number of scans were taken, they were layered into one Photoshop file, and the sections with the most image information were masked out of each layer" (see **figure 7.15**).

3. Each layer was color corrected and, after rebuilding the image, Sean added a new layer and chose (Option) [Alt] Layer > Merge Visible to create a new working layer where he worked on the fine details of the restoration.

4. The woman's tintype had been hand-colored, which was common, and Sean had to repaint the colors of the make-up, dress, and jewelry, as shown in **figure 7.16**. For additional information on hand-coloring, please see Chapter 8, "Refining and Polishing the Image."

Lifting the Subject off the Photograph

In the example in **figure 7.17**, the couple had their photo taken during the wedding reception. Many years later, they wished that they had a professional studio portrait, and as you see in **figure 7.18**, the photo now looks as though it were taken in a studio. In an example like this one, by Laurie Thompson of Imagination Studios, the background replacement is rather straightforward. Laurie used a shot of an empty generic studio backdrop to form the new background (see **figure 7.19**), on which the couple was added.

In a case like this, taking the time to make a good selection around the wedding party is the most important step to creating a realistic composite in which the edges aren't harsh, jagged, or obvious. Believe me, spending a few more minutes at the initial selection stage will save you time later because you won't have to tediously retouch all the edges to cover up a bad selection.

Photoshop has numerous tools to make a selection, including the Magic Wand, Pen tool, Color Range, and the Extract command. No matter which one or combination of these tools you choose to use, I recommend saving the selection into an alpha channel as you go, enabling you to return to the channel to refine the edges of the selection with the painting tools.

🌐▷< **ch7_BW_wedding.jpg**

🌐▷< **ch7_BW_wedding_backdrop.jpg**

1. Make your initial selection by tracing along the edges of the couple with the selection tool you are most comfortable with. Don't worry about getting the selection 100% perfect with your first attempt because you'll use the alpha channel to refine the selection edges in the next step.

BEFORE

figure 7.17

AFTER

figure 7.18

figure 7.19

The studio background.

2. Use either the Lasso tool or, as I prefer, the Pen tool. After activating the Pen tool, make sure to click the Paths button on the Pen tool's options bar and use the Pen tool to outline the couple. After turning the path into a selection, save the selection into an alpha channel by clicking the new channel icon at the bottom of the Channels palette, as shown in figure 7.20.

figure 7.20

After making the path into a selection, I saved the selection into an alpha channel.

3. With the Alpha 1 channel active, click the Show/Hide icon of the primary channel and use a brush to refine the edges. If you used the Pen tool, you would use a hard-edged brush, and if you used a selection tool with a feather to make the initial selection, you need to use a soft-edged brush to match the quality of the edges.

4. When refining the bottom edge of the bride's wedding dress, keep one finger near the X key. Tapping it toggles between the foreground and background color—in this case black and white—enabling you to quickly switch the color of the brush as you refine the edges.

5. When working with a softer image like this one, blur the mask with a low-setting Gaussian Blur to soften the selection. As you can see in **figure 7.21**, the original alpha channel is active and is being slightly blurred.

Tip

Before applying a filter to an alpha channel, duplicate the alpha channel to make a backup insurance copy. That way you can experiment with blurring the alpha channel mask and still have the backup mask in case you over-softened the edges.

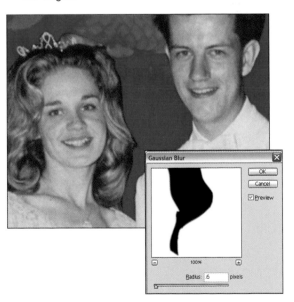

figure 7.21

Applying a subtle Gaussian Blur softens the edges slightly and makes the resulting image look less like a cutout.

6. Make the grayscale image active (Cmd + 1) [Ctrl + 1]. If you are working with an RGB or CMYK file, use (Cmd + ~) [Ctrl + ~].

7. Load the blurred mask as a selection by dragging it down to the Load Channel as Selection icon on the Channels palette.

8. Select Layer > New > Layer via Copy (Cmd + J) [Ctrl + J] to copy the bride and groom onto their own layer. Name the layer.

9. Open the backdrop file and drag it into the bride and groom file. Position it under the bride and groom layer, as shown in **figure 7.22**. If necessary, use Edit > Transform to scale it to match.

figure 7.22

Scale the backdrop to fit the wedding couple file.

10. Zoom in to a 100% or 200% view and double-check the edges of the bride and groom. Use a small, soft-edged eraser to erase any remaining edge artifacts that would show up as dark pixels against the lighter backdrop. In the cases where you place a light subject against a dark backdrop, you'd look for telltale light edges.

Tip

When replacing backgrounds, it is helpful to use a similarly toned or colored background. Using backgrounds that are very different will make the edges much harder to match.

Creating the Drop Shadow

The detail that makes this composite realistic is the subtle shadow underneath the bride's wedding gown. A slight drop shadow gives the figures the needed visual weight to make them seem as though they're really standing on the new background.

1. Select the bottom part of the dress with the Lasso tool, as shown in **figure 7.23**.

figure 7.23

Selecting just a portion of the area you want to shadow will keep the file size down.

2. Select Layer > New > Layer via Copy or (Cmd + J) [Ctrl + J] to float the selected area onto its own layer.

3. Double-click the layer with the hem of the dress to open the Layer Style palette, as shown in **figure 7.24**. Use the distance, spread, and size to add a subtle drop shadow under the dress. Because the lighting in the original image was diffuse, the shadow should be soft and subtle to match.

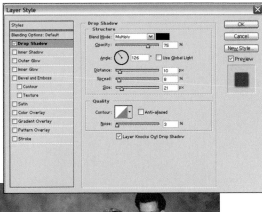

figure 7.24

Use Photoshop Layer Styles to add a slight drop shadow underneath the bride's wedding dress.

4. Photoshop has added a drop-shadow effect around the entire layer, and it looks as though the dress has a dirty tear in it. Move the dress bottom layer to fall under the bride and groom layer, as shown in **figure 7.25**.

 Tip

When creating shadows, mimic the direction and quality of the light in the original photograph. If there are existing shadows in the image, look at them and use them as your reference as you create new digital shadows. You don't want the new shadow to conflict with existing shadow information.

figure 7.25

Position the layer with the shadow underneath the object—in this case, the dress—that is casting the shadow.

To polish the image, Laurie hand-colored the couple to finalize the photograph, as seen in **figure 7.26**.

figure 7.26

The final colorized version is ready for framing.

FINDING SUITABLE REPLACEMENT MATERIALS

In some cases, the ravages of time may have claimed entire chunks of a photograph, or a photo may have been taken in a less-than-attractive environment. In **figure 7.27**, the original image was taken in the basement of a community center, and the woman's head is uncomfortably cropped off. The final version in **figure 7.28** is an artful repair and replace job that took advantage of Laurie Thompson's retouching and creative borrowing skills.

BEFORE

figure 7.27

© Laurie Thompson, Imagination Studios

AFTER

figure 7.28

The two primary challenges Laurie faced were to replace the less-than-pleasant basement environment and to rebuild the woman's head. Starting with the bigger problem—the background—Laurie looked through her slide collection and found this oddly focused and softened snapshot of a gift shop porch (see **figure 7.29**).

figure 7.29

Just the porch.

1. Laurie started by selecting the woman and little girl with the Lasso tool and selected Layer > New > Layer via Copy to lift the figures onto their own layer.

2. She then dragged the porch file and positioned the porch layer underneath the figures, as shown in **figure 7.30**.

3. As you can see in **figure 7.30**, the porch background is too magenta and vibrant. To match the background with the figures, Laurie added a Hue/Saturation Adjustment layer and reduced the saturation and adjusted the hue to tie the background and the figures together visually.

4. To complete the woman's head, Laurie referenced Hermera's Photo Object image collection and found a woman with a similar bouffant hairdo, which she separated from the head, as shown in **figure 7.31**.

figure 7.30

The woman and girl are placed on their own layer, above the porch layer.

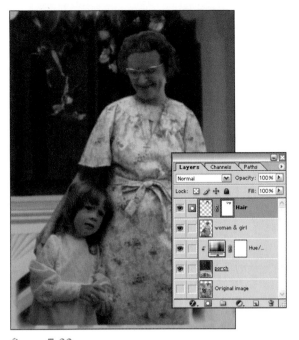

figure 7.32

The hair image copied into place.

figure 7.31

Just the hair.

5. Laurie then dragged the hair into the image reconstruction file and used a layer mask to blend the edges (see **figure 7.32**). To match the new hair to the woman's original hair color, Laurie added a grouped Hue Saturation Adjustment layer by holding (Option) [Alt] and clicking the image adjustment button and selecting Hue/Saturation. When you check Group with Previous, Photoshop creates a clipping group based on the pixel information of the underlying layer. This ensures that the Hue/Saturation changes will affect only the woman's hair without impacting the rest of the image.

6. Laurie fine-tuned the image by moving the hair behind the woman's head to maintain her original hairline and, with the addition of a final Levels adjustment layer shown in **figure 7.33**, the image is ready for the final crop and framing.

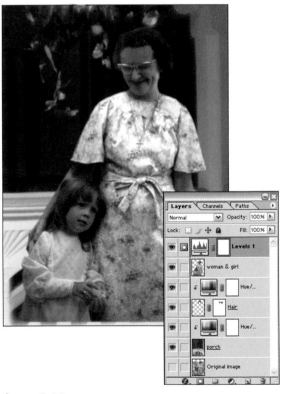

figure 7.33

After moving the hair layer and a final adjustment layer.

The Beauty Is in the Details

I love catching continuity mistakes in Hollywood productions—the clock that never changes time; the glass that is full, empty, and then full again in the same scene; or the shirts that change color from take to take. You can avoid continuity mistakes in your portrait and background retouching by being aware of the following issues:

- Color and contrast: Make sure to match the color and contrast of the pieces you are compositing.

- Film grain and texture: Double-check to see whether the grain and texture match.

- Focus and focal plane: Verify that the focus of a newly placed image background matches foreground elements. Use the blur filters to soften backgrounds to visually push them further back.

- Lighting and shadows: Every image has at least one light source. Sometimes it's the sun, other times a studio light, or perhaps even reflected light, illuminating your subjects. Study how the light is falling in an image and use that information when creating shadows. Look for colors that might be reflected into your image from surrounding areas, such as brightly colored walls or trees.

- Edges and transitions: Mimic the softness or hardness of the edges in the original image to create seamless edges between retouched areas.

- Size relationships: Match the size of dropped-in objects with the people and objects in the original scene.

- Reflections: If someone has glasses on or there are windows in a scene, double-check that the reflections in these surfaces actually reflect the environment in the picture.

- Hollow areas: If someone is standing with his hands on his hips or with his legs spread apart, make sure to mask out the hollow triangle so that the new image background can show through.

Picky, picky, picky. When reconstructing images and backgrounds, keep these details in mind to create seamless and invisible retouching.

BUILDING A DIGITAL BACKGROUND COLLECTION

Image elements and backgrounds are everywhere for you to create or use. The easiest and least expensive replacement backgrounds are the ones you create from scratch with Photoshop. Start with a new file the same size and resolution as the image for which you need a background. Fill the image with a Gradient Blend, as seen in figure 7.34. Choose a lighter and darker version of a color to simulate the light fading toward the bottom. Then add some monochrome noise. The digital noise will give you additional tooth and texture to work with. Once you've made the background you need, simply drag it into your working image.

figure 7.34

Using similar colors when making the Gradient Blend helps to mimic a photo studio backdrop.

In this example, I used the Motion Blur filter and then used the Dust & Scratches filter to mottle the background as though it was a studio linen backdrop, as seen in figure 7.35. Experimenting with filters and color combinations to create your own backdrops is free, easy, and a great way to doodle away a bit of time. Additionally, you can scan pieces of cloth or artistic papers to create your own backgrounds.

Collect your own backgrounds by carrying a camera with you. Whenever you see a pleasant scene or suitable background, take a picture of it—that way you can build your own unique image background library. Very often, the image background should be out of focus. It is better to take the picture out of focus instead of using the Blur filters in Photoshop.

In case you can't create, scan, or photograph an optimal background, turn to the web and CD stock photo collections. Online companies, such as PhotoDisc (www.photodisc.com) and GettyOne (www.gettyone.com), and CD stock companies, such as Hemera Photo Objects (www.hemera.com) and Visual Language (www.visuallanguage.com), offer royalty-free image collections. Always read the usage conditions of the image collection before using the images for commercial purposes. Some collections will not allow you to make calendars or other products for resale or use the images in a pornographic or offensive manner.

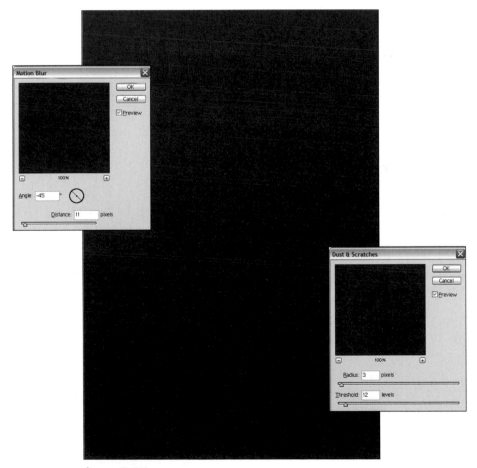

figure 7.35

Combining filters enables you to create unique backgrounds.

Working with Substitute Body Parts

Sometimes fixing an image requires more than a new background or a bit of healing to bring it back to life. In **figure 7.36**, you see the sad scrap that a client handed to Art Johnson of Memories in Minutes with the request that he make the image suitable for framing. As Art explained, "I was stymied with this job, as I had done it a year earlier and the client didn't like it. On that first attempt, I used flowers to fill in the missing corner, which just didn't look right. The client also provided me with another photo of the same person for me to see the woman's hair." (See **figure 7.37**.) With this additional reference, Art was able to create a finished image the client loved, as seen in **figure 7.38**.

figure 7.37

The client provided an additional reference of what the woman's hair looked like.

1. As Art explains, "While I was working on this, I decided to try something new. One of my employees was wearing a spaghetti strap blouse one day, so I took her into the photo studio, wrapped her in cloth and tulle, and did several shots with and without flowers (**figures 7.39** and **7.40**). While I was taking the pictures, I tried to position her like the original.

figure 7.36

The original print remnants.

figure 7.38

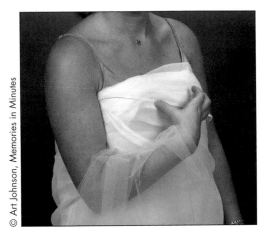

© Art Johnson, Memories in Minutes

figure 7.39

Art took several photos of a model posed like the woman in the photo.

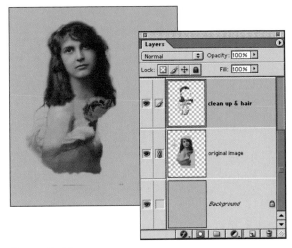

figure 7.41

Art first repaired the damaged original.

© Art Johnson, Memories in Minutes

figure 7.40

Art's modern-day replacement model holding flowers.

2. Art started the restoration process by repairing the damage with the Clone Stamp and Healing Brush (see **figure 7.41**). Then he added the new photographs and used both the image with and without the roses, which enabled him to position them as needed (see **figures 7.42** and **7.43**).

As Art finishes, "The customer loved this new version, and I've used this 'photograph to fix' technique on several orders now. I'm also busy building a stock file of body parts and clothes from both contemporary and antique photographs for me to use as a library."

figure 7.42

The repaired image combined with the modern model.

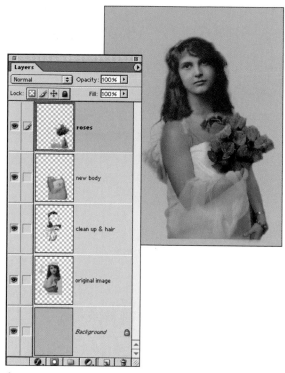

figure 7.43

Compositing the model holding the roses separately allowed Art greater freedom in positioning.

Beg, Borrow, and Steal Image Information

If you don't have access to a photo studio to re-create body parts, follow the lead that Patrick O'Connell did to rebuild the images in **figure 7.44** (before) and **figure 7.45** (after).

Working with Photoshop 6, Patrick used the Clone Stamp tool to repair the most obvious damage first. After hours of cloning, mostly in the sky, the grass, the roof, and the dark siding of the house, he had a cleaner image to better assess the serious damage to be repaired. More importantly, he now had large, clean areas he could use to replace the missing areas.

Then he started repairing the building, borrowing whole sections of window and roof-line. Each new section was copied and pasted into its own layer and then sized, rotated, or flipped to fit. He used Levels to match the tonality of each to its new location.

The coat on the boy at the far right was too damaged for cloning, so Patrick borrowed a new lapel, part of a shirt, and collar from the boy on the left and then resized and rotated them to fit the smaller boy. The boy on the right was also missing half of his face, so Patrick again borrowed from another boy. He resized it somewhat, to make him look a little chubbier than his brother, just to prevent them from looking too identical. Finally, he repaired the boy in the background, borrowing the arms and legs of the larger boy in the foreground and then resizing.

As you can see, different Photoshop artists approach image problems with a variety of strategies. I personally would fix the people first. Patrick used a different strategy of carefully building up image information to work with and refer to as he repaired the image. In the end, the results are what matter.

BEFORE

figure 7.44

AFTER

figure 7.45

© Patrick O'Connell

REBUILDING A PORTRAIT

When retouching damaged portraits, you might have to finesse a face out of nearly nothing, which requires careful use of the Healing Brush, Patch, and Clone Stamp tools. In extreme situations, you might need to "borrow" facial pieces from other photographs or sketches to re-create the face. If this all sounds as though you're playing Dr. Frankenstein, just keep in mind how emotionally valuable the retouched photo will be once it is artfully re-created.

Even an image that is as fungus-ridden as the one in figure 7.46 has enough information and potential to be transformed into the stunning portrait in figure 7.47, which was restored by Maggie Burnett from Auckland, New Zealand.

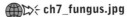 ch7_fungus.jpg

1. Maggie decided she was better off replacing all of the image color rather than trying to restore it. She duplicated the background layer and desaturated it using Image > Adjustments > Desaturate (see figure 7.48). She notes that she did not do tonal adjustments at this stage because she would only be accentuating the tonal variations she sought to remove.

figure 7.46

BEFORE

figure 7.47

AFTER

© Maggie Burnett

figure 7.48

Maggie started by duplicating the background layer and
desaturating it with Hue/Saturation.

2. Maggie used her time and energy wisely. By
    separating the subject from the damaged back-
    ground and placing her on a faux studio back-
    drop, as seen in **figure 7.49**, she avoided a lot
    of tedious repair work.

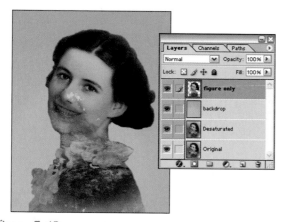

figure 7.49

Placing the separated figure above the faux studio backdrop.

3. Much of the image was obscured by damage,
    and Maggie found it very distracting. As she
    explained, "The jaw line was a problem, and I
    actually visited the lady now in her late eight-
    ies and sketched the line of her jaw. When I
    scanned the sketch, it did not quite fit in with
    what appeared to be the jaw line in the photo.
    I went with my sketch and memory, as the
    sketch seemed a more accurate jaw line of
    that lady's features than did the misleading

lines showing through the damage. I felt that
the damage was possibly showing me an inac-
curate jaw line. I feel the end result proved
this to be the correct thing to do." After scanning and tracing the jaw line as seen in **figure
7.50**, the areas needing restoration were much
clearer. As the restoration proceeded, this
layer was discarded.

figure 7.50

A temporary painted layer to hide the distracting damage.

4. Maggie had large areas of skin to reconstruct.
    She started by making a new layer and using
    the Clone Stamp tool to borrow good skin
    information from the forehead and one good
    cheek. As she assembled enough information
    to cover the damaged areas, she switched to
    the Healing Brush and Patch tool to help
    define contours. This process is depicted in
    the progression shown in **figure 7.51**.

5. Maggie continued rebuilding the face and, to
    keep her work organized, she placed the layers
    in progress into layer sets and color-coded
    them, as shown in **figure 7.52**. As Maggie
    told me, "The hardest thing I found was to
    keep realistic texture to her skin. I have to
    confess that I painstakingly cloned texture
    into the good parts of her face as well as her
    damaged areas in my efforts to get as near
    perfect texture match as I could."

figure 7.51

Maggie cloned undamaged skin information onto a new layer and then used to Healing Brush and Patch tool to define contours.

figure 7.52

Layer sets kept Maggie's work organized.

6. To avoid creating a strong demarcation line between hair and skin, Maggie used the Clone Stamp and Smudge tools with a spatter brush setting to create a soft and wispy transition between the woman's forehead and hairline. She filled out the back of the hair with the Clone Stamp tool to improve the contours, as shown in **figure 7.53**.

figure 7.53

Improving the shape of the hair.

7. Because Maggie has visited the woman, she had the first-hand experience to emphasize her special characteristics. "One thing that was very noticeable about this lady was the brilliance of her eye color; I tried to replicate this color and retain the brightness of the eyes. They are today as they must have been as a young woman: beautiful eyes. I found that although the eye color was correct, there was something radically wrong with the eye area. I left the work alone for a week and did other jobs. When I opened up the file after a week's break, the problem was glaring—her eyelashes were barely visible. Taking a one pixel hard brush, I painted in eyelashes in color mode with an off-black shade. I also changed the shape of the catchlight and the shading of the iris somewhat."

8. Maggie copied the flowers to a new layer and used the Clone Stamp tool and Healing Brush to repair them and bring out the details, as shown in **figure 7.54**.

figure 7.54

The repaired flowers.

9. The original photograph had been hand-colored, and Maggie did a fantastic job applying color back to the image, as shown in **figure 7.55**. Layer by layer, Maggie painted color back into the image by adding a new layer for each color. Changing its Blending Mode to Color allows the tonal information of the photograph to show through. She chose realistic colors and painted small amounts of skin tones onto the contours of the face. She used a similar but warmer color around some of the blush areas and shadowed parts of the face. Turning down the layer opacity softened the color application and provided a more realistic coloration. For additional hand-coloring techniques, please see Chapter 8.

figure 7.55

Refining the hand-coloring.

Flattening Your Image

When a retouch is made up of numerous layers, it can be less confusing to work on a flattened version—a Work in Progress, WIP—while maintaining the working layers. Working on one layer simplifies the process of making selections, applying color correction, and cloning information. There are three ways you can go about creating a flattened image:

- To create a flattened version saved on your hard drive, use File > Save As with the Layers option unchecked. Photoshop automatically adds the word *copy* to the existing name to avoid overwriting your original file. Then open your original file and continue working.

- To merge all working layers while keeping the layered document intact, add a new layer on top of the layer stack and, with all layers visible that you want to merge, hold (Option)[Alt] while selecting Merge Visible from the Layers palette menu. Make sure to keep the (Option)[Alt] key depressed until the layer is flattened and visible.

- To merge the layers in a layer set without merging all the working layers, highlight the set to be merged and hold down (Option) [Alt] as you select Merge Layer Set from the Layers palette menu. Photoshop will automatically create a new layer with the merged layer set.

Shan Canfield, a highly energetic Photoshop expert, teacher, and passionate artist, restored the very damaged painterly portrait shown in figure 7.56 and created a wonderful image by rebuilding and painting on many layers (see in figure 7.57), as Maggie Burnett did in the previous example.

figure 7.56

figure 7.57

Restored by Shan Canfield

Perseverance and Patience

Some restoration projects can feel daunting and endless. If you ever feel overwhelmed by a restoration challenge, look to Leigh-Anne Tompkins of Graphics Afoot Studio Design for inspiration. She started with a tiny, tattered print of a friend's grandmother taken in 1909 (see **figure 7.58**) and worked and reworked the image to create the final image in **figure 7.59**.

The first version Leigh-Anne completed, shown in **figure 7.60**, was much too painterly, and her friend asked her to keep trying. The next time she showed her friend the file, her friend thought that the skin was too splotchy (see **figure 7.61**). Finally, after using dozens and dozens of layers to rebuild the file, both Leigh-Anne and her friend were happy (see **figure 7.59**).

BEFORE

figure 7.58

figure 7.60

Too much like a painting.

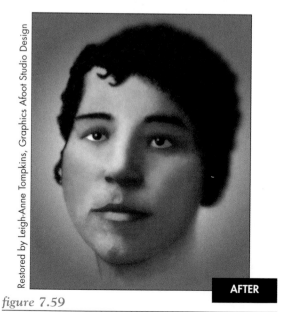

Restored by Leigh-Anne Tompkins, Graphics Afoot Studio Design

AFTER

figure 7.59

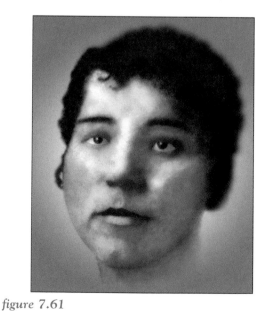

figure 7.61

The skin was too splotchy.

The reason I suggest that you look to Leigh-Anne for inspiration is because she is a successful graphic designer and multimedia specialist. The reason she named her company Graphics Afoot is that Leigh-Anne is a quadriplegic. She uses a Kensington trackball on the floor to move the mouse cursor with her right foot. She also has a head stylus, which allows her to type on the keyboard. So the next time you face a disheartening or complex restoration, think about this example and Leigh-Anne's perseverance to take a tattered scrap of a tiny photo and work with it to create the final image.

figure 7.62

BRINGING PEOPLE CLOSER TOGETHER

Once-in-a-lifetime moments—by definition—can never happen again. This was a situation where the wedding couple did not have a shot of just the two of them after the day was over (figure 7.62). Wayne Palmer of Palmer Multimedia Imaging copied the bride onto her own layer and covered up the grandfather with some of the background that was already in the picture to create an image of the memory of that day as seen in figure 7.63.

1. Wayne started by covering up the grandfather by extending the existing background. He used the Lasso tool to select large areas of the background and then chose (Cmd + J) [Ctrl + J] to copy the selected information onto its own layer. He selected and duplicated the selected area two more times, each time moving it into place until the entire area to the groom's left was covered, as shown in figure 7.64.

2. Now the bride and grandfather were covered with background information, but the transitions between each layer were rather obvious. To make things look more natural, Wayne made a new merged layer and used the Healing Brush to hide the seams between the pieces, as shown in figure 7.65.

figure 7.63

© Erika Kyle

figure 7.64

Wayne selected a section of background, copied it three times onto new layers, and then moved them into place.

figure 7.65

Wayne used the Healing Brush on a merged layer to hide the seams.

3. The groom was a bit lopsided, and Wayne replaced the missing area of the groom by selecting his right side (to our left) with the Lasso tool. He then copied and pasted it onto a new layer, and used Edit > Transform > Flip Horizontal to give it the correct orientation. After moving it into place, he used a layer mask to blend the edges, as shown in **figure 7.66**.

figure 7.66

The missing left sleeve was replaced with a flipped copy of the right sleeve.

4. Now the groom was complete, but the newly created background on his left didn't really have the same atmosphere as the original background on his right. Plus, the skyline transition was very abrupt, and there was a repeating pattern in the background from pasting the same information multiple times. Wayne made a new layer, and with the Clone Stamp tool set to Use All Layers, he constructed a new skyline and added some variations to conceal any obvious patterns.

5. Using the Lasso tool, Wayne copied the bride to a new layer. He used a layer mask to refine and soften her outline and moved her into place next to the groom. He used a temporary black fill layer to hide the distracting background while working on her mask. Notice that the grandfather's hand, which was around the bride's waist, now appears to be the groom's hand (see **figure 7.67**).

6. Rather than cropping the layered file, Wayne used File > Save As and unchecked the Layers option to create a separate flattened version, which he then opened and cropped to create a vertical image.

figure 7.67

The bride is copied onto her own layer, refined with a layer mask, and moved into place.

7. Wayne refined the final image contrast with two Levels Adjustment layers and used a gradient Layer Mask to even out the tonality, as shown in figure 7.68.

figure 7.68

The image is cropped and a layer mask is used to blend two Levels Adjustment layers.

 N o t e

Matching the focus or sharpness of image elements is a challenge. I prefer to soften the sharper image to match the softer image. Sharpening an out-of-focus image is usually a futile undertaking.

Figure 7.69 shows a portrait with the bride and her parents, who then requested a portrait be made of them as seen in figure 7.70. Carrie Beene of H&H Color Labs did a fantastic job of covering the bride up with pieces of the mantelpiece (figure 7.71), selecting and bringing the couple closer together (figure 7.72), and paying attention to the details such as the flowers in the mother's hands, narrowing her arm and waist, and cleaning up the background.

Figure 7.69

Figure 7.70

figure 7.71

Covering up the bride with pieces from the environment.

© First Image Photography

figure 7.72

Moving the parents closer together.

figure 7.73

figure 7.74

In the next original photograph, shown in **figure 7.73**, the four generations of women are simply sitting too far apart. In **figure 7.74**, by repositioning the women, Art Johnson brought the four generations together and created a much better image composition.

 T i p

When you're matching color and contrast between elements, look away from the monitor every few minutes to clear your visual memory. Then look back at the monitor, and you should be able to see any problems with a fresh eye.

RECONSTRUCTING COLOR

Correcting overall color casts as described in Chapter 4, "Working with Color," can alleviate many problems, but often the actual color information of the file is extremely damaged by light leaks, chemical staining, or dye coupler failure, causing severe color splotches or radical color shifts.

The damage seen in **figure 7.75** could have been caused by opening the camera back before the film was entirely rewound or by light leaks in the camera or on the film roll. Or the image might be the first exposure, which may have been partially exposed to light when the film was being loaded into the camera. The image in **figure 7.76** has been repaired and recolored—of course a repaired image will never be as perfect as one that wasn't damaged to begin with.

figure 7.75

BEFORE

figure 7.76

AFTER

© Susan Oakes

⬤▷✂ **ch7_lightleak.jpg**

When you are facing an extreme color problem, the very first thing to do is to repress the impulse to fix the obvious. For example, the extreme red damage may be luring you into thinking, "I need to get rid of that awful red area." And you would diligently add an Image Adjustment layer in the hope of neutralizing the red. But with a problem as extreme as this one, you need to dig deeper and be a more resourceful Photoshopper. When facing difficult or extreme color damage challenges, the best method of correction involves rebuilding the damaged color channels. The first step is to inspect the three individual color channels to identify exactly what is causing the problem. Simultaneously, you are looking for image information to use to repair the damage.

Take a look at **figure 7.77**, which shows the three separate color channels. Can you see how damaged the right side of the red channel is? Now take a second look to identify the image channel that has the most image information. The green channel has the best detail and luminance information.

Red channel

Green channel

Blue channel

figure 7.77

Examining the separate color channels shows you which one has the most damage.

Even if the green channels' damage is as bad as the red channel's, as soon as you can find intact image information, you can breathe a sigh of relief and get to work rebuilding the actual image information. The goal is to take good image information and use it to replace the damaged information. In this case, the right side of the red channel needs to be replaced with good green channel information.

 T i p

To increase the size of the channel's thumbnails, simply select the channels Palette Options and choose the larger thumbnail size.

1. Activate only the green channel. (Cmd + 2) [Ctrl + 2] and choose Select > All and Edit > Copy.

2. Activate the red channel by clicking on its icon in the channels palette or (Cmd + 1) [Ctrl + 1].

3. To define where the green channel information you copied should go, take advantage of the Quick Mask tool and the Gradient tool. Press Q to enter the Quick Mask mode. Press G to activate the Gradient tool, and be sure that the first option, Linear Gradient, is selected. Press D to reset your colors to black and white. Press X to exchange colors, making white the foreground color.

4. Draw a gradient from left to right—start the gradient just to the left of the damage, and drag and release to the worst part of the damage. In this case, I started the gradient by the girl's shoulder and dragged and released, as shown in **figure 7.78**.

5. Because you are in Quick Mask mode, the right side of the image will look red. Don't be distracted by this. The area turned red by the mask will be protected from what is going to be corrected. The purpose of the mask is to protect image areas that do not need fixing.

6. Press Q again to exit Quick Mask mode to create the active selection shown in **figure 7.79**. Click the word *red* in the channel palette, so that only the damaged channel is active and visible, as shown in **figure 7.80**.

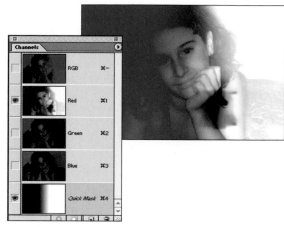

figure 7.78

Using the Gradient tool in Quick Mask mode.

figure 7.79

Exiting Quick Mask mode to create an active selection.

figure 7.80

Viewing only the red channel with the active selection.

7. Choose Edit > Paste Into. Please note: It is very important that you select Paste Into, which really means "Paste into the Active Selection," but Adobe couldn't fit that sentence into the Edit menu. If Paste Into isn't active, there isn't an active selection.

8. This pastes the green channel into the damaged area of the red channel. Click the RGB channel icon or press (Cmd + ~) [Ctrl + ~) to return to the RGB image to see how well the repair worked (see figure 7.81).

figure 7.82

Improving skin tones by painting on a new layer set to Color Blending Mode.

figure 7.81

Clicking the RGB icon shows how well the repair worked.

Many times, after rebuilding image information, you may need to fine-tune specific areas. For example, after repairing the red channel, the image is still a bit flat, and the girl's skin tone looks a little pasty.

9. Add a Levels Adjustment layer and improve the image contrast by moving the highlight slider to the left.

10. To improve her skin tones, add a new layer and change its Blending Mode to color. Use the Eyedropper to sample good skin color, and select a soft-edged brush and paint over the girl's face, as shown in figure 7.82. For this image, I opted to keep her rosy and tan, making her look like she has been outside, because the T-shirt she is wearing attests to the summer season.

11. Sample some hair color and paint over the last vestiges of red on her hair. Add a new layer, change its Blending Mode to Color, and paint the walls of the room with a white brush, as shown in figure 7.83.

figure 7.83

Neutralizing the wall's color cast by painting with white on a new color layer.

12. Add a new layer on the top of the layer stack and hold down the (Option) [Alt] key and Layer > Merge Visible. Use the Healing Brush on this layer to clean up the remaining dust and dirt from the image.

If the damage to an image is not along a straight line like this one, the repair process is very similar. Start by inspecting the channels and copy the best channel information. Then select the damaged area with either the Lasso tool or by painting on a Quick Mask. Make sure that the damaged channel is active, and select Edit > Paste Into. As you can see, the photo in **figure 7.84** has terrible, ragged damage right in the middle of the file. **Figure 7.85** shows the three channels, and **figure 7.86** shows the channels and layers I used to rebuild this file to create the final image in **figure 7.87**.

figure 7.84

The original image has terrible damage right in the middle.

Red channel

Green channel

Blue channel

figure 7.85

The individual color channels.

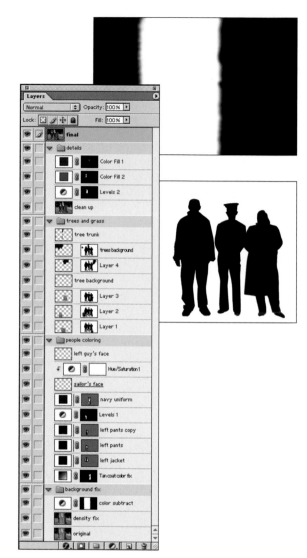

figure 7.86

The alpha channels and layers used to rebuild the file.

figure 7.87

The final image.

ALLEVIATING EXTREME COLOR DAMAGE

Photographic color prints and Father Time rarely make a good partnership, and too often colors fade, shift, or disappear altogether. Take a look at the yellow cowboy image in **figure 7.88**. As far as we can tell, the yellow dye couplers broke free from their oil-based encasing molecules and fogged the entire print with a hideous yellow stain. Lloyd Weller, Director of the Photography Program at Everett Community College, was kind to share this image resurrection with me to include in the book. Reconstructing the color in the image as seen in **figure 7.89** involved swapping channels, working with Levels, and using digital coloring techniques.

Replacing the Damaged Channel

When an image has a blatant color problem like this cowboy image, start by inspecting the individual channels by clicking them in the Channels palette. As shown in **figure 7.90**, the blue channel doesn't have useful image information, but it is required to reconstruct the color, and we'll need to replace it.

figure 7.88

figure 7.89

figure 7.90

The blue channel doesn't hold useable image information and needs to be replaced.

 **ch7_cowboy.jpg**

1. Duplicate the damaged file by selecting Image > Duplicate and then select Image > Mode > Lab Color. The Lab Color mode separates the color information from the lightness (also called luminance) information.

2. In the LAB file, activate the Lightness channel as seen in **figure 7.91** and Select > All and Edit > Copy.

figure 7.91

Duplicate the original file and convert it to Lab Color mode to separate the color information from the lightness information.

3. Return to the original RGB file, activate the blue channel, and Select > All. Use Edit > Paste Into to place the luminance information into the blue channel.

4. **Figure 7.92** shows that the ugly yellow cast is gone. Although the resulting image is still off-color, it certainly looks better than the original jaundiced image.

5. To bring the rest of the color into reasonable balance, use a Levels Adjustment Layer (see **figure 7.93**). Adjust the shadow point slider of the red channel to where the true red channel information begins, thus reducing some of the gross overcast. The Levels Input values Lloyd used on the red channel were 84, 1.00, and 255.

figure 7.92

After replacing the blue channel, the image might still have a color cast that needs to be corrected.

figure 7.93

Adjusting the red channel in a Levels adjustment layer reduces the magenta color cast.

6. Select the green channel in the Levels dialog box and adjust the highlight slider to where the majority of the true green channel information begins (see **figure 7.94**). This will eliminate some of the extreme highlight value information. The midtone gamma slider is also adjusted slightly to assist with the correction. The Levels values Lloyd used on the green channel were 0, 1.05, and 238.

figure 7.94

Adjusting the green channel in a Levels adjustment layer further corrects the color.

7. Select the Blue channel in the Levels dialog box and bring the shadow slider up to the right to eliminate the blue color cast in the background, as seen in figure 7.95. (Try Input Levels settings of 64, 1.00, and 246).

figure 7.95

Adjusting the blue shadow point to the right enables the greens of the background to show through.

Fine-Tuning Individual Color

At this point, the image is starting to look believable—a cowboy in (perhaps) a green shirt on a chestnut horse. The hand-coloring process involves selecting the area to be colored, adding a new layer, filling the selection with the appropriate color, and changing the layer's Blending Mode to Color. By reducing the opacity of the channel, you can control the color saturation of each image element.

1. Start by making a rough selection around the area to be selected. In figure 7.96, I used the Marquee tool to frame the jeans, which will limit the Color Range command to look only inside that selection.

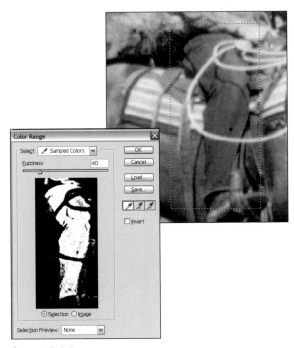

figure 7.96

The Color Range command looks only at specified colors inside the initial selection.

2. When using the Color Range command, you can add colors to the selection with the plus eyedropper or by Shift + clicking the desired colors. In this case, I was careful to select the jeans but not the leather reins or lasso rope.

3. If the selection seems ragged or inexact, press Q to enter Quick Mask mode. Paint in the mask with black (to delete) or white (to add) until the mask is refined, as seen in **figure 7.97**.

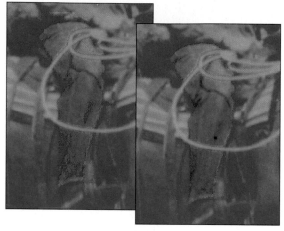

figure 7.97

Check the quality of your selection in Quick Mask mode and refine the mask with the painting tools.

4. Press Q again to activate the selection, add a new Color Fill layer via Layer > New Fill Layer > Solid Color, and choose an appropriate blue for the jeans.

5. Changing the layer's Blending Mode to Color changes the color while letting the black-and-white tonal information show through (see **figure 7.98**) Reduce the layer's opacity as needed to avoid an inappropriately over-saturated look. If you don't like the results, choose a different color by double-clicking on the Color Fill icon and selecting a new color, or try other Blending Modes, such as Multiply, Overlay, or Soft Light.

6. Lloyd made individual selections and used Color Fill layers for each area to transform the seemingly hopeless yellow version to a realistic color photograph that is a pleasure to look at.

figure 7.98

Adjusting the Blending Mode and Opacity enables the tonal information to show through the color.

Using Apply Image to Rebuild Color Channels

Referring to the yellow image in **figure 7.99**, Lloyd Weller explains, "The significant yellow shift throughout the image is due primarily to age and the destruction of the colored couplers in the original blue layer of the early 1950s Kodacolor print film. The yellow dye color is the likely result of a breakdown of the blue layer colored couplers, creating an indiscriminate yellow dye throughout the image. As these dyes are essentially clear when in their original form, once they are exposed to air and light, they break down and they turn yellow." Reconstructing the color in the image as shown in **figure 7.99** involved using the Apply Image command to rebuild channels, working with levels, selections, and hand-coloring techniques to create the charming image in **figure 7.100**.

ch7_yellow_baby.jpg

1. Upon inspecting the three image channels, you can see that the blue channel is so damaged that it is useless (see **figure 7.101**). You will need to rebuild this channel with undamaged image information.

figure 7.99

figure 7.100

Red channel

Green channel

Blue channel

figure 7.101

Examining the individual channels shows the Blue channel has no usable information.

2. The red channel maintained the most image information and can be used to replace the blue. Although this will not give you a perfect correction, it will provide a better foundation upon which other corrections can by applied.

 N o t e

As Lloyd explains, "Using Image > Apply Image allows you to replace a channel with another channel or a percentage of another channel. You can also apply this correction with many of the Blend Modes commonly used in Photoshop. I've found that using the Apply Image command allows me to correct image problems with less chance of creating spiky histograms or banding in the shadow areas."

3. Activate the blue channel, the one that needs repair. Select Image > Apply Image and choose the red channel as the source, as seen in **figure 7.102**. To rebuild the channel, use Normal mode at 100%. The resulting image has a distinct purplish cast.

figure 7.102

Using Apply Image to replace the blue channel with the red channel gives the image a purple cast.

4. The next step will boost the strength of the red channel. In the Channels palette, click the red channel and select Image > Apply Image. Use the red channel with Multiply at 80%. The result is shown in **figure 7.103**.

figure 7.103

Using Apply Image to boost the red channel.

5. In the Channels palette, click the blue channel prior to using the Apply Image command, and add some of the green channel to the blue with Image > Apply Image, with green channel to blue target channel at 100% and Multiply as seen in **figure 7.104**.

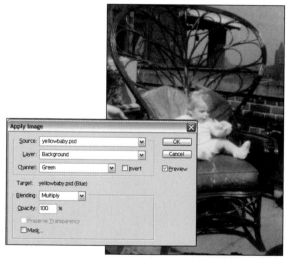

figure 7.104

Further boosting the blue channel using the green channel.

6. In the Channels palette, click the red channel and add some green to red with Image > Apply Image with the green channel to red target at 30% and use Multiply, as shown in **figure 7.105**. These channel corrections give the best sense of the image's original colors.

figure 7.105

One last adjustment to the red channel using information from the green channel.

7. Contrast correction is accomplished by defining the black and white points of the image using Levels or Curves. The white point that seems to work best is a highlight on the baby's shirt. To set the black point, find the darkest shadow in the roof areas behind the chair. Activating the black point eyedropper and clicking this area intensifies the darker values a little without changing the color balance very much (see figure 7.106).

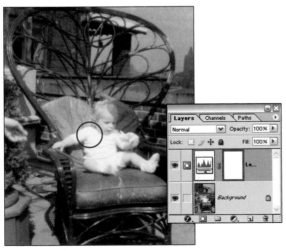

figure 7.106

Setting a new white and black point intensifies tonal values without changing the color balance much.

8. To individually color correct and improve individual image areas, use hand-coloring techniques. Make a new layer and call it *Skin*. Select a skin tone from the Color Swatches palette; Lloyd chose one from the default color palette (232R 173G 98B), and with an appropriately sized brush, he painted in the child's face.

9. Set the Blending Mode in Layers to Color and adjust the opacity for the layer to approximately 24%, as shown in figure 7.107.

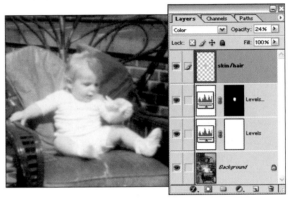

figure 7.107

Painting on a color layer adds realistic color to the child's face.

10. Mix a light gray using the Color palette: 200R 200G 200B, add a new Color layer, and paint the clothing in with 100% opacity, as shown in figure 7.108. This neutralizes the magenta shift, turning the light shadows to a gray.

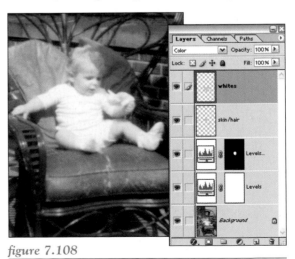

figure 7.108

Painting with gray on a color layer neutralizes the magenta in the clothing.

11. Continue adding new layers, changing the Blending Mode to Color and painting with appropriate colors. To paint in the sky, select a light Cyan color and paint in the sky, adjusting opacity to taste (see figure 7.109).

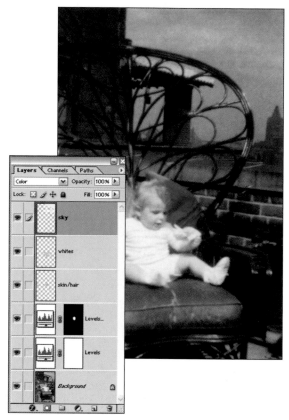

figure 7.109

Painting the sky with light Cyan.

12. For the bricks, add a new layer set to Color Blending Mode and select a light brown from the bottom-left corner of the Swatches palette. Paint in the floors and bricks as needed. You can use a separate color for the brick if you like. Also, use a different color for the window areas. Again, lower the layer opacity as needed.

13. Lloyd continued to use new layers of the pillow, the cushions, and the chair.

14. To refine the retouch work necessary, Lloyd added a new layer on the top of the layer stack and chose (Option) [Alt] Layer > Merge Visible and used the Healing Brush and Clone Stamp tool to clean up any remaining dust or ragged edges.

CLOSING THOUGHTS

Replacing, rebuilding, and re-creating missing image elements requires creative problem-solving skills, the willingness to dig around in a file to look for useful material, and the ability to appropriate suitable pieces from other photographs and scenes. The search will result in new images that are much more pleasing and meaningful to display and cherish.

8

REFINING AND POLISHING THE IMAGE

After perfecting an image's color and contrast and repairing the ravages of time, it's time to apply the final polish, the frosting, the cherry on top. Finishing an image can be as simple as converting a so-so color image into a snappy black-and-white photograph or colorizing a black-and-white photo. You can make the difference between "Ho-hum" and "Wow!" by adding just the right amount of sharpening or a subtle filter effect or by experimenting with creative exposure and edge techniques to accentuate the image.

All in all, this chapter is about experimenting, dabbling, exploring, and adding a touch of pizzazz to retouched images or forgotten snapshots to make them stand out. Here you learn how to do the following:

- Convert color images to black and white
- Add color to black-and-white images
- Work with soft and selective focus
- Add frames and vignetted edges
- Sharpen images to add snap

CONVERTING COLOR TO BLACK AND WHITE

A fine black-and-white photograph has an abstractness and aura that full-color images often just don't have. They remind us of the rich heritage of the photographic masters—Edward Steichen, Alfred Stieglitz, Ansel Adams, and Edward Weston, to name a few.

If black and white is so attractive, why do most of us use color film? Because we see in color, it's easier to take a color picture than to figure out how the colors will translate into shades of gray. In fact, I never use black-and-white film anymore, but I do make beautiful black-and-white prints. How, you wonder? I shoot color slides or color negative print film and scan them. In more and more cases, I use a digital camera and then use Photoshop to convert the color file into a beautiful black-and-white image.

As with many techniques in Photoshop, there are numerous methods of converting an RGB file from color to grayscale, ranging from a one-click solution with no control to a multi-step process with infinite control.

Of course, I'd like you to avoid the one-click method because it removes important image information. However, please don't jump to the last, most involved method because you think it must be the best. It may not be the best for the images you're working with. All of the techniques I describe here will work with both RGB and CMYK images. Your numeric values will vary depending on your color and separation setup.

Converting to Grayscale Mode

The fastest (but worst) way to convert a color file to grayscale is to select Image > Mode > Grayscale, which just discards color information without giving you control over the process. As benign as this process seems, the behind-the-scenes math is rather complicated. Photoshop references your color and ink settings and then takes approximately 30% red, 59% green, and 11% blue to make the single-channel grayscale file. The worst part of this conversion process is that there's no preview and you have no control over the percentages or the final outcome.

To simplify this, Photoshop takes all three channels and smashes them down into a single channel. If one of the channels is damaged or excessively noisy, as shown in figures 8.1 and 8.2, those artifacts go into the grayscale file as well. Although this method is fast and easy, I cannot recommend it for either RGB or CMYK files because you can achieve better results with the following methods.

ch8_costume.jpg

figure 8.1

The original image.

figure 8.2

In this digital camera file, the blue channel shows excessive noise that would degrade the quality of the grayscale file if you chose Mode > Grayscale and flattened the three RGB channels into one.

Using a Color Channel

A second way to convert from color to grayscale gives you a chance to choose the best channel before discarding the color information. Inspect the quality and characteristics of each channel and decide which one has the best tonal information. (Remember that pressing (Cmd)[Ctrl] along with 1, 2, 3, and (for CMYK images) 4 will activate channels individually.)

In most cases, it will be the green channel, but for some pictures, such as creative portraits, the red channel may offer a pleasingly glowing alternative. In either case, make the best channel active (as shown in **figure 8.3**), and select Image > Mode > Grayscale. The less-useful channels are thrown away, and the channel you consider the best becomes the grayscale image. Many newspaper productions use this technique to convert a color image to grayscale quickly.

figure 8.3

Converting to grayscale with the best channel active will delete the two (or three) weaker channels.

Using the Luminance Channel

A third method to convert a color image to grayscale starts by converting it from RGB or CMYK to Lab, as shown in figure 8.4. Then, make the L channel (lightness) active and select Image > Mode > Grayscale. Like the previous example, you will see a dialog box asking whether you want to discard the other channels. This method maintains the luminance value of the image more closely than using a single channel from an RGB or CMYK file (see figure 8.5).

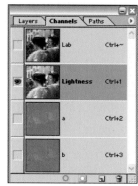

figure 8.4

Converting a color image to Lab color separates the tonal information from the color information.

figure 8.5

The resulting grayscale file doesn't have any of the noise artifacts that the original color image had.

Using the Channel Mixer

The Channel Mixer enables you to add and subtract varying amounts of each color channel to build grayscale files with a wide tonal and interpretive range. This is by far the best balance of ease of use and quality of results for converting color images to grayscale. It's my favorite way to get very good results quickly.

1. Add a Channel Mixer Adjustment Layer and make sure that the monochrome (another word for *grayscale* or *single channel*) check box is checked.

2. Adjust the color sliders to create a grayscale image that uses tonal attributes from the desired channels. To maintain tonality when converting, the sum total of the numeric values should not exceed 100. However, if your

goal is to create the best grayscale image possible, experiment with the sliders until you're satisfied with the results (see **figure 8.6**). I rarely use the Constant slider because it applies a linear lightening and darkening effect like Brightness/Contrast. I'd rather use Levels or Curves to finesse the final tonality of the image after conversion.

figure 8.6

Using a Channel Mixer adjustment layer to create quality black-and-white images from a color file gives you tremendous control.

3. Remember to keep an eye on the Info palette, and don't let the highlights go over 245, 245, 245 so they don't get blown out to pure white. Click OK to close the Channel Mixer dialog box.

 T i p

You can open the Info palette by pressing the F8 key. Press it again to hide the palette. This works even while you're in the Channel Mixer dialog box (or any Adjustment Layer interface).

4. Once you've created the black-and-white image you want, flatten the layers, and select Image > Mode > Grayscale. Photoshop will bring up the Discard Color Information warning, which you can disregard because all three channels are identical now. Select File > Save As and save it as another filename to preserve your original color image.

 T i p

When using the Channel Mixer, you can start with the 100% green channel rather than the default 100% red channel by pressing (Cmd + 2) [Ctrl + 2] before checking the Monochrome box.

 T i p

To speed up production when converting similar color files to grayscale, you can either save and load the Channel Mixer settings or drag the Channel Mixer Adjustment Layer between files.

🌐 ⊳⊱ **ch8_sunflower.jpg**

The Channel Mixer enables you to interpret and influence how the color values are translated into black and white. In **figures 8.8**, **8.9**, and **8.10**, I've created three interpretations of the color image shown in **figure 8.7**. Working from left to right, I created subtle to dramatic interpretations of the sunflower scene by changing the Channel Mixer settings.

figure 8.7

The original image.

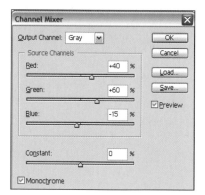

figure 8.8

The Channel Mixer can be used to create a classic black-and-white image…

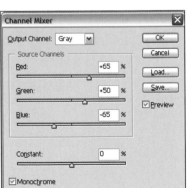

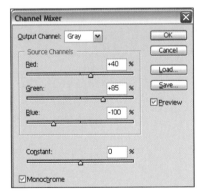

figure 8.9

…*or something a little more dramatic…*

figure 8.10

…*or something quite stormy.*

Mimicking Photographic Film and Filters

I learned the following technique from Russell Brown (www.russellbrown.com), the ultimate Photoshop evangelist. It uses two Hue/Saturation image adjustment layers—one acts as a filter on the lens, and one is the black-and-white film. By combining these layers with Blending Modes, you can mimic how black-and-white photographers use filters and film types to influence scene rendition.

ch8_poppy.jpg

1. To create the photographic filter layer, add a Hue/Saturation Adjustment Layer and simply click OK without changing anything in the dialog box. Change the Blending Mode to Color, as seen in **figure 8.11**.

figure 8.11

The filter layer starts as an unadjusted Hue/Saturation layer set to Color Blending Mode.

2. To create the film layer, add a second Hue/Saturation Adjustment Layer and set the saturation to –100, as shown in **figure 8.12**. To reduce possible confusion, you may want to name the top layer *film* and the lower layer *filter*.

figure 8.12

The film layer is another Hue/Saturation layer, this time set to –100 saturation.

3. After you've added these two layers, the fun and creativity can begin. Double-click the filter layer and adjust the Hue slider. Notice how the color values are translated into black and white. **Figure 8.13** shows a variation in which I emphasized the shadows in the image, and **figure 8.14** is a brighter, less ominous interpretation of the image.

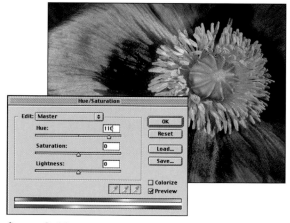

figure 8.13

Adjusting the Hue slider on the filter layer to emphasize the shadows.

figure 8.14

Changing the Hue setting for a brighter version.

4. You also can adjust the saturation, which emphasizes that area of the color wheel even more (see **figures 8.15** and **8.16**).

figure 8.15

Adjusting the Saturation slider to emphasize changes made to the shadows with the Hue slider.

figure 8.16

Adjusting the Saturation slider in the brighter version emphasizes the highlights.

5. For additional control, you can drop down to a specific color in the filter Hue/Saturation layer and make further adjustments on specific colors, as seen in **figure 8.17**.

This technique avoids a common downfall of the simpler Channel Mixer technique in that it is nearly impossible to over-influence the image and blow out the highlights to pure white.

figure 8.17

Adjusting individual colors offers very fine control over the grayscale representation.

Blending Channels

Black-and-white photography has such a rich history that it comes as no surprise that there are numerous methods to convert beautiful color images like figure 8.18 into beautiful digital black-and-white images like figure 8.19. Lee Varis (www.varis.com) showed me this method, which takes advantage of layer Blending Modes and layer masks to create an image using the best parts of an image's channels. Before beginning this technique, I cannot emphasize enough that you need to work on a duplicate or a backup of your color file. Okay, you've been warned—let's get started.

figure 8.18

BEFORE

© Katrin Eismann

figure 8.19

AFTER

Caution

Before splitting the color channels into individual files, you must flatten the color image, delete all alpha channels, and duplicate the image.

ch8_newmexico.jpg

1. Open a color image. In the Channels palette, select Split Channels from the palette menu. This will separate the three channels into individual files (see figure 8.20) that are named after the channels from which they originated.

figure 8.20

Selecting Split Channels separates each channel into a separate grayscale file.

2. With the Move tool, drag the green channel file onto the red channel file. To ensure perfect registration, hold down the Shift key while dragging the files on top of one another. Drag the blue channel file on top of the red channel file and name the layers to reflect their origins, as shown in figure 8.21. Close, without saving, the separate green and blue channel files.

3. Take a moment to look at the three layers and decide which tonal attributes you like. In this example, I prefer the building rendition in the red layer and the sky in the blue and green layers.

figure 8.21

Holding the Shift key while using the Move tool to drag one file onto another will add it as a perfectly registered layer.

4. Drag the red layer to the top of the layer stack, as shown in figure 8.22. To concentrate on the clouds, turn off the view icon (the eye) of the red layer and activate the green layer.

5. Change the Blending Mode of the green layer to Soft Light to add contrast to the clouds, which you can adjust using the opacity sliders. I used 60% opacity to allow the tones of the blue channel layer to shimmer through.

figure 8.22

Place the layer with the least amount of desired tonal information on top of the layer stack.

6. To add the building from the red layer back into the image, use a layer mask to hide and reveal image areas that you want to interact. Make the red layer visible again and add a layer mask. To conceal the clouds on the red layer, use the Gradient tool with black as the foreground color and select the black to transparent gradient, as shown in figure 8.23. In this instance, I clicked on reverse in the options bar to allow me to protect the building while fading out to the clouds.

figure 8.23

Using a black-to-transparent gradient enables the use of multiple gradients on one layer mask.

7. Start the gradient just within the top building edge and draw it out to the edge of the image (see figure 8.24). Repeat with a gradient on the left side of the building, as shown in figure 8.25.

figure 8.24

Using the gradient to mask out the sky.

figure 8.25

Adding a second gradient to the same layer mask.

8. (Option + click)[Alt + click] the layer mask to make it visible, as shown in **figure 8.26**. As you can see, wherever the mask is white, the building will show through, and where the mask is black, the clouds are hidden, allowing the green layer clouds to be seen.

9. As a final tweak, I changed the red layer's Blending Mode to Lighten, as shown in **figure 8.27**.

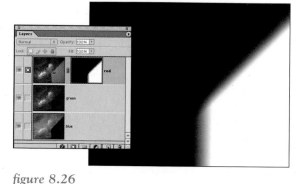

figure 8.26

(Option + clicking) [Alt + clicking] the layer mask icon displays the mask. Repeat to return to your image.

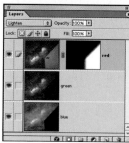

figure 8.27

Changing the Blending Mode of the red layer to Lighten adds the finishing touch.

All of these changes are purely subjective, and your interpretation of a file may vary greatly from mine. Experimenting with Blending Modes and layer position can create wonderful tonal juxtapositions that are sure to surprise and intrigue the viewer.

Using Calculations

The final method of converting an image from color to grayscale is to use the Calculation functions. Besides color management, mastering this feature is the one thing that separates the Photoshop weenies from the meisters. Similar to Channel Mixer, the Calculations command enables you to mix individual channels with all the benefits of Blending Modes, opacity settings, and masks. Unfortunately, you can combine only two channels at a time. The following technique is especially useful when you're converting a CMYK file to grayscale. Figure 8.28 shows an attractive portrait; after converting it to black and white with calculations, figure 8.29 has an understated yet classical feeling.

BEFORE

figure 8.28

© Ablestock

AFTER

figure 8.29

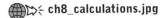 **ch8_calculations.jpg**

1. Inspect the color channels to see which ones carry the attributes you would like either to accentuate or minimize. Avoid using channels that are too contrasty, noisy, or posterized.

2. Select Image > Calculations.

3. Use the pull-down menus to select the two channels you want to combine, as shown in figure 8.30.

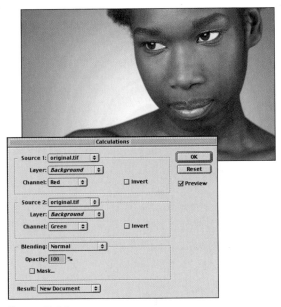

figure 8.30

Start by selecting the channels you want to combine.

4. Change the Blending Mode to influence the interaction between the channels. As you can see in figure 8.31, changing the Blending Mode to Hard Light changes the tonal character of the portrait.

5. Adjust the Opacity setting to 75%. This controls how strongly the topmost channel (in this case, the red channel) is used in the calculation.

6. Make sure that Result is set to New Document and click OK.

7. The resulting document is a Photoshop multichannel document. To save the document as a standard grayscale file, select Image > Mode > Grayscale.

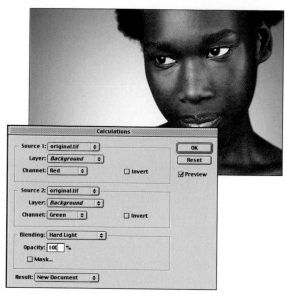

figure 8.31

Changing the Blending Mode, opacity, and order of Source 1 and 2 channels influences the final outcome.

8. By using the red and green channels with the Softlight Blending Mode, I was able to reduce the contrast, to create a softer interpretation of the portrait shown in **figure 8.32**.

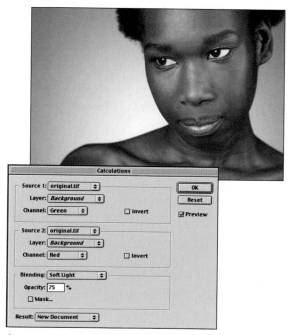

figure 8.32

Working with Image Calculations to create another image interpretation.

 C a u t i o n

When you're calculating with separate images, each image must be the same size, pixel for pixel; otherwise, the Calculations interface won't recognize the file.

All in all, I've shown you seven different ways to convert a color file to grayscale, and I hope that you take the time to experiment to see which one gives you the most pleasing results.

COMBINING COLOR AND BLACK AND WHITE

You can draw a viewer's eye to an element by making it the only color object in the picture. This effect is used all the time in advertising campaigns. (For example, a pair of blue jeans are in color and the rest of the picture is black and white.) Experiment with desaturating an image and painting back a few color elements to create a painterly or nostalgic look.

I was drawn to this café in New Mexico by the juxtaposition of the Madonna and the Coke sign (see **figure 8.33**). Isolating and accentuating the two, as shown in **figure 8.34**, emphasizes the intended character of the photograph.

ch8_cafe.jpg

1. Add either a Hue/Saturation or Channel Mixer Adjustment Layer to a color image. If you use Channel Mixer, adjust the channel sliders to create a pleasing black-and-white image, as described previously. If you use Hue/Saturation, move the saturation slider all the way to the left, as shown in **figure 8.35**.

2. Click the layer mask and use a soft-edged, black brush to block out the desaturation or, said differently: Paint over the areas where you want to bring color back (see **figure 8.36**).

figure 8.33

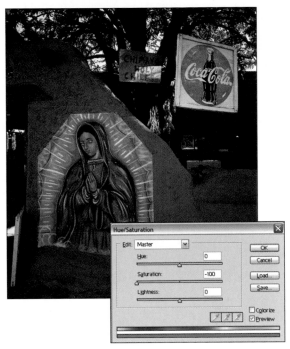

figure 8.35

Use a Hue/Saturation Adjustment Layer to remove all of the color from the image.

© Katrin Eismann

figure 8.34

figure 8.36

Painting with a soft, black brush on the layer mask reveals the original color.

4. Experiment with using shades of gray to fill the selection in order to maintain a hint of color. I duplicated and inverted the Hue/Saturation layer, double-clicked it, and saturated the Madonna and Coke sign by 15% to accentuate their color even more (see figure 8.37).

PJ Leffingwell specializes in wedding photography and uses Photoshop to accentuate the mood of a wedding. In the beautiful image in figure 8.38, PJ used a Channel Mixer Adjustment Layer to convert the image into black and white; then he painted on the layer mask to bring back the color of the flower bouquets.

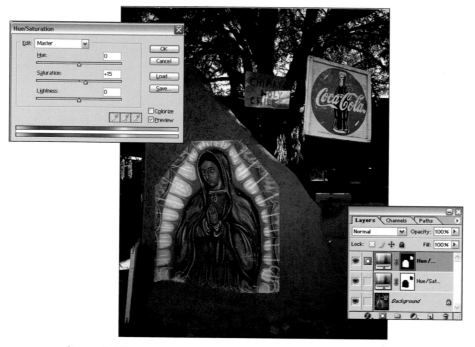

figure 8.37

Duplicating and inverting the original Hue/Saturation layer lets you make further refinements to just the color areas.

© PJ Leffingwell

figure 8.38

Combining Sepia with Color

You can combine more than back and white and color. In fact, as PJ Leffingwell shows, you can combine sepia and color to create very romantic images (see figure 8.47 at the end of this section) or to create very popular images from a color photograph to sepia with color, as seen in figures 8.39 and 8.40.

figure 8.39

© PJ Leffingwell

figure 8.40

To achieve this effect, which, PJ says, "my customers just love," use the following technique. Use a flattened, color image of your own:

1. From the Action palette menu, select Image Effects.atn to load the Image Effects Actions (see figure 8.41).

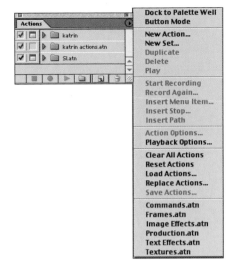

figure 8.41

Clicking the fly-out menu in the Actions palette reveals the many action sets that come with Photoshop.

2. Load the Image Effects actions by clicking the small triangle next to the Image effects folder and click Sepia Toning (layer). Click the Play button at the bottom of the Actions palette, as circled in figure 8.42.

figure 8.42

After selecting a specific action, clicking the Play button starts it.

3. As the Layers palette reveals in **figure 8.43**, Photoshop duplicated the image to a new layer, converted it to black and white, and used a Hue/Saturation layer to add the sepia toning.

figure 8.43

The Sepia Toning (layer) action creates a desaturated duplicate layer and a grouped Hue/Saturation Adjustment Layer.

4. Apply the sepia effect by selecting Layer > Merge Down to create a sepia layer on top of the color layer. Add a layer mask to the sepia layer.

5. By painting with a soft-edged, black brush on the layer mask, PJ is able to reveal the original color image below the sepia layer. In this example, PJ painted back the yellow bouquet and the blue of the little girl's dress, as shown in **figure 8.44**.

figure 8.44

Painting with a soft, black brush reveals the color layer below.

6. To darken the edges of the image, PJ added a Curves Adjustment Layer and set the Blending Mode to Multiply, which darkened the entire image, as shown in **figure 8.45**.

figure 8.45

A Curves Adjustment layer set to Multiply darkens the entire image.

7. PJ inverted the Curves layer mask via Image > Adjustments > Invert (Cmd + I) [Ctrl + I] and then very slyly used a white-to-transparent gradient to reveal the darker edges. By setting the Gradient tool to use white to transparent, PJ could drag over each edge with the Gradient tool to darken the edges (see **figure 8.46**).

figure 8.46

Inverting the Curves layer lets you reveal the darker edges with a white-to-transparent gradient.

require a great deal of guesswork on your part because Variations gives you a preview of the finished image. For more details on the Variations dialog box, see "Understanding Color Correction with Variations" in Chapter 4, "Working with Color."

Figure 8.48 shows the original image, and figure 8.49 shows the toned version. To me, the bluer version is much more attractive and fitting to the subject.

figure 8.47

Combining sepia and color to create a romantic effect.

figure 8.48

TONING IMAGES WITH COLOR

Photographers tone their prints for a number of reasons. Selenium toners add warmth to a print and make it last longer. Ferric oxide toners add a beautiful blue tone, and gold toners add richness that is hard to resist. But toning prints in a traditional darkroom can also pose both health and environmental hazards. Unless you have proper ventilation and chemical disposal options, traditional darkroom toning is not recommended. But with Photoshop, you can tone images to your heart's content without having to clean up messy sinks and smelly trays or dispose of noxious chemicals.

Toning with Variations

The Variations dialog box is the easiest way to experiment with image toning options. The original image is shown, along with a collection of variations (hence the name) created by strengthening or weakening the colors in the image. It doesn't

figure 8.49

ch8_lion.jpg

1. Select Image > Adjust > Variations.

2. The ring of six color options enables you to experiment by clicking the color you want to add to the image. I recommend reducing the strength of the effect by moving the Fine to Coarse slider to the left, as shown in figure 8.50.

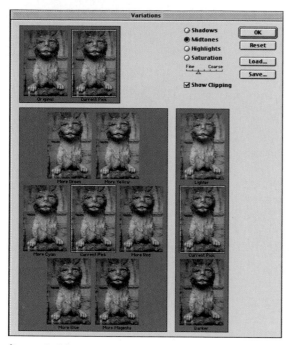

figure 8.50

The visual feedback you get from Variations is often a good place to start when toning a black-and-white image.

3. You can click a color more than once to strengthen the effect, or click the opposite color to subtract the first color.

T i p

When working with Variations, you can zero out the effect by clicking the original thumbnail in the upper left of the Variations interface.

C a u t i o n

For any black-and-white image to be colorized or toned, the file must be in either RGB, CMYK, or Lab color mode. Before you begin, convert the file from grayscale to a color mode, preferably RGB or CMYK.

Monocolor Toning

Variations is very easy to use, but that simplicity comes with a price because your changes aren't applied to a separate layer or added as an Adjustment Layer. In other words, you're changing the actual image data and not working on a separate layer. To maintain control and flexibility, I prefer to work with separate layers and do my toning with the tools described here and in the next section, "Multicolor Toning." Monocolor toning is a straightforward method of adding one color to an image (as shown in figures 8.51 and 8.52) and can be used to tie a group of images together visually or to add an interpretive mood to an image.

 **ch8_facade.jpg**

1. Select Layer > New Fill Layer > Solid Color and select a color from the Color Picker.

2. Change the layer's Blending Mode to Color, Overlay, or Pin Light to create the effects shown in figures 8.53, 8.54, and 8.55.

3. The advantages to using the Color Fill layer, as shown in figure 8.56, are that you can work with the Opacity and Blending Modes to reduce the effect; take advantage of the Layer Mask to control where the effect takes place; and, by double-clicking the Solid Color layer, select new colors. If you don't like the results, you can just throw the entire layer away and start over again.

figure 8.51

figure 8.52

figure 8.53

The Color Blending Mode.

figure 8.54

The Overlay Blending Mode.

figure 8.55

The Pin Light Blending Mode.

figure 8.56

Placing the color on a separate layer enables you to fine-tune the effect with Opacity and Blending Mode settings.

Multicolor Toning

The world is your Photoshop oyster when you work with Adjustment Layers. The Color Balance tool enables you to tone and color highlights, midtones, or shadows separately, just as a fine art photographer would do in a traditional darkroom.

The original chapel photo used in this example is a black-and-white RGB file, as shown in **figure 8.57**. **Figure 8.58** shows how adding complementary colors into the highlights and shadows makes the image more dimensional and attractive.

 ch8_chapel.jpg

1. To add subtle colors to the shadows, midtones, and highlights, add a Color Balance Adjustment Layer and click shadow, midtone, or highlight, depending on the area you want to tone.

2. Adjust each area so that it complements and offsets the others. Often, I tone the shadows and highlights and don't alter the midtones. This adds color tension to an image.

3. As shown in **figure 8.59**, I toned the shadows blue-cyan. In **figure 8.60**, I chose to contrast the cool tones with warm tones in the highlights.

The only correct setting for any of these techniques is what looks good to you. So have fun, experiment, and bring those black-and-white images to life.

BEFORE

figure 8.57

AFTER

figure 8.58

© Katrin Eismann

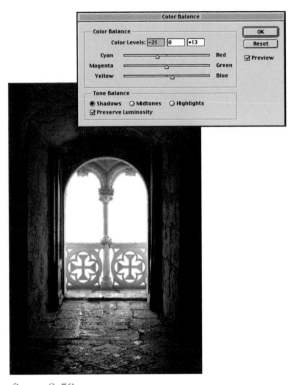

figure 8.59

Adding cyan and blue to the shadows.

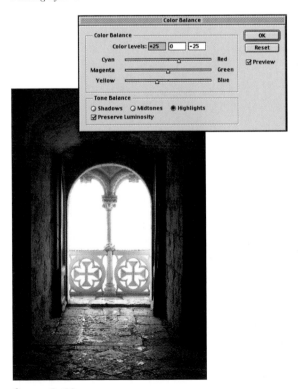

figure 8.60

Adding red and yellow to the highlights.

HAND-COLORING A BLACK-AND-WHITE IMAGE

Since the advent of photography, photographers and artists have hand-colored photographs to add realism. Even in today's era of computers and Photoshop, there are many professional retouchers and photo enthusiasts who still enjoy working with Marshall Oils to add a handcrafted look to their photos. I've never been very good at hand-coloring traditional darkroom prints, which is why I especially like doing it on the computer.

The most straightforward method of hand-coloring an image entails adding an empty layer that has been set to the Color Blending Mode and using any painting tool to color it, as shown in figure 8.61.

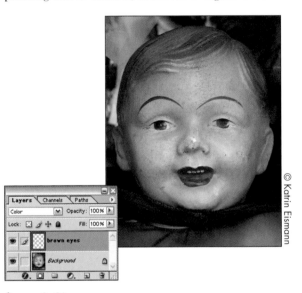

figure 8.61

By painting on an empty layer that has been set to the Color Blending Mode, you can hand-paint details in the eyes of this window mannequin.

You also can hand-color an image by making selections and using Color Fill Layers, as illustrated by the black-and-white image shown in **figure 8.62**, which Frank Eirund, a Munich-based computer specialist but self-proclaimed Photoshop beginner, has hand-colored (well, mouse-colored) beautifully, as shown in **figure 8.63**. This coloring method requires a bit more patience, but the flexibility of working with Color Fill Adjustment Layers is well worth the effort.

Before you start hand-coloring an image, take a moment to visualize and plan out your color scheme. After scanning in the original photograph of his parents' wedding photo from August 1963, Frank decided to turn the black-and-white photo into a color one as a gift for their 40th wedding anniversary celebration. Frank took a moment to decide which colors he would use. Of course, the

flower bouquet needed to be red and green and he decided to make the background blue to frame the couple wonderfully.

1. Select the first element of the image you would like to hand-color. Frank started by selecting the roses with the Lasso tool, as shown in **figure 8.64**.

2. Add a Solid Color Layer by clicking the Adjustment Layer button on the bottom of the Layers palette and selecting Color Fill, or select Layer > New Fill Layer > Solid Color.

3. Use the Photoshop Color Picker to select a color (most likely in the red family) for the roses. The Fill Layer is automatically filled with the color (see **figure 8.65**). Set the layer's Blending Mode to Color to let details from the original image show through.

figure 8.62

BEFORE

© Frank Eirund

figure 8.63

AFTER

figure 8.64

The roses are the first element selected for coloring.

figure 8.66

Using different shades of red and green makes the bouquet more realistic.

figure 8.65

The image after the selection has been filled with color and the layer's Blending Mode has been changed to Color.

4. Frank selected the green leaves of the bouquet, added a new Color Fill layer with green, and set the Blending Mode to Color. Of course, the entire flower bouquet won't all be an identical shade of green, so he made another selection and filled this with a darker shade of green (see **figure 8.66**).

5. If a color is too strong, you can double-click the Color Fill Adjustment Layer icon and select a new color with the Color Picker. Or, you can reduce the opacity of the layer.

With the patience of a saint, Frank continued selecting his way up the image, using individual layers for elements as small as individual flowers and his parents' eyes for a total of 24 Color Fill layers to create the final image.

Because the Color Fill layers are based on selections and have masks with them, you can refine where the coloring takes place by painting with a black or white brush on the Color Fill's layer mask.

🖐 *Hand-Coloring Tips*

Hand-coloring can be both tedious and rewarding. Here are a few tips to help you work a little faster and make your results more realistic:

- As Wayne Palmer explains, "When you mix color with white, you get white. When you mix color with black, you get black. For the best results, you need shades of gray that the color can interact with." As shown in figure 8.67, where the red strip is over the darkest or lightest areas of the gradient, you cannot see the red.

figure 8.67

When using a Color Fill layer, the very dark and very light areas aren't visibly affected.

- To speed up hand-coloring work, press (Option) [Alt] while adding a new Solid Color layer from the Layers palette. This brings up the New Layer window where you can change the Blending Mode to Color before selecting the color.

- Use reference photographs from CD stock collections or from your own photos to collect, record, and select colors.

- Due to the many, many layers that a good colorization requires, it is imperative that you name your layers, as Diane Trembley illustrates in figure 8.68.

© Diane Trembley

figure 8.68

Naming your layers is essential when colorizing a complex image.

- When you're coloring skin tones, make sure to vary the shades of colors to make your hand-coloring look more realistic. Figure 8.69 shows a close-up of the beautiful colorization that Diane Trembley did. As you can see, the woman's face, cheeks, and lips are of a similar color palette, yet they offer enough visual distinction to be effective.

- Save your colors into your color swatches and use the Preset Manager to name them, as shown in figure 8.70.

- Finally, as Wayne Palmer so aptly says, "Colorization is very subjective. Even though your customer has told you which colors to put into a picture, it is common for them to change their minds according to their recollection. For this reason, I always use Color Fill layers and masks, which give me the ability to easily change colors."

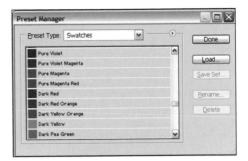

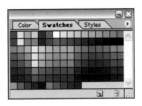

figure 8.70

Photoshop's Preset Manager is useful for naming and organizing your Swatches palette.

figure 8.69

Vary the shades of skin tones to make your hand-coloring look more life-like.

From Traditional to Digital

Lorie Zirbes is a traditionally trained restoration artist with more than 20 years of experience. A traditional retoucher or restoration artist would work directly on a film negative or paper print with dyes and chemicals to enhance an image. As you can imagine, the realm of the traditional retoucher is shrinking, and Lorie is learning to work with Photoshop. I find it interesting that she approaches a hand-coloring job differently than I would.

Figure 8.71 shows the original image and figure 8.72 shows the hand-colored image of Lorie's great aunt. Now take a look at the layers palette and the isolated layer (see figure 8.73). Rather than working with selections and Color Fill layers, Lorie has developed a technique in which she duplicates the layers and isolates the essential image information with layer masks. She then paints directly on the image information with a soft-edged brush set to Color Blending Mode.

Once again, I am surprised as to how many ways there are to accomplish similar results with Photoshop. In the end, whatever achieves the best results for you is what works the best. Figure 8.74 shows another original and hand-colored image by Lorie.

BEFORE

figure 8.71

The original image.

AFTER

figure 8.72

Lorie paints directly on the image with a soft brush set to Color.

figure 8.73

Lorie uses layer masks to isolate each part to be colored on its own layer.

WORKING WITH SOFT AND SELECTIVE FOCUS

Photoshop users either love filters or hate them. The haters snub their noses at filters, saying that they're just canned effects that anyone with a mouse could use, in the same way a roomful of chimps with a typewriter would eventually be able to peck out a *Hamlet*. The filter-lovers insist that they use them to apply creative and painterly effects to an image.

Actually, both factions are right. Playing around with Photoshop filters doesn't take any talent, but applying them in an intelligent fashion does. By combining filters, layers, and Blending Modes, you can create unique effects and add a special touch to your images. Entire books have been written on Photoshop filters, so I've chosen to concentrate on the more photographic filters here.

To control the filter's effect and protect the original image, always duplicate the layer to be manipulated before applying filters. Working on a duplicate layer lets you experiment with filters and Blending Modes without having to worry about ruining your original image. Best of all, if you really don't like the effect you've created, you can simply delete the layer and start over again.

figure 8.74

Another example of Lorie's hand-coloring technique.

Subjective Focus and Exposure

Selective focus also can be used as an interpretive tool to add a hint of mystery or intrigue to an image. As you can see in figure 8.75, the color and quality of light give the winter scene an interesting character. But I took the image further, as shown in figure 8.76. This is a more fitting interpretation of how I perceived the scene on that winter evening in the Black Forest. The softening effect was created in a similar fashion to what was just described in the "Selective Focus Controls" section. To accentuate the mood even further, I also darkened and lightened contrasting image areas.

figure 8.75

figure 8.76

 ch8_rest.jpg

1. Duplicate the background layer and run the Gaussian Blur filter to soften the image.

 T i p

Avoid filters that don't give you control. Use the ones that bring up an interface window that enables you to adjust settings. For example, you have a number of options under the Blur filters (see figure 8.77). The first two options apply a blur effect over which you have no control. The following four options are followed by ellipses, meaning that an interface will pop up and you'll be able to adjust the settings to suit your image.

figure 8.77

Selecting the filters that give you more control will produce better results.

2. Add a layer mask and use a large, soft gray brush to paint onto it, as shown in figure 8.78. If need be, erase any painted areas on the mask by painting with white.

3. Add a new layer and change the Blending Mode to Soft Light. Choose black as your foreground color. Select the Gradient tool and choose the Foreground to Transparent gradient from the gradient options. Drag the Gradient tool from the edge of the image to the center, as shown in figure 8.79.

© Katrin Eismann

4. You can build up density by using the Gradient tool repeatedly or by painting with black to add a random, dappled effect.

5. To lighten the figure of Jesus Christ, add a neutral layer. (Option + click) [Alt + click] the New Layer icon. Set Mode to Color Dodge and check the Fill with Color-Dodge-Neutral Color (Black) option.

6. Paint with a light-opacity white Brush with 2–4% Pressure to selectively lighten image areas on the crucifix figure, as shown in figure 8.80.

figure 8.78

Painting on the layer mask determines which parts are in focus and which ones aren't.

figure 8.80

Carefully lighten the figure to draw the viewer's attention to the crucifix.

figure 8.79

Using a foreground-to-transparent gradient on an empty Soft Light layer will darken the exposure on the edges of the image.

Creative Combinations

Throughout the retouching and enhancement process, it's very important to keep in mind the people in the images. Figure 8.81 shows a compelling composite that photographer Mark Beckelman created by combining a picture of his father as a young boy (see figure 8.82) with a more recent photograph of his father looking into a pool of water cupped in his hands.

Mark started by scanning the photograph of the football team. After looking at the scan, he realized that it didn't contain the amount or quality of image information that he required. He made a 4×5 copy negative of the original print and scanned it (see figure 8.83). Mark then took a photograph of a stream and one of his father's cupped hands, as shown in figures 8.84 and 8.85.

With great skill, Mark composited the images. Figure 8.86 shows how he employed the many lighting and softening techniques described in this chapter to create a sensitive portrait of his father looking back through time.

© Mark Beckleman

figure 8.81

This image combines old and new images very effectively.

figure 8.82

The original print.

figure 8.85

A contemporary image that was blurred to make it recede into the background.

figure 8.83

A crop of the 4×5 copy negative.

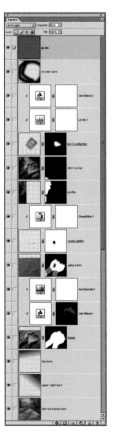

figure 8.84

A picture of Mark's father's hands holding water.

figure 8.86

You can see how layer-intensive image creation work is.

CREATIVE AND VIGNETTE EDGES

The edges of an image are critical visual elements that define the image and ground the composition. In painting, the edge of a composition is defined by the right angles and parallel lines of the frame, which often is a decorative piece of gold-leafed craftsmanship. In other painterly media, such as etching and printmaking, the edges are often defined by the artist's hand; each is unique and as precise or rough as the artist desires. In these instances, the edges are as integral to the final image as any element in the composition.

Photography is a photochemical medium in which the edges of an image are created by the four blades of the easel that holds the paper in place during exposure. Many photographers, desiring to show the entire negative, have been known to file out the negative carriers so they can print a black border around the image. Using the easel, the photographers could create a precise black line around an image. Or, by pulling the easel blades out further along the same black line, they could give the edge a dappled, abstract appearance. Still other photographers use hand-painted emulsions of platinum and palladium and let the brush strokes define the image.

Of all the image-making processes, digital image creation is the most precise. The computer lets us change a single pixel or make radical global changes to the entire image. But the power and precision of the computer can give many images a machine-made feel. Simply put, the perfection of the image-making process eliminates any sense of the human craft—those interesting imperfections and unique qualities that come with handwork. Using creative edges can be an effective way to give computer-generated images a handmade appearance.

Vignetting a Portrait

Using softness or texture to frame an image can often be the finishing touch when you're working with antique images, as shown in **figures 8.87** and **8.88**.

figure 8.87 **BEFORE**

figure 8.88 **AFTER**

 **ch8_vignette.jpg**

1. Select the center part of the image with the Elliptical Marquee tool.

2. Press Q to enter Quick Mask mode so that you can see the selection and select Image > Adjust > Invert to protect the center of the image. Add a very large Gaussian Blur (see **figure 8.89**) to the mask.

figure 8.89

Running the Gaussian Blur filter on the Quick Mask gives you a preview of the softening effect.

3. To avoid banding in the soft transitions, apply Filter > Noise > Add Noise and add a small amount of noise to the mask (see figure 8.90).

figure 8.90

Adding a hint of noise can offset banding problems.

4. Press Q again to return to Standard mode, and then activate the selection.

5. Add a new layer, fill the selection with white, and crop as needed.

 Tip

If you want added flexibility, build your vignette on a separate layer. This will allow you to reposition it, move it to other documents, or throw it away if you decide you don't like it.

Vignetting an image isn't just for antique images; it also can be very effective for contemporary images, as shown in **figures 8.91** and **8.92**.

figure 8.91

figure 8.92

After retouching this portrait, photographer Phil Pool wanted to bring the viewer's attention to the young woman's face by using the soft white frame as described here.

1. Phil added a new layer.

2. He set the foreground color to white, activated the Gradient tool, and selected the Foreground to Transparent gradient from the options bar.

3. Working in full-screen mode, Phil drew in a gradient from each side of the image, as shown in figure 8.93.

4. To reduce the white effect on the girl's head, Phil added a layer mask, and with a large, soft-edged black brush, he painted over her hair to create the final image shown in figure 8.94.

figure 8.93

On a new layer, Phil drew in a gradient from each edge.

figure 8.94

Because the vignette is on its own layer, it can be finessed with a layer mask.

Adding Creative Edges

Working with Quick Mask to break up edges is a quick and easy way to add texture to the edge of any image (see figures 8.95 and 8.96). Best of all, everything you need to use this technique is already in Photoshop.

figure 8.95

BEFORE

figure 8.96

AFTER

⊕ ▷ᡃᠼ **ch8_frame.jpg**

1. Duplicate your background layer and select the area of the image that you do not want to be affected.

2. Press Q to enter Quick Mask mode.

3. Press (Cmd + I) [Ctrl + I] to invert the mask. Apply a Gaussian Blur of 5 to the mask to soften the edge, as shown in figure 8.97. Higher-resolution files might need a larger blur.

figure 8.97

Adding the Gaussian Blur to the initial mask will give the next filter in the process more shades of gray to work with.

4. Experiment with the built-in filters in Photoshop to change the edges of the softened Quick Mask. Good filters to try out include the following:

   - Filter > Brush Strokes > Spatter
   - Filter > Distort > Glass
   - Filter > Sketch > Torn Edges
   - Filter > Texture > Craquelure

5. Run more than one filter on the Quick Mask to create unique edges.

 C a u t i o n

When you're experimenting with filters, keep an eye on the center part of the Quick Mask. Some filters are so aggressive that they may also affect the area of the image you're trying to frame.

6. When you have the effect you want, press Q again. The Quick Mask becomes an active selection.

7. Add a new layer and fill the active selection with your color of choice.

SHARPENING FILTERS

I wish I had a megabyte of RAM for every time I was asked whether Photoshop can focus or sharpen an image that's soft, blurry, or out of focus. Photoshop can't transform poor images into sharp, crisp images that would look as good as well-focused originals. We're working with pixels here, and too many Hollywood spy thrillers have made it look as though a computer can enhance any out-of-focus photograph into a recognizable image. Keeping your expectations within reason, this section provides you with techniques to sharpen your images to make them look their best.

When to Sharpen

"To sharpen or not to sharpen, that is the question: Whether 'tis better to sharpen during scanning or before printing, or suffer the slings and arrows of outrageous sharpening artifacts...."

Believe me, many a raucous debate has been ignited over the best time to sharpen an image. Rather than joining in, I take my cues from Bruce Fraser and David Blatner, authors of *Real World Adobe Photoshop 7* (Peachpit, 2002), and Richard Benson, who is a MacArthur fellow, a brilliant printer, and chair of the Yale School of Art. They say you should sharpen either as the next-to-last step in the printing process, just before converting to CMYK, or the very last step, after converting to CMYK.

If you're outputting your images to inkjet, thermal dye transfer, film recorders, or other direct digital output that accepts RGB data, I recommend sharpening as the very last step. If you're working in or going out to CMYK, do all of your color correction, retouching, and resizing in RGB, convert the file to CMYK, apply sharpening, then target the black-and-white points for your specific CMYK output.

For a retoucher who's going to RGB output, the sharpening workflow entails the following steps: color correction, retouch, save as, flatten, size image for output, duplicate background layer, sharpen, mask out areas that do not benefit from sharpening, and save as a flattened version into your Finals folder. Sharpening on a duplicate layer enables you to mask out areas that don't require sharpening, such as large surfaces of sky or skin pores, which should rarely be sharpened.

Although Photoshop comes with four sharpening filters, all in the Filter > Sharpen menu, you should use only the Unsharp Mask filter (also referred to as USM). In the following section, you'll learn about applying the Unsharp Mask filter, smart sharpening methods, faux sharpening with the Emboss filter, interactive sharpening with the High Pass filter, and working with the Custom filter to sharpen images. All sharpening methods are edge-detection processes, and wherever an edge is found, it is exaggerated by making the dark and light areas of the edge darker or lighter.

The Unsharp Mask Filter

The worst part of the Unsharp Mask filter is its name. If you haven't worked in a traditional darkroom or prepress shop, you might not realize that something called "Unsharp" is actually excellent for sharpening. In the dark pre-digital days of not too many years ago, a separator would make a pin-registered contact negative of an original. To soften the mask, the repro artist would place a sheet of frosted mylar between the original and the masking film. This soft "un-sharp" mask increased edge contrast, making the image look sharper. Similarly, the Unsharp Mask filter looks for edges and differences to accentuate, making the image look sharper. There are three controls you use with the Unsharp Mask filter:

- Amount: This is similar to the volume dial on a radio—the higher you crank the knob, the stronger the sharpening becomes. For offset printing, start with a high amount, from 120%–200%, and control the results with the radius and threshold controls. If you're outputting to CMYK offset, you should oversharpen the image by finding visually pleasing settings and then going a bit further. Direct

digital output devices, such as film or photographic paper writers, require a lower amount setting (in the range of 40 to 80%) and should not be oversharpened. Sharpening for the web or screen display is the easiest because you can judge the results on your monitor.

- Radius: This controls how far out Photoshop looks and determines the width of the edge contrast increase. An accepted rule of thumb for offset printing is to divide the printer's output resolution by 200 and use that as your starting point for the radius setting. This is the most critical setting—pushing it too high will cause ugly dark or light halos to appear along the edges of the image.

- Threshold: This scale goes from 0 to 255. Use it to tell Photoshop to ignore image tones that are very similar. For example, a threshold setting of 5 will ignore all tones that are within 5 level values of each other. Using a setting between 3 and 6 will protect tonally similar areas from being sharpened. This is especially useful to avoid sharpening image shadows and skin pores, wrinkles, and blemishes (you really don't want to sharpen someone's pores), as well as the grain in images that were shot on higher-speed film.

To really understand what the Unsharp Mask filter does, download the sunflower image (shown in **figure 8.98**) from the web site and apply various amounts of the USM filter to the entire image. Keep an eye on the differentiation between the sunflower seeds, the edges of the petals against the blue sky, and the grayscale on the bottom of the image. The grayscale is a clear indicator of how the USM filter accentuates edge differences. **Figure 8.99** shows the image with the right amount of sharpening, and **figure 8.100** is an example of sharpening gone too far.

🌐▷< **ch8_sharpen.jpg**

figure 8.98

The original image.

figure 8.99

Just the right amount of sharpening has been applied here.

figure 8.100

The artifacts around the edges indicate that the image is oversharpened.

Unsharp Mask Workflow

Lee Varis introduced me to the following Unsharp Mask workflow that offers great control. If you are working along on a flattened file, duplicate the background layer. If you're working with a layered file, click the very top of your layer stack, add a new layer, hold (Option)[Alt] and select Layer > Merge Visible to flatten all layers onto a new layer.

1. Duplicate the background layer (or flattened layer) and set the Blending Mode to Luminosity, as shown in **figure 8.101**. The Luminosity Blending Mode helps you avoid the color fringing that the Unsharp mask may cause. For our visual system, it is more important to sharpen the luminous information rather than the color information.

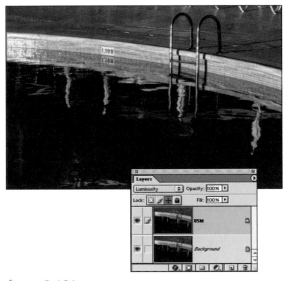

figure 8.101

Sharpening on a duplicate layer set to Luminosity helps avoid color fringing.

2. Zoom out so that you are viewing the image at 50%. As Lee explains, "When you're zoomed out to 50%, you're looking at the size of the image at approximately 150 pixels per inch. Most of the time, you're printing to 300 pixels per inch, and viewing at 50% is a compromise so that you can see how the image will look like printed."

3. Adjust the Unsharp mask settings, as shown in figure 8.102. It is most important to set the radius and the amount high enough to adequately sharpen without creating obvious halos.

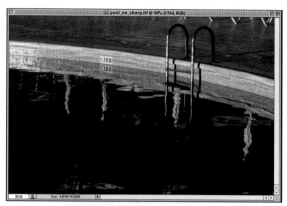

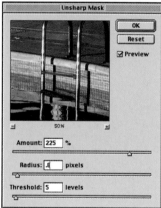

figure 8.102

Viewing at 50% helps you visualize how the sharpening will look when printed.

4. In figure 8.103, you can see that the specular highlights on the swimming pool ladder are too sharp and almost look posterized. To finesse the transitions, use the Advanced Blending options in the Layer Style palette. Double-click the top layer's name in the layer palette or choose Layer > Layer Style > Blending Options > Advanced Blending Options, as shown in figure 8.104.

figure 8.103

At this point, the image is too sharp.

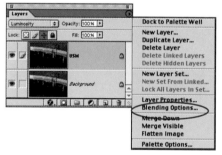

figure 8.104

Sharpening on a separate layer enables the use of Blending Options.

5. By sliding the Underlying Layer highlight slider to the left (figure 8.105), Photoshop shows the highlights of the underneath layer or, in this example, of the original layer. To create a smooth transition, press (Option) [Alt] while dragging to separate the triangular sliders, as shown in figure 8.106.

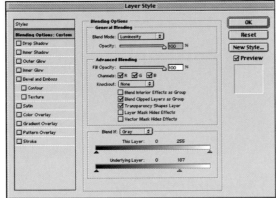

figure 8.105

Moving the lower highlight slider reveals the highlights of the layer below.

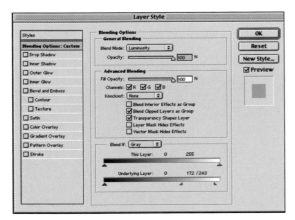

figure 8.106

Splitting the sliders creates a smooth transition.

If your image has noise in the shadows that the Unsharp Mask filter has accentuated, move the black Underlying Layer slider to let the original unsharpened image information show through, as explained in step 5. Before making a lot of prints or sending a service bureau numerous digital files, ask them what they recommend for USM settings. If they don't have recommendations, run a test by ganging strips of the same image on one page with various USM settings and have it output. The USM filter is a powerful tool that can make your images stand out, either positively (crisp) or negatively (ugly USM halos).

Unsharp Mask Tips

- Images that are uniformly sharp seem unnatural; blurring parts of an image will draw the eye to the sharper image areas.

- In the USM dialog box, click and hold the Preview box to see the image with and without the sharpening effect.

- Experiment with selective sharpening by masking out image areas that don't need to be sharp.

- Print your sharpening tests with the printer and paper that you'll use for the final document.

- Avoid resizing or retouching a sharpened file.

- When you send files to a service bureau, tell them whether you've already applied sharpening or you want them to do it. Too much sharpening can be just as bad as no sharpening.

- Use USM on individual channels. This is especially useful when one channel is noisy or when you're sharpening CMYK files.

- To apply a different Blending Mode or change the opacity of the USM filter after running it, select Edit > Fade Unsharp Mask and change the settings. Or better yet, sharpen on a duplicate layer and control the intensity with layer opacity and Blending Modes.

Smart Sharpening

Smart sharpening is a term that Photoshop insiders use for a process that allows you to sharpen image edges without sharpening noise, film grain, pores, or out-of-focus areas. This method may seem like too much trouble, but keep it in mind for those noisy and grainy images and files that are suffering from JPEG artifacts. (Although this technique requires 10 steps, it can be scripted to run as an action, which I have included in Chapter 8 of the book's supplemental web site.) The subtlety that is possible is especially effective with digital camera files, as shown in figures 8.107 and 8.108.

figure 8.107

figure 8.108

🌐▷⊰ **ch8_smart_sharpen.atn**

🌐▷⊰ **ch8_lisbon.jpg**

1. Duplicate the background layer.

2. Duplicate the channel with the highest image contrast. I duplicated the red channel, as shown in figure 8.109.

figure 8.109

Duplicate the channel with the highest image contrast.

3. Select Filter > Stylize > Find Edges.

4. Invert the channel (Cmd + I) [Ctrl + I].

5. Select Filter > Noise > Median and use a value of 2 to accentuate the edge lines (see figure 8.110).

figure 8.110

Use the Median filter to thicken the lines.

6. Select Filter > Other > Maximum and use a value of 2 to spread the edge lines even more (see figure 8.111).

7. Select Filter > Blur > Gaussian Blur and apply a value of 2.

8. Return to the composite view (Cmd + ~) [Ctrl + ~] in the Channels palette.

9. Load the channel mask (Cmd + Option + 4) [Ctrl + Alt + 4].

figure 8.111

The Maximum filter spreads the lines further.

10. Apply the Unsharp Mask filter to sharpen only the edges of the subject while avoiding sharpening noise and grain, as shown in figure 8.112.

figure 8.112

Use the Unsharp Mask filter as the final step.

High Pass Sharpening

No matter how careful I am with the Unsharp Mask filter, when I'm still not happy with the results, I turn to the High Pass filter to enhance image edges. That filter turns all non-edge areas to neutral gray but leaves image edges intact. This, combined with Soft Light or Overlay Blending Modes, yields a sharpening effect that avoids ugly artifacts created when the standard sharpening filters are over-used. Lee Varis has developed and put this technique to fantastic use, especially with digital camera files that do not benefit from the Unsharp Mask Threshold controls because digital camera files don't have film grain.

Figure 8.113 shows a before image of a simple garlic and onion still-life taken with the Nikon CoolPIX 990. Figure 8.114 shows the sharpened file created with the High Pass filter.

figure 8.113

figure 8.114

🌐▷⟨ **ch8_garlic.jpg**

1. Duplicate the background layer.

2. Select Filter > Other > High Pass and use the Radius slider to bring out the image edges. A very high Radius setting is less effective than a lower setting. Start with a setting between 2 and 5 and experiment with the Radius slider to increase or decrease the edge enhancement effect, as shown in **figure 8.115**.

3. Change the filtered layer's Blending Mode to Overlay or Soft Light to make the neutral gray disappear while maintaining the edge accentuation, as shown in **figure 8.116**. Using the Overlay Blending Mode adds a bit more contrast to the image than using Soft Light will.

4. If the image is too sharp, decrease the filtered layer's opacity to achieve just the right amount of sharpening.

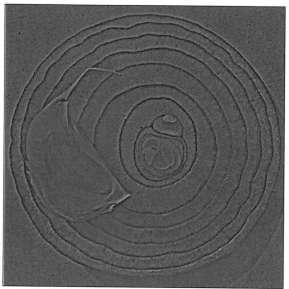
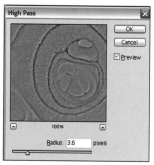

figure 8.115

Use the Radius slider to bring out edge differences.

figure 8.116

Changing the Blending Mode and opacity offers tremendous control of the strength of the sharpening effect.

Emboss Sharpening

I learned this method from Greg Vander Houwen, a talented digital artist and illustrator in Seattle. Greg has devised a method to bring soft-focus images like figure 8.117 into focus; it creates faux edges that fool the eye into seeing a sharper image, as seen in figure 8.118. This technique works best for images that were shot with a soft-focus filter or are slightly out of focus.

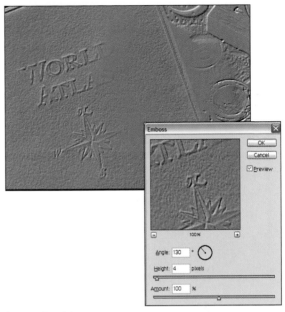

figure 8.119

Use the Emboss filter on a duplicate layer.

figure 8.117

3. Change the embossed layer's Blending Mode to Overlay. The edges are accentuated, as shown in figure 8.120. It's a Photoshop miracle!

figure 8.118

1. Duplicate the background layer.

2. Select Filter > Stylize > Emboss. Set the Angle to mimic the direction of light in the image, keep the Height between 2 and 4, and keep the Amount near 100% (see figure 8.119). Click OK.

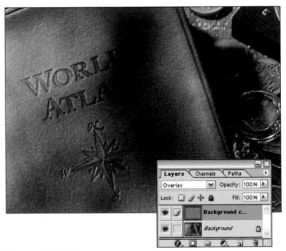

figure 8.120

Change the embossed layer's Blending Mode to Overlay.

Custom Sharpening

The Filter > Other > Custom filter features a 5×5 matrix of edit boxes, into which you type numbers ranging from +999 to –999. It's hardly obvious which numbers you should type to achieve a desired result, or what will result from a given matrix of numbers. Chris Tarantino, who specializes in high-end catalog color correction and retouching, has spent many hours investigating the Custom filter to develop brightening, softening, and sharpening filters for high-end prepress file preparation. As Chris explains, "The advantage of the Custom filter is that I can sharpen without adding artifacts or halos, and if need be, I can brighten and sharpen in one fell swoop."

The Custom filter calculates pixels against one another in response to the typed-in values. In the following figures, I've shown some of Chris's most useful Custom filter settings. Use these values as a starting point for your investigation of the Custom filter. Figure 8.121 is the original scan that Chris started with. After masking out the individual image areas (sweater, scarf, purse, and background), Chris used his own Custom settings to bring out each image area, as shown in figure 8.122. Figure 8.123 shows a Custom setting for strong brightening and sharpening. Figure 8.124 shows a Custom setting for subtle sharpening.

ChrisCustomKernels

To access Chris's kernels, download ChrisCustom Kernels to your hard drive, open an image and select Filter > Other > Custom, click on the Load button, and navigate to where you saved his kernels.

Once you've experimented with Chris's Kernels and found settings that work for your purposes, remember to click the Save button and save your settings into Photoshop's Filter folder. This way you can save, load, and share Custom filter settings. To make your Custom settings compatible across platforms, save them in the 8dot format—an eight-letter filename with the file extension .acf, such as bright.acf.

BEFORE

figure 8.121

AFTER

figure 8.122

figure 8.123

A *Custom filter setting that increases both brightness and sharpness.*

figure 8.124

A *Custom filter setting for sharpening without brightening.*

CLOSING THOUGHTS

All in all, digital tools and techniques give you tremendous control and creative possibilities. The most important thing to do is to duplicate your background layer and then go to town with these techniques to interpret your images to your creative heart's content.

IV

Putting the Best Face Forward

9

PORTRAIT RETOUCHING 273

10

GLAMOUR AND FASHION RETOUCHING 325

9

PORTRAIT RETOUCHING

The first step of successful portrait retouching is to identify the character of the person and determine which facial features you can accentuate or minimize to help that person shine through the picture. Imagine that you had to retouch three portraits: a fashionable teenager, a professional athlete, and a successful senior executive. Each of these people has different characteristics you need to recognize and enhance. The teenager's skin might need to be cleaned up, whereas the professional athlete's sweat and muscle tone could be accentuated for greater effect. In the senior executive's portrait, you wouldn't want to take out every wrinkle or gray hair because lines in the face and gray hair are signifiers of wisdom and experience. Before you pick up the mouse, take a moment to look at the portrait and recognize which type of person you're working with.

As a retoucher, it's your job to bring out the best in each person. In this chapter, you learn to work with contrast, color, and detail to make people look their best. The areas we'll concentrate on in this chapter are

- Developing a portrait retouch strategy
- Removing distractions and improving contours
- Improving skin texture
- Enhancing facial features

As a portrait retoucher, your role is to accentuate the person's natural features while minimizing the blemishes that can detract from a pleasing portrait. Most importantly, you want to maintain the individuality of the person. Not every person will have the Hollywood ingénue's flawless skin or a lion's head of hair. So study the character of the person in the picture and decide which attributes to accentuate and which to minimize before you begin to click your mouse.

Note

If by chance you jumped to this chapter first, please understand that the very first step to working with any digital image is to apply global exposure and color correction, as explained in earlier chapters. When those problems are solved, you can move on to correcting and enhancing selective areas as described in this chapter.

LEVELS OF RETOUCHING

Retouching a person's face can be a sensitive undertaking. You don't want to take away important characteristics or accentuate less-than-flattering features. Additionally, you don't want to put time and effort into a portrait retouch that the client isn't willing to pay for. Before you begin any retouching, it is imperative that you discuss with your clients exactly what they want done to the portraits.

Clients may have a hard time envisioning the possibilities of retouching. To avoid any confusion or miscommunication, create a sample portfolio of your retouching services. As clients page through the portfolio, explain that you can remove blemishes and wrinkles for X number of dollars; if they would like additional retouching as seen in your more advanced examples, it will cost them X dollars. Not all clients will want the full treatment, and knowing this before you begin will save you time, effort, and money.

Rick Billings (www.photowave.com) has developed a three-level approach to retouching, shown in figures 9.1 through 9.4:

- Level 1: Removes obvious blemishes, wrinkles, and distractions with a process similar to applying a little make-up.

- Level 2: Continues where Level 1 stops and uses lights and darks to create volume and shape; this draws the viewer's eye into the subject's face.

- Level 3: Finely sculpts the face with contrast, color, and detail to accentuate the eyes, lips, and facial contours just as a classic painter would use light and shadow to define important details.

A three-level approach enables you to develop a plan as to the amount of retouching you will do, which in the end determines how much you will charge the client. A straightforward blemish removal or subtle wrinkle reduction can be accomplished in 2 to 10 minutes, whereas applying chiaroscuro lighting requires a master's time and touch—which both add much more to the final bill. Communicating with your client and knowing what your final outcome will be before lifting a mouse will help you work economically and efficiently.

 Looking Behind the Curtain Costs Extra

In the movie *The Wizard of Oz*, the great and wondrous wizard insisted that no one look behind the curtain because that would reveal that he was really just a bunch of hot air and noisy machinery. Digital retouching is not smoke and mirrors, but it *is* magical, and I highly recommend that you keep the process magical for your clients.

Don't let the client watch while you're retouching. Letting clients see how quickly you can work and the magic you can create with Photoshop is a sure way to deflate your position and have them ask for more and more retouching for possibly less money. I've heard it over and over: "Oh, you make it look so easy! While you're at it, can't you just straighten out my nose or remove the dark circles under my eyes?" Well, the answer is of course you can, but doing it quickly while they watch will cheapen your value and skills.

Clients seem to forget that you had to practice long into the night to develop your skills or that you may still be paying for your equipment. In addition, you can work much more efficiently without having a nervous client watching or distracting you. The only clients who I permit to watch me are the art directors hired and paid for by the client or agency to direct a project.

Tip

Retouching is more than a skill; it is an art form. Don't rush through any job, and try to avoid working when you're over-tired. Remember that you're working with a person's face and identity—something that requires your full concentration and empathy.

figure 9.1

Original portrait.

figure 9.2

Level 1 retouch with exposure improvement and blemish removal.

figure 9.3

Level 2 retouch with shaping face and smoothing of skin by modeling the lights and darks.

figure 9.4

Level 3 finish, using painterly techniques to model the face and draw attention to the eyes.

DEVELOPING A PORTRAIT RETOUCH STRATEGY

Mapping out a portrait retouch strategy will make your retouching time more efficient and effective. Before beginning to work on a portrait, use the following checklist to plan out your retouch workflow:

- Distractions are image elements that draw the viewer's eye away from the portrait. To find them, look at the portrait while squinting or defocusing your eyes and notice what your eyes register. Distractions include high-contrast areas, background elements (as shown in **figure 9.5**, which are removed in **figure 9.6**), splotches of sunlight, light areas by the image edge, bra straps, and unattractive folds of clothing.

© Kimberly Phillips

figure 9.5

Examining the original image reveals distracting elements.

figure 9.6

Removing the tree and smoothing the contours of the dresses focuses the attention on the girls. Adding the dog effectively covers up the awkward posing.

- Contours of the person's hair, face, neck, and body should be smooth and flattering, as shown in **figure 9.8**. Fly-away hair or bulges caused by awkward posing (as seen in **figure 9.7**), body position, weight, or age should be carefully reduced or smoothed out.

© Studio G Photography

figure 9.7

An awkward pose created an unflattering jawline.

figure 9.8

Contouring the neck created a cherished wedding photograph.

- Skin needs to be appropriate to the person. The goal is not to smooth the skin so much that it looks like plastic wrap. Rather, the goal is to reduce wrinkles, remove blemishes (see **figures 9.9** and **9.10**), and smooth the skin to make the person look like a well-rested and well-lit version of themselves.

- Facial features include the eyes, lips, teeth, and nose. The eyes are the most important facial attribute to emphasize, followed by the mouth, as shown in **figures 9.11** and **9.12**.

© Hooper Photography

figure **9.11**

The eyes and mouth can disproportionately affect our memories of a person's appearance.

© Wagner Portrait Group

figure **9.9**

Portraits can unfairly accentuate temporary skin blemishes.

figure **9.12**

Reducing the wrinkles and brightening the athlete's teeth lets his personality shine through.

figure **9.10**

Reducing the skin blemishes of this high school portrait provides a fairer and actually more representative image.

All in all, my final goal when doing portrait retouching is to make people look as though they have just come back from a relaxing vacation. They should look well rested, alert, and positive. By removing the distractions, flattering the contours, cleaning up the skin, and accentuating the eyes and mouth, you help your clients look their very best.

Note

Special thanks to H&H Color lab (www.hhcolorlab.com) in Raytown, Missouri, for providing the examples to illustrate this section and an extra thank you to Carrie Beene whose sensitive eye and artistic touch masterfully completed the retouches. Due to copyright and privacy issues, a number of the featured images in this chapter are not available for download.

REMOVING DISTRACTIONS

Start the portrait retouch by looking at the entire image—too often I've seen people dive into a retouch by randomly removing blemishes or whitening teeth without first understanding the overall image. Our visual system perceives contrast, focus, and color. Our eyes go from light to dark, sharp to soft, and more color to less color. In other words, you need to emphasize or downplay these three image attributes to keep the viewer's eyes on the portrait.

Squint your eyes and take a look at the teenager in figure 9.13. Do you notice any distractions? The contrast of the black ribbon against her light skin and covered crucifix is screaming, "Look at me!" and the bra strap, which is peeking out by her neckline, interrupts the visual flow of the neckline. Now take a look at figure 9.14 and squint your eyes—notice how your eye keeps coming back to her face. By removing the dark against light contrast of the black ribbon, the visual interest has been removed from the unimportant ribbon and returned to her face.

figure 9.13

The cluttered neckline draws attention away from the face.

figure 9.14

Cleaning the neckline focuses attention on the face.

In most cases, removing distraction involves duplicating the background layer and using the Clone Stamp, Healing Brush, and Patch tools to remove the distractions just as you would remove scratches and damage (as explained in Chapter 6, "Damage Control and Repair," and Chapter 7, "Rebuilding, Rearranging, and Re-creating Portraits").

FLATTERING THE CONTOURS

The second step in the portrait retouch is to let your eye follow the contours of the person to find anything that breaks up the smooth flow. Primary items to watch for are fly-away hair, uncomfortable arm or shoulder angles, unsightly bulges in clothing, wide heads, unflattering body contours, double chins, and the folds of skin in an older person's neck. The Liquify command, cloning, and pinching are useful for smoothing contours or narrowing a person.

The Digital Seamstress

Photographing a person can often cause the oddest folds in her clothing to become noticeable. In figure 9.15, you see a studio portrait of yours truly. As soon as I saw the scans, I was bothered by the way the pockets jutted out and the lack of waistline. I don't go to the gym to look like that. Figure 9.16 shows me wearing a custom-tailored jacket and with a slightly narrower face. To custom tailor clothing in Photoshop, follow these steps:

figure 9.15   *figure 9.16*

 **ch9_tailor.jpg**

© Daryl-Ann Saunders, dasaunders.com

1. Duplicate the background layer. Use the Pen tool to draw in the desired body contour, as shown in figure 9.17. If you are not comfortable with the Pen tool, you can also use the Lasso tool to outline the desired contour.

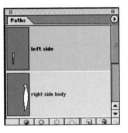

figure 9.17

The Pen tool provides a smooth selection for the new contour.

2. Turn the path into a selection by dragging it down to the Load Path as Selection icon on the Paths palette. Choose Select > Feather > 1 to soften the transition slightly.

3. Use the Clone Stamp tool to clone the studio background over the selected jacket pocket, as shown in figure 9.18.

figure 9.18

Cloning the background into the selected area leaves a realistic new contour.

4. After deselecting, use the Healing Brush and Clone Stamp tools to clean up any telltale signs, as shown in **figure 9.19**.

figure 9.19

The Clone Stamp tool alone leaves telltale signs that need cleaning up with the Healing Brush.

5. Repeat the procedure on the right side with the path shown in **figure 9.20** to create the final jacket shown in **figure 9.21**.

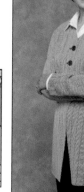

figure 9.20

The procedure is repeated on the other side.

Keep the digital seamstress handy to clean up wrinkles in suits, straighten crooked collars, or repair uneven seams.

figure 9.21

A final cleanup with the Healing Brush completes the digital suit alteration.

You Don't Need to Be a Brain Surgeon

Narrowing people's faces is a common request, and with Photoshop, you achieve remarkable results without a medical degree. The man's head in **figure 9.22** is rather broad, while the same man in **figure 9.23** still looks like himself, but there is just a bit less of him. You can use the following technique on a person's head or his entire body—it relies on the flexibility of the layer mask to create a seamless transition between the head and body pieces as they are brought closer together.

© John Warner Photography

BEFORE

figure 9.22

figure 9.24

When selecting the area, avoid essential details such as eyes and jewelry.

2. (Cmd + J) [Ctrl + J] to duplicate the selected information onto its own layer. Activate the Move tool and, while holding Shift, press the left arrow key two or three times to move the layer 20 or 30 pixels. In this example, I moved the right side of his head with three Shift-taps, which moved the layer 30 pixels to the left, as you see in **figure 9.25**.

AFTER

figure 9.23

1. Use the Lasso tool with a 5-pixel feather to select one side of the person's head or body. Make sure not to go through essential image areas, such as a person's eyes or jewelry (see **figure 9.24**), and include the background in the selection.

figure 9.25

Moving the selected image area to a more flattering locale.

3. Zoom in on the image to check for artifacts such as the chunk of missing hand or oddly nibbled shoulder, both noted in **figure 9.26**.

figure 9.26

Examine the transition area closely for telltale artifacts.

4. Add a layer mask to the moved layer. Use a soft-edged black brush to trace over the transition areas and artifacts. Toggle between a black and white brush by tapping X when painting to hide and reveal the image areas as needed (see **figure 9.27**).

figure 9.27

Use layer masks to hide artifacts and create a more realistic transition.

5. Repeat the select, duplicate, move, and mask technique on his shoulder to reduce his overall mass.

6. Add a new layer and used the Clone Stamp tool and Healing Brush to refine any telltale signs of the digital surgery.

7. Often, narrowing a person's head can make the face look unnaturally long. To restore the proper proportions, Edit > Free Transform and scrunch down the head ever so slightly. In this example, I transformed the height by 2.5%, as seen in **figure 9.28**.

figure 9.28

Correcting image and facial proportions.

Please note: I'm not saying that everyone needs to wear a size 8 or fit into blue jeans with a 28-inch waist—I am saying that as a portrait retoucher, it is your job to make clients look their best.

Adjusting Posture

As often happens when a person is holding a baby, as in **figure 9.29**, the arms form a cradle, and in this case, the left shoulder looks uncomfortably high. **Figure 9.30** shows the lowered shoulder, which looks much more comfortable—for both mother and child.

Myke Ninness

figure 9.29

figure 9.30

1. Duplicate the background layer.
2. To use the Liquify command most efficiently, generously select the area to be shaped with the Marquee tool, as shown in figure 9.31, and select Filter > Liquify, which opens the dialog box.

figure 9.31

Selecting the area to be Liquefied ensures a large and fast preview.

3. To avoid distorting background elements—in this case—the flowers, use the Freeze Tool to paint a Quick mask over all areas that should not be changed, as seen in figure 9.32.
4. I selected the Shift Pixels tool (S), chose a 64-pixel brush, lowered the pressure to 10, and gently pushed her shoulder down by stroking along the top contour of the shoulder, as seen in figure 9.33. The Shift Pixels tool moves pixels perpendicular to the stroke direction. Brushing to the left shifts pixels downward, and brushing to the right moves pixels upward.

5. You can compare the new shoulder to the original by checking the Backdrop option (circled in **figure 9.34**) in the lower-right corner of the Liquify dialog box and selecting the layer with the original information. In this case, I viewed the background layer to see how much to reduce the shoulder.

6. After clicking OK to apply the Liquify command, check the results by turning the layer on and off.

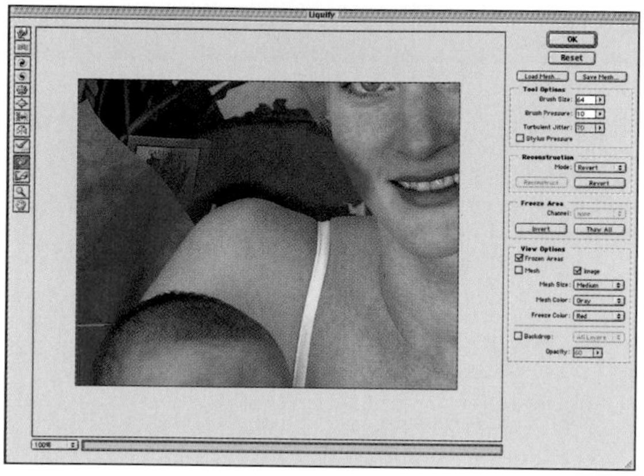

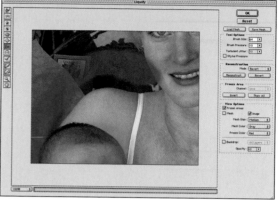

figure 9.32

Freezing areas guarantees that they will not be distorted.

figure 9.33

Shifting her shoulder down into a more comfortable position.

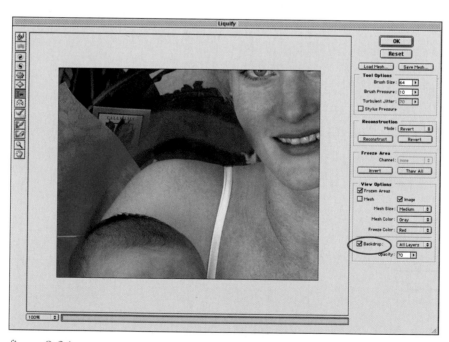

figure 9.34

Checking the Backdrop option lets the unaltered image area show through for comparison.

The Digital Diet

It goes without saying that not everyone can or should fit into the pages of *Vogue* or look like a cast member on *Friends*. The problem with taking a photograph is that often in the process of flattening three-dimensional people down to the two-dimensional film plane, they looks wider than they may be in reality—additionally, the person may be self-conscious of some gained weight.

As Eric Kuaimoku explained, "Over the last year, the bride had put on some extra weight. I wanted to create wedding pictures she would cherish over the years, rather than reminding her of the period in her life where she gained weight. The main focus of the retouch was to reduce her weight to make her look like her true self. These pictures were taken on the beach in Santa Cruz, California with my Canon G3 digital camera." (See figure 9.35.)

Eric used a combination of Free Transform, Liquify, Warp, and Pucker brushes and the Clone Stamp tool to create the wedding album photos seen in figures 9.36 and 9.41.

1. Eric started by duplicating the background layer and then selected the entire left side of the photograph, including the bride, with the Lasso tool with a one-pixel feather, as shown in figure 9.37.

2. He chose Edit > Free Transform and used the handle on the left side of the selection to narrow down the image area by 10%, as shown in figure 9.38.

© Eric Kuaimoku

BEFORE

figure 9.35

AFTER

figure 9.36

3. After accepting the transform, Eric selected Filter > Liquify and used the Warp tool (W) to carefully give the bride's waist and hips greater definition (see figure 9.39). The Warp tool pushes pixels forward as you drag. With a low brush pressure, the changes occur slowly, making them easier to control.

In the bride and groom photograph shown in figure 9.40, Eric used the Free Transform technique to achieve the initial narrowing of the bride seen in figure 9.41.

4. Then Eric entered Liquify and used the Pucker tool (P) to reduce the bride's arms, back, and feet, as seen in figure 9.42. The Pucker tool moves pixels toward the center of the brush as you hold down the mouse button.

figure 9.37

Selecting the entire left side of the image avoids potential artifacts.

figure 9.38

Dragging a Free Transform handle to narrow the selected area.

figure 9.39

The Liquify filter's Warp tool pushes pixels forward as you drag.

BEFORE

figure 9.40

AFTER

figure 9.41

figure 9.42

The Liquify filter's Pucker tool moves pixels toward the center of the brush area.

IMPROVING SKIN TEXTURE

Many people are self-conscious about their skin. Perhaps we suffered through the teenage years of acne, we're older and can already see the first crow's feet, or we didn't get enough sleep and look puffy and pale. It's a wonder we even get out of bed at all! Improving the appearance of skin in a portrait can be as simple as covering a few blemishes or as global as softening the entire portrait and then using the History Brush or a layer mask to paint back areas of selective focus.

Skin Blemishes... the Teenage Years

Why is it that blemishes seem to pop up when you're about to have your picture taken, need to go for a job interview, or are about to have a first date? Photoshop can't help you with the job interview or the date, but removing blemishes in a photograph is a snap.

Healing Good over Bad

This method of removing blemishes (see figure 9.43) is similar to removing dust or mold from an old photograph (and there were plenty of examples of those problems in Chapter 5, "Dust, Mold, and Texture Removal"). By working on a duplicate layer with the Healing Brush tool, you can quickly remove blemishes while maintaining skin texture, as shown in figure 9.44.

🌐 ▷⯈ **ch9_blemish1.jpg**

1. Duplicate the background layer and name it *Blemish Removal*.

2. Set the Healing Brush to lighten (as circled in figure 9.45) and select a brush size that is slightly larger than the blemish. Using the Lighten Blending Mode tells Photoshop to change only those pixels that are darker than the source area and makes the healing even less visible than when working with the Normal Blending Mode.

figure 9.43

figure 9.44

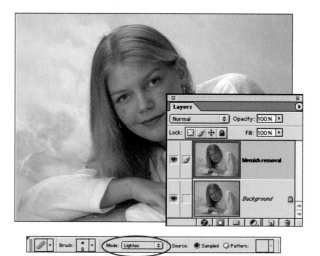

figure 9.45

Working on a duplicate layer to remove blemishes protects your original and guarantees you the ability to throw away the retouch and start over again if necessary.

3. Make the Blemish Removal layer active. Set your healing source by (Option + clicking) [Alt + clicking] good skin information to sample good skin texture, as seen in figure 9.46.

figure **9.46**

Remember to use a hard-edged brush when working with the Healing Brush.

4. If you slip or the blemish removal is too obvious, step back via the History palette and then redo the healing.

 T i p

If the Healing Brush is not working as expected, double-check the tool's Blending Mode in the options bar. Often, I use Lighten or Darken for a retouching project and forget that I've changed the Blending Mode when I return to work the next day.

Patching Good over Bad

The most important aspect to skin retouching is to maintain the original skin and image texture. You don't want a person to have soft or artificial-looking spots on her skin. And as much as I love the Healing Brush, it does require that I pay attention to where I am sampling and painting (boy, do I sound spoiled!). To remove numerous blemishes or moles like those in figure 9.47 quickly, use the Patch tool for the results shown in figure 9.48.

figure **9.47**

figure **9.48**

1. Duplicate the background layer and select the Patch tool. In the options bar, make sure that Source is clicked.

2. Zoom in on the blemish or mark to be removed and circle it with the Patch tool, as shown in figure 9.49.

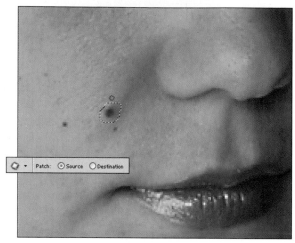

figure 9.49

Circle the blemish to be removed with the Patch tool.

3. Drag the selected area to good skin information and release the mouse, as shown in figure 9.50. Repeat this process for each blemish.

4. Zoom in and fine-tune any telltale areas with the Healing Brush.

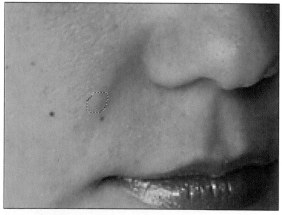

figure 9.50

Release the mouse to patch the blemish.

Patch Tool Tips:

- You do not need to deselect between patching one blemish and another, so you can work very quickly. Using the Patch tool to remove blemishes is much more efficient than using the Healing Brush.

- When making a new patch selection, start the selection of the new patch outside the current selection.

- If a black smudge appears inside your patch, then you overlapped your current patch with the last area you patched.

- If a white smudge appears, the tool is averaging from outside the image.

Using the History Brush and Blending Modes

I learned this method from Eddie Tapp (www. eddietapp.com). It combines the Gaussian Blur filter, History Brush tool, and Blending Modes to enhance a portrait. His technique will take you from the original shown in figure 9.51 to the enhanced version in figure 9.52. This method requires that you do the first three steps in the exact order described in the following text. As Eddie explains, "Try this technique several times and at various opacities to get the results you like."

09_colorportrait.jpg

1. Start by using the Gaussian Blur filter. The objective of the blur is to create a smooth transition between the specular and diffused highlights and the diffused and reflected light shadows, as pointed out in figure 9.53. For women, I use between 30- and 60-pixel blur radius, and for men, I use 15 to 30 pixels. In this example, I used a 40-pixel blur.

2. Take a History Snapshot by (Option + clicking) [Alt + clicking] the Create New Snapshot icon and name the snapshot *Blur*.

3. Select Edit > Undo Gaussian Blur.

© Eddie Tapp

BEFORE

figure 9.51

AFTER

figure 9.52

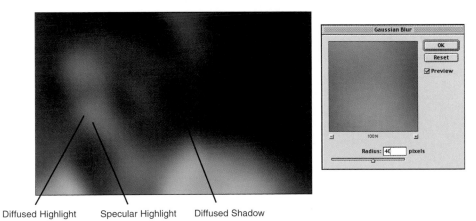

Diffused Highlight   Specular Highlight   Diffused Shadow

figure 9.53

Use the Gaussian Blur filter to soften the entire portrait.

4. Select the History brush tool, set the Blending Mode to Darken, and use 30% opacity. Set the History Source to the Blur snapshot, as shown in **figure 9.54**. Paint the entire skin tone, including the neckline, with multiple strokes of the History brush. Avoid painting over the hair, eyes, and lips. You may notice that the specular highlights get duller, but we'll bring those back a little later.

figure 9.54

After undoing the Gaussian Blur, use the History brush in Darken mode to paint over all the skin tones.

5. Switch the Blending Mode to Lighten and repeat the process by painting only the skin tone again at 30% opacity. Here, you'll notice the freckles and small blemishes diminishing, and the skin tone takes on a beautiful look (see **figure 9.55**). Make sure to avoid areas such as the hair, lips, teeth, and eyes, because you'll want to retouch them separately.

After Eddie enhances the skin texture with this method, he then removes any visible blemishes with the Healing Brush and cleans up the eyes as described in this chapter in the "Careful Cleanup" section later in this chapter.

figure 9.55

Switch the History brush to Lighten and repeat the process.

Caution

When working with the History palette, you must finish the retouch process before closing the file. The History States and Snapshots are forever purged if you close the file or quit Photoshop or if the computer crashes. You can salvage some of this work by saving your file with a new name at various stages of the retouching process.

Reducing the Marks of Time

As people get older, gravity, sun exposure, and changes in skin structure cause wrinkles. Every wrinkle is not created equal, and rather than removing all of them, I suggest you remove only the most distracting ones. Horizontal lines, such as the lines on our foreheads when we raise our eyebrows in surprise, are friendly and require the least amount of work. Vertical lines are caused by age and worry; if they are dark or deep, they should be reduced. Diagonal lines make a person look tense and anxious, and these are the wrinkles you should reduce the most.

In a photograph, a wrinkle is not a wrinkle; it's actually a dark area against a lighter area. By lightening the wrinkle, you are reducing the contrast of that part of the face and thereby reducing the visual interest that the viewer will have. Their eyes will seek out areas in the portrait that have more contrast, detail, and visual interest.

As people age, their wrinkles become longer and deeper. By shortening the length of the wrinkle, you can "take off" a few years without making people look as though they had plastic surgery. To reduce the length of the wrinkle, start at the youngest (the narrowest) end, not its origin (see figure 9.56), and use the techniques described in the following text to turn back the clock.

BEFORE

figure 9.57

Youngest   Oldest
part of the   part of the
wrinkle   wrinkle

figure 9.56

For effective wrinkle reduction, retouch wrinkles from the youngest part in toward the older part of the wrinkle.

In the portrait of a retiring judge, Joel Becker of Becker-Cline Digital Photography used a Kodak DCS 460c digital camera to take the original picture. Figure 9.57 shows a cropped view of the original portrait, and figure 9.58 shows the retouched version. Notice that after retouching and reducing the wrinkles, the judge still looks experienced and wise, without looking plastic or fake.

I have devised three methods to remove or reduce wrinkles—using a duplicate layer, a neutral overlay layer, and the Patch tool—and I usually end up using a combination of these three techniques to melt the years away.

 **ch9_judge.jpg**

AFTER

figure 9.58

Working on a Duplicate Layer

1. Duplicate the background layer (or the layer with the person's face) and change the duplicate's Blending Mode to Lighten.

2. Set the Dodge tool to 5–15% exposure and the range to Midtones.

3. Set the brush size to match the width of wrinkle to be removed.

4. Zoom in on the wrinkle, and, starting at its youngest end, dodge inward toward the origin of the wrinkle. Reduce the newest, narrowest part of the wrinkle first because this is the part that appeared most recently. As you can see in **figure 9.59**, the judge is looking less imposing.

figure 9.59

Using the Dodge tool on the youngest part of the wrinkle makes it appear shallower and softer.

Working on a Soft Light Neutral Layer

Working with a Soft Light neutral layer has three advantages. If you over-lighten an area, you can paint over problem areas with 50% gray and then rework the area again with the 3–5% white brush. Adding a neutral layer does not double the file size as does duplicating the background layer in the first method. Finally, the Overlay neutral layer enables you to lighten up darker areas, such as the shadow areas of the judge's eyelids.

1. (Option + click)[Alt + click] the New Layer icon on the Layers palette.

2. Select Soft Light from the Mode menu and click Fill with Soft-Light-neutral color (50% gray), as shown in **figure 9.60**.

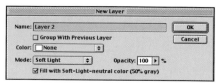

figure 9.60

Setting up the Soft Light neutral layer.

3. Set the foreground color to white, the Paintbrush tool to 5–10% opacity, and the brush size to match the width of the wrinkle to be reduced.

4. To lighten the dark areas of the wrinkles, paint with white on the Soft Light neutral layer with the Paintbrush tool set to a low opacity (see **Figure 9.61**). Start the wrinkle-removal process at the end of the wrinkle to lessen the youngest part of the wrinkle first.

figure 9.61

Use the Paintbrush tool with white paint and a soft brush on the Overlay neutral layer to reduce the darkness and contrast of the wrinkles.

Reversing the Aging Process

Working with Photoshop can feel like a late night TV advertisement that chirps, "As seen on NBC, CBS, and CNN, and even *Oprah*! The health discovery that actually reverses aging while burning fat, without dieting or exercise! Forget aging and dieting forever!"

- Reduce body fat and build lean muscle without exercise

- Enhance sexual performance

- Remove wrinkles and cellulite
- Lower blood pressure and reduce cholesterol
- Improve sleep, vision, and memory
- Restore hair color and growth
- Increase energy and cardiac output
- Turn back your body's biological time clock 10 to 20 years in 6 months

It seems that we can accomplish this entire list of medical wonders—well, almost all of them—with careful use of layers and this Patch tool technique. To reduce the signs of aging, work on a duplicate layer and use the Patch tool to quickly decrease wrinkles and furrows. **Figure 9.62** shows an attractive and mature woman. After a bit of patching, **figure 9.63** retains her warmth without making her look artificial.

© Ablestock

BEFORE

figure 9.62

AFTER

figure 9.63

🌐 **ch9_maturewoman.jpg**

1. Duplicate the background layer.
2. Set the Patch tool to source and circle the wrinkle, as shown in **figure 9.64**. Move the selection to a good skin area—in this case, I moved the patch selection to the woman's cheek. At 100% layer opacity, the patch is too apparent, as shown in **figure 9.65**.

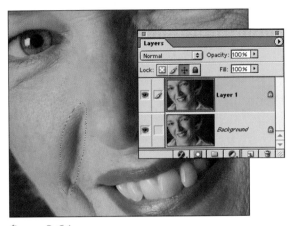

figure 9.64

On a duplicate layer, select the wrinkle with the Patch tool.

figure 9.65

The Patch tool completely removes the wrinkle, leaving an unnatural look.

3. By reducing the layer opacity (see **figure 9.66**), the original image information blends with the patch layer. This makes the wrinkle removal blend in and also helps you to avoid the over-retouched look that would not be appropriate for a mature woman.

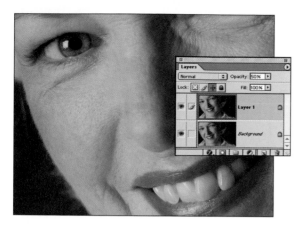

figure 9.66

Reducing the layer opacity blends the original and patched versions.

4. To adjust the opacity of an individual patch, after using the Patch tool immediately select Edit > Fade Patch Selection (Shift + Cmd + F) [Shift + Ctrl + F] and adjust the opacity slider, as shown in **figure 9.67**.

5. Continue selecting and patching her furrows and wrinkles.

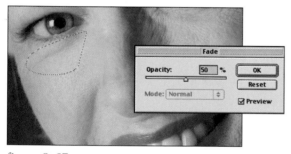

figure 9.67

Fading the patch to restore initial skin texture.

6. In most cases, you will need to refine the details with the Healing Brush. Add a new layer and select (Option) [Alt] Layer > Merge Visible. Carefully refine the details, as shown in **figure 9.68**.

figure 9.68

Use a merged layer to refine the details with the Healing Brush.

I prefer the Patch tool over the Healing Brush to reduce wrinkles because it is faster and easier to use.

Note

Removing blemishes and wrinkles requires a careful hand, and it is better to apply a little bit of good retouching than to overpower the portrait with a lot of bad retouching.

Dealing with Five O'Clock Shadow

On a rugged outdoorsy photograph, beard stubble can be quite attractive. On a formal portrait of a U. S. Navy Rear Admiral (see **figure 9.69**), the five o'clock shadow has a tendency to make a man look unrested. By using the Healing Brush and the Dust & Scratches filter, you can give the toughest beard a quick trim, as shown in **figure 9.70**.

ch9_beard.jpg

1. Duplicate the background layer.

2. Select Filter > Noise > Dust & Scratches and use a radius setting high enough to obliterate the beard, as shown in **figure 9.71**.

3. Choose Edit > Define Pattern and name the new pattern, as shown in **figure 9.72**.

4. Select Edit > Undo to undo the Dust & Scratches filter.

BEFORE

figure 9.69

AFTER

figure 9.70

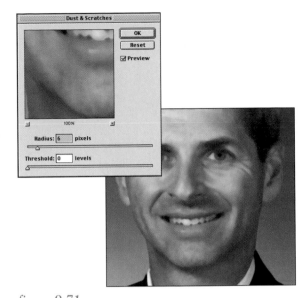

figure 9.71

The Dust & Scratches filter removes the stubble.

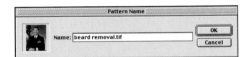

figure 9.72

Give the new pattern a distinctive name.

5. Set the Healing Brush to Pattern and Aligned, and make sure that the correct pattern is selected as circled in **figure 9.73**. Reduce the duplicated layer's opacity to 50% and then brush over the man's beard, as shown in **figure 9.74**.

figure 9.73

Set the Healing Brush source to the saved pattern.

Tip

Use this Dust & Scratches method to soften away wrinkles, blemishes, or deep furrows.

figure 9.74

When using a pattern source, simply brush in your corrections with the Healing Brush.

Warning

Delete unneeded patterns to reduce the size of the pattern preference file in the System Folder. Select Edit > Preset Manager > Pattern to delete unnecessary patterns.

Reducing Double Chins

Gravity has a way of sneaking up on us. All of a sudden, we have a double chin or jowls that we just don't like to see in the mirror—or in a photograph. Some people may turn to plastic surgery, but I prefer to turn to Photoshop because it doesn't hurt at all.

The goal is to reduce the contrast of the shadows of the wrinkles and to form a more flattering neckline. In **figure 9.75**, you see Joy—a woman full of energy, good will, and Senior of the Year for the Thousand Oaks, California City's Senior Program. When we asked whether we could feature her photograph in the book, her spontaneous response was, "Anything I can do to help others learn is fine by me." I hope to be that open and positive when I am older. By reducing the visual information on her neck, the viewer's eye is drawn to her wonderful face, as you can see in **figure 9.76**.

© Forrest Friends Photography

figure 9.75   **BEFORE**

figure 9.76   **AFTER**

 **ch9_chin.jpg**

1. Duplicate the background layer.

2. Select Filter > Liquify and use the Warp tool to gently push the neckline in and the wrinkles up, as shown in **figure 9.77**. Don't try to repair the entire neck, because Dr. Patch will follow this initial Liquify surgery. **Figure 9.78** shows the effectiveness of the Liquify tool.

3. Add a new layer and choose (Option) [Alt] Layer > Merge Visible to create a new working surface for the Patch tool to use. Set the Patch tool to work from source and select one wrinkle, as shown in **figure 9.79**. Drag the selection to good skin information and release the mouse. Repeat the patching of the other wrinkles to achieve the results in **figure 9.80**.

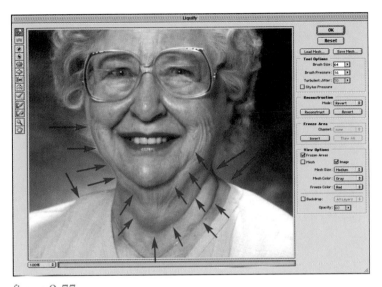

figure 9.77

Use the Liquify filter's Warp tool to gently push in the neckline.

figure 9.78

After Liquify surgery.

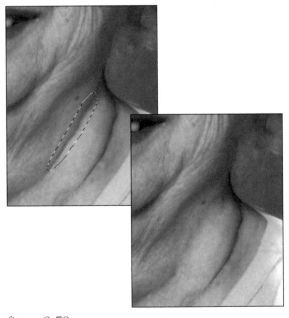

figure 9.79

Use the Patch tool to remove one wrinkle at a time.

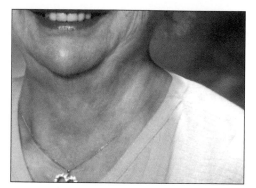

figure 9.80

Repeat until all wrinkles are removed.

4. If the patching looks too artificial, select Edit > Fade Patch Selection and reduce the opacity to allow some original skin structure to show through.

5. Often, fine jewelry can disappear between skin folds, as is the case here. Select the intact gold chain with a 5-pixel feathered Lasso tool, Edit > Copy, Edit > Paste and then move and transform the existing gold chain to rebuild the rest of the chain, as shown in **figure 9.81**.

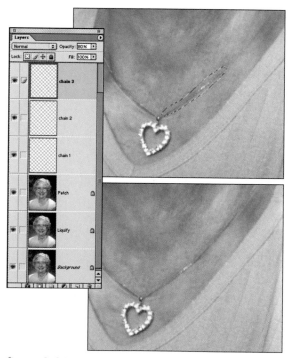

figure 9.81

Rebuild the chain by copying and pasting from existing sections.

6. Add a new layer and select (Option) [Alt] Layer > Merge Visible to create a final working surface. Use the Healing Brush to clean up remaining wrinkles or patch artifacts, as shown in **figure 9.82**.

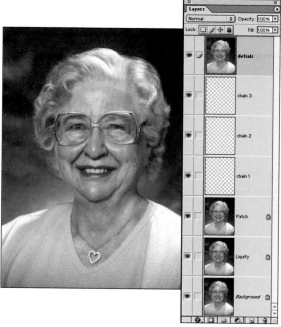

figure 9.82

Use the Healing Brush on a merged layer for final cleanup.

Reducing Shiny and Hot Spots

Over-exposed areas, usually found in the protruding areas of the face—nose, cheeks, forehead, and chin—can be very distracting (see **figure 9.83**). By using the Patch tool on a separate layer, you can reduce the shininess very quickly, as shown in **figure 9.84**. This technique also works on bald heads.

ch9_shinyskin.jpg

1. Duplicate the Background layer.

2. Use the Patch tool set to Source and select the hot spot.

3. Move the selection to an area of good skin information and release the mouse.

© Ablestock

BEFORE

figure 9.83

AFTER

figure 9.84

4. Continue patching all of the hotspots. Finally, adjust the duplicated layer's opacity. In this example, I set the patch layer to 65% (see **figure 9.85**) to allow the tonality of the original portrait to shimmer through. In most cases, you do not want to leave the patched layer at 100% because this can make a portrait look dull and flat.

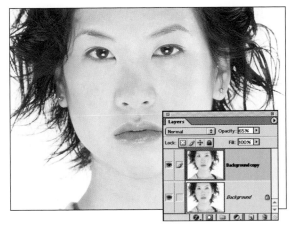

figure 9.85

Reduce the opacity of the patched layer to let the tonality show through.

ACCENTUATING FACIAL FEATURES

After you've removed distractions, shaped contours, and improved a person's skin texture, it's time to get into the nitty-gritty details of portrait retouching. In most cases, this involves working on a person's eyes and mouth.

We look into peoples' eyes to see their soul, to see whether they are speaking the truth, and to make one-on-one contact. The eyes are the most important aspect of most portraits and require special care. Accentuating a person's eyes can make the portrait more intriguing, and by increasing contrast, color, and detail in a person's eyes, you also draw the viewer's eye away from less interesting aspects of the portrait. I use a variety of methods to retouch a person's eyes. In the following examples, we'll work with layers, the Dodge and Burn tool, and the painting tools to bring out the very best in a person's eyes.

Eyeball Fundamentals

Our eyes are spheres, and you should avoid overworking them with over-zealous cloning or lightening of the whites or darkening of the iris. Being heavy-handed in the eyes will flatten them out and make them appear lifeless. Before you retouch a person's eyes, take a moment to study the light origin so that you can work with the light and not against it. **Figure 9.86** shows that the lightest part of the eye whites are in the lower half of the eyeball and that the lightest part of the iris is always opposite the primary light source. To keep the eyes lively and interesting, it is essential to maintain moisture and highlights and to keep the red tones in the corners by the tear ducts.

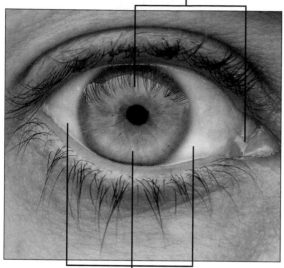

Make sure to keep moisture
and highlights in the eye.

The lightest areas of the eye whites and
irises are opposite the main light.

figure 9.86

Our eyes are round and translucent, and light plays off and through them.

Accentuating Contrast with the Dodge and Burn Tools

There are numerous methods to enhance a person's eyes—from working with Dodge and Burn, Clone Stamp, and Paintbrushes, to working with Levels and Curves (as described in Chapter 10, "Glamour and Fashion Retouching"). In addition to accentuating the natural beauty in a person's eye, you may be asked to remove redeye, reduce catchlights, and take out reflections in eyeglasses.

After softening and correcting the skin tones of the black and white portrait in **figure 9.87**, I needed to accentuate her eyes by lightening the eye whites and carefully darkening the eyelids—just as though we were applying eyeliner or mascara to her eyes (see **figure 9.88**).

© Katrin Eismann

BEFORE

figure 9.87

AFTER

figure 9.88

Whenever you lighten or darken an aspect of a person's features, you can strengthen the effect by using the opposite tone in the adjacent area. For example, if you lighten the eye whites, you should also darken the iris (as described in the example after this one) or accentuate the eyelashes with a bit of digital mascara to contrast the lighter eye areas.

ch9_BWeyes.jpg

1. Activate the layer that has eye information for you to accentuate. Generously select the eyes with the Marquee tool, as shown in figure 9.89.

figure 9.89

Select the eyes with the Marquee tool.

2. Select Layer > New > Layer via Copy (Cmd + J) [Ctrl + J] to place the eyes onto their own layer.

3. Select the Dodge tool and set the exposure to 5% and Range to Highlights.

4. Zoom in on the eyes and carefully lighten the eye whites. As you can see in figure 9.90, the left eye is already brighter and more interesting than the right eye, which hasn't been retouched yet. Don't over-lighten or take out every bit of tonality to avoid the frozen-in-the-headlights look (see figure 9.91).

figure 9.90

Working on the eye layer, use the Dodge tool to lighten the eye whites. In this example, the eye on the left has been enhanced and the eye on the right is still in its original state.

figure 9.91

Being heavy-handed with either lightening or darkening will make the eyes look lifeless and dull.

5. Use the Dodge tool on the other eye to balance out the eye whitening effect.

 C a u t i o n

When using the Dodge and Burn tools, use a very low exposure (5–10%) and build up the effect slowly. The default setting of 50% is like trying to retouch with a sledgehammer.

6. Working on the same eye layer, select the Burn tool and set it to Shadows and 10%.

7. Use a brush that is the same size as the edge of the eyes to which you are going to apply eye-liner and carefully trace the edges of the eye, as shown in **figure 9.92**.

figure 9.92

Use the Burn tool to gently outline the eyes.

8. Carefully apply similar darkening to the other eye.

9. If the retouch is too strong, reduce the opacity of the eye layer to create the desired effect.

Careful Cleanup

The Dodge and Burn tools as previously described can also be used on color portraits. If the eyes need more aggressive cleanup, use a combination of the painting and Clone Stamp tools as described here. In the color portrait by Eddie Tapp, the woman's eyes are very pretty but a bit blood-shot (see **figure 9.93**). By enhancing the eyes with careful cloning and a bit of painting, Eddie cleaned up her eye whites and enriched the natural color without making her eyes look artificial, as shown in **figure 9.94**.

1. Create a new window (Window > Documents > New Window) so that you can position one at 100% zoom ratio and make the other, where you will do the actual work, larger on your screen. The 100% window will allow you to see quickly the quality of work you're doing, because you'll be zoomed in fairly close to work on the eyes (see **figure 9.95**).

figure 9.93

BEFORE

figure 9.94

AFTER

figure 9.95

Work in a zoomed window while monitoring progress in a 100% view.

2. Duplicate the background layer and name it *Eyes.*

3. To remove discolorization in her eye whites, use the Brush tool set to Color mode and 70% opacity. With the brush active, (Option + click) [Alt + click] to temporarily change the brush into the Eyedropper tool to sample good eye white color. Carefully paint away the discoloration in the whites of the eyes, as you see in figure 9.96. Be careful when working in the whites of the eyes because overdoing it and taking out every bit of color or definition will make them look fake.

figure 9.97

Add color depth by tracing around the iris with the Burn tool.

6. Switch to the Dodge tool to create a little gleam (half-moon shaped) on the opposite side of the catchlight, as shown in figure 9.98.

figure 9.96

Sample good eye white color and paint over the discolored areas with a low-opacity brush set to Color mode.

4. Select the Clone Stamp tool and set the tool's Blending options to Lighten and 20%. Clone out any blood vessels or dark regions and then switch over to the Clone Stamp tool's Darken mode and minimize the light in the white of her left eye. Be sure to uncheck Aligned in the options bar, because the source region is very small.

5. To add a bit of sparkle and color to her eyes, use the Burn tool set to shadow and 10% opacity and trace around her iris rim, as shown in figure 9.97.

figure 9.98

Add a half-moon shaped gleam with the Dodge tool.

7. Finally, select the Sponge tool, set it to saturate, and use 20% flow. Sponge over the iris to strengthen the natural colors, as shown in **figure 9.99**.

figure 9.100

figure 9.99

Use the Sponge tool to saturate the colors of the iris.

 T i p

The shortcut key to access the Dodge tool is O ("oh," not zero). Use Shift + O to cycle between the Dodge, Burn, and Sponge tools.

Painterly Accentuation

The final method I use to accentuate eyes takes a painterly approach that emphasizes the play of lights, shadows, and colors. The best aspect of this technique is that all of the enhancements are built up on separate layers, giving you tremendous control over the intensity of the retouch. As you can see in **figure 9.100**, the original eyes are attractive, but the enhanced ones in **figure 9.101** have a romantic, painterly quality to them. In the following technique, you lighten the eye whites and rim, enhance the iris, fine-tune the catchlights, darken the eyelashes, and warm the eyes to draw in the viewer's eye.

figure 9.101

🌐⤴️ **ch9_coloreyes.jpg**

1. Zoom in to 200% on the eye to be retouched, create and position a new view (Window > Documents > New Window), and make sure that the Layers palette is visible.

2. Add a new layer.

3. Set the Brush tool to work at 5–10% opacity and make sure that the foreground color is set to white. The brush should be almost as large as the individual eye whites, as you see in **figure 9.102**.

4. Lightly paint a hint of white onto the eye whites to the left and right of the iris. Don't worry about staying "inside the lines" because you can use the Eraser tool to clean up any color spill.

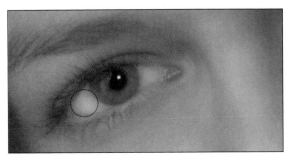

figure 9.102

By adding a hint of white to either side of the iris, her eyes become lighter and clearer.

5. Add another new layer and use the Brush tool set to black and a small diameter to carefully trace the rim of the iris with a very low opacity, as shown in **figure 9.103**.

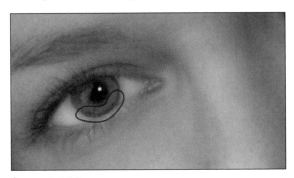

figure 9.103

On a designated layer, trace the rim of the iris with the Brush tool set to 10% opacity.

6. Add a new layer. Use the Clone Stamp tool set to Use All Layers to remove any bothersome catchlights. In this example, the small catchlight in the woman's pupil is distracting.

7. On the same layer, paint in a soft light that mimics the larger catchlight in the upper-left side of the iris (see **figure 9.104**).

 N o t e

Eyes are translucent spheres, and light travels through them. Adding a touch of white on the opposite side of the primary light source accentuates the roundness and liveliness of the eye.

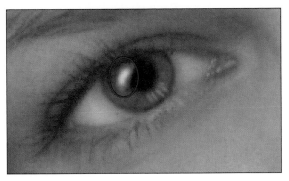

figure 9.104

Simplify the eyes by removing harsh and distracting catchlights.

8. As shown in **figure 9.105**, use a very small white Brush set to 20% opacity to add a hint of the highlight on the iris opposite the catchlight. I often soften these lines with a touch of the Smudge or Blur tools.

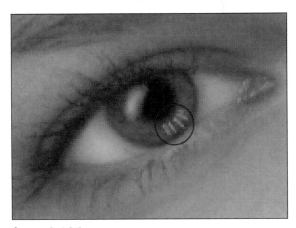

figure 9.105

Opposite the main catchlight, draw in hints of light and use the Blur or Smudge tools to soften them.

9. To accentuate the natural color of the eyes, sample the color of the iris, open the Color palette, and switch the palette to HSB mode. Boost the Saturation by 30–50% and the Brightness by 15–25%. HSB is a useful color mode to work in when you need to strengthen colors without shifting them.

10. Add a new layer and paint over the iris with a large soft brush set to 5% opacity. Change the Blending Mode of the iris color layer to Color to make the color translucent and natural (see figure 9.106). Use the Eraser tool to clean up any color spill.

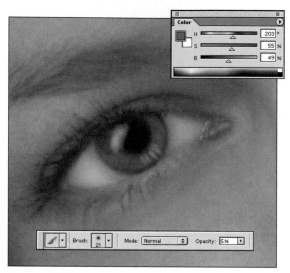

figure 9.106

Brighten the eyes by painting with a more saturated and brighter version of the original color.

11. Not all portraits will need to have the eyelashes accentuated, but in many cases, framing the eye with darker eyelashes adds a heightened contrast in relationship to the eye whites.

12. Add a new layer and name it *eyelashes*. Use a 10% opacity, soft, black brush to swoop around the entire eye.

 N o t e

For more realistic eyes, warm the tear ducts with a touch of red. As Jane Connor-Ziser, a classically trained painter and retoucher who has been working digitally for over a decade, explains, "In some cases, retouching the eye can make the image too cool and unfriendly. You can offset this by dabbing just a touch of red into the tear duct area."

13. Use a smaller Eraser to erase any spill in the eyes and to separate the lashes. Lower the opacity of the eyelash layer to your liking for results like those shown in figure 9.107.

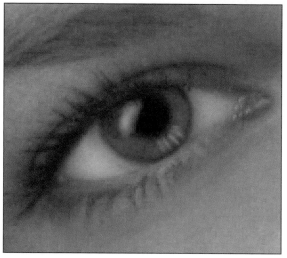

figure 9.107

Use the Brush and Eraser tools on a new layer to make the eyelashes darker and thicker.

14. Add a new layer and name it *tear ducts*.

15. Choose a bright red from the swatch window. Jane likes the default warm red in the upper-left corner of the Swatches palette, as shown in figure 9.108.

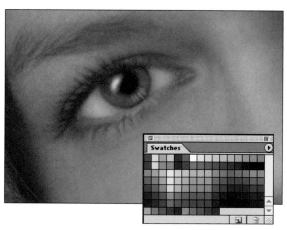

figure 9.108

Adding a touch of red to the small corners of the eye adds warmth to the eye and the portrait.

16. Use the Brush tool to daub a hint of the red over the tear ducts and in the outside corners of the eyes. Clean up any overspill with the Eraser tool and reduce the opacity of the layer if need be.

17. Finally, look away from the portrait for a few moments to clear up your visual memory and to refresh your eyes. Look at the portrait again and check your work with contrast, color, and detail in mind.

Tip

Get a second opinion. After working on a portrait, you become very familiar with it and might not even notice problems or areas that are overworked or don't look right. Ask someone to take a look at the portrait and tell you what he or she notices or thinks about the image.

Removing Reflections in Glasses

Removing reflections in glasses can be as straightforward as simply reducing them with a bit of burning and cloning as Joel Becker did in the portrait of the judge (refer to figure 9.58). In the example in figure 9.109, the photographer's flash—seen in both pairs of eyeglasses—is distracting. In figure 9.110, you see the retouch that Carrie Beene did to remove the reflections via painting and cloning good information over the bothersome reflections.

Tip

Portrait photographers take more than one exposure. Ask your client for these additional exposures—they might contain information you can use to rebuild the image.

1. Start by studying the image. Notice where the light is coming from and where there is information you can take advantage of to hide the reflections.

2. Add an empty layer and use the Elliptical Marquee tool to define the new iris, as shown in figure 9.111.

© Photographic Images

figure 9.109

figure 9.110

figure 9.111

Defining the iris with a selection.

3. Sample existing eye color, and with a small brush, paint in the new iris. Our eyes are multicolored, so vary the eye color and, make the outer rim of the iris a bit darker.

4. Paint in the pupil. In portraits, a large pupil is a sign of openness and friendliness. It is important to keep at least one catchlight in the eye, or the eyes will look flat and lifeless.

5. If the painting looks too flat, use Filter > Add Noise to give the iris a bit of texture. Use monochrome noise.

6. Deselect and use the Clone Stamp set to Use All Layers to clean up any artifacts and the eye whites, as shown in figure 9.112.

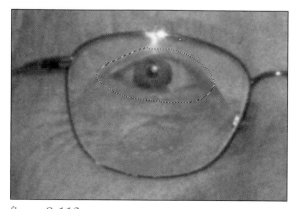

figure 9.113

Select the entire eye area with the Lasso tool.

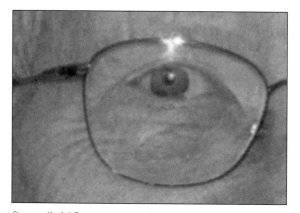

figure 9.112

After painting in the iris and pupil, use the Clone Stamp tool to clean up.

7. Generously select the entire eye with a 5-pixel feather lasso, as you see in figure 9.113. Duplicate the eye onto a new layer using Edit > Copy Merged and then Edit > Paste.

8. Move the duplicate eye over the other eye and add a layer mask to this new layer. Use a black brush on the layer mask to hide unneeded parts of the eye, as shown in figure 9.114. When working on eyes, pay careful attention to make sure that the person doesn't suddenly have two sets of tear ducts on the second eye.

figure 9.114

Use the arrow keys to move the replacement eye precisely into position. Even a slight difference in apparent position can create a disturbing appearance.

9. Add a new layer to the top of the layer stack and choose (Option) [Alt] Layer > Merge Visible to create a new working surface.

10. Removing the distracting flash reflections on the man's glasses is a straightforward select, duplicate, position, and blend technique. Select the good eyeglass information with a one-feather pixel Lasso tool, as shown in figure 9.115.

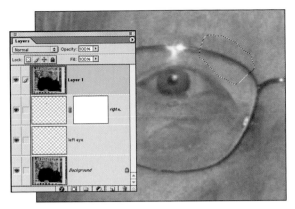

figure 9.115

On a merged layer, select a section of eyeglass frame with no reflections.

11. Copy the selected section of eyeglass frame onto its own layer using Layer > New > Layer via Copy or (Cmd + J) [Ctrl + J]. Then rotate using Edit > Free Transform and, as **figure 9.116** shows, place the pivot point of the bounding box on one edge of the eyeglass frame to rotate on that point.

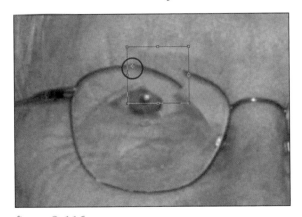

figure 9.116

Rotate the duplicate eyeglass section into place.

12. Rotate the top of the eyeglass frame into position and if need be, use the (Control + click) [right mouse click] to access the context sensitive menu of the transform. In this example, I needed to flatten out the curve of the eyeglass frame with a subtle distortion, as seen in **figure 9.117**.

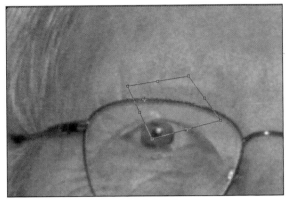

figure 9.117

Drag the handles of the Free Transform bounding box to rotate and distort the section of eyeglass frame into place.

13. Add a layer mask and use a black brush on the layer mask to paint over the transition areas of the skin to create a smooth transition, as seen in **figure 9.118**. You may be thinking, "Can't I just use the Eraser tool to erase extraneous skin?" Well, you could; but I'm a conservative Photoshopper who would rather hide and reveal pixels with layer masks than erase them. You never know when you will need that pixel back.

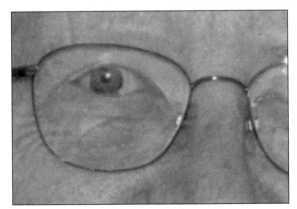

figure 9.118

Use a layer mask to blend the edges of the replacement frame section.

14. Repeat the select-and-duplicate repair on the other eyeglass frame. Use the Clone Stamp tool set to Use All Layers to do any final cleanup to achieve the final results shown at the beginning of this section.

Tip

When photographing people with glasses, ask them to take off their glasses and take one or two photos. These exposures may provide useful information to use to replace large reflections.

Taking out reflections is similar to repairing damaged photographs as described in Chapter 6. It involves begging, borrowing, and stealing information from other parts of the person's face, the image background, and in some cases, other images.

In the portrait in figure 9.119, the window reflections in the baby's eyes are rather disturbing. Compare this to the final photograph in figure 9.120, which makes the portrait look as though it were taken with professional flash equipment.

© Debbie Daanen Photography

BEFORE

figure 9.119

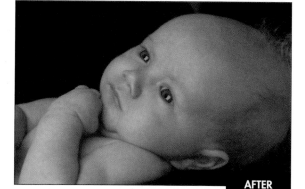

AFTER

figure 9.120

Removing Redeye... or Becoming a Digital Exorcist

Redeye occurs when the flash bounces off the back of the eyeball. Redeye makes people and pets look as though they are possessed by Linda Blair demons. Redeye has a higher chance of occurring if the flash is on the camera or very close to the lens. This is the case for most consumer point-and-shoot or low-end digital cameras. Redeye is also more likely to be a problem if the subject is in a dark room and the pupils are wide open. Taking it out is one of the most common retouching jobs.

Avoiding Redeye

To prevent redeye, use any or all of following photographic techniques:

- Move the flash off the camera using a sync cable or radio slave.

- Increase the ambient light or move the subject into a better-lit position. This will cause the pupils to shrink, reducing the possibility of redeye, and you might not need to use flash at all.

- Some cameras offer a redeye reduction mode that tricks the iris into closing down by firing a pre-flash before the main flash. Personally, I'm not a huge fan of this pre-flash method because people think that you've taken the picture when the pre-flash fires, and they have a tendency to look away.

As every Photoshop user knows, a number of different ways are often available to accomplish the same task. The following text outlines two techniques for removing redeye. Although the results are similar, I've spelled out two techniques so that you can pick one—or perhaps combine them—to come up with what works best for you. Experiment with combining these techniques to save the world from red-eyed aliens. For additional redeye information, please visit the book's web site, Chapter 9 section to download the file ch9_redeye_removal.pdf.

Figure 9.121 shows a true dragon child; with a little Photoshopping, the demonic redeye is removed in figure 9.122.

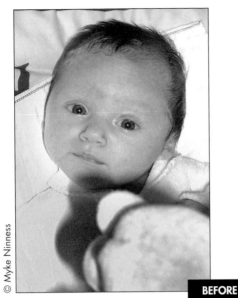

© Myke Ninness

BEFORE

figure 9.121

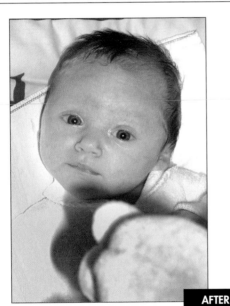

AFTER

figure 9.122

Select and Desaturate

This method quickly removes the offending redeye. I'm often asked when to use each method, and as you can imagine, there are no hard and fast rules. Experiment with each one, and I'm sure you'll develop techniques of your own that work well for different image scenarios.

ch9_redeye.jpg

1. Zoom in on the eyes and press Q to enter Quick Mask mode.

2. Use a soft, black brush that is a bit smaller than the pupil. With the brush in place, click repeatedly. With each mouse click, you'll see that the black circle enlarges toward the edges of the pupil. Repeat this step for the second pupil (see figure 9.123).

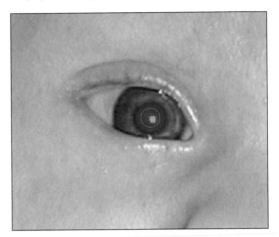

figure 9.123

Working in Quick Mask mode, use a soft, black brush to paint over the redeye.

3. Press Q to activate the selection and inverse (Select > Inverse) it.

4. Add a Hue/Saturation Adjustment Layer.

5. Move the Saturation slider all the way to the left to draw out all the color (see figure 9.124). In many cases, this will at least look better, but the pupils may now look washed out. (This is the same effect achieved by desaturating with the Sponge tool.) When you change the Blending Mode of the Adjustment Layer to Multiply, Photoshop darkens the desaturated layer to a rich, dark tone.

6. Adjust the opacity to taste, to the point that the pupils are enhanced without looking unnatural.

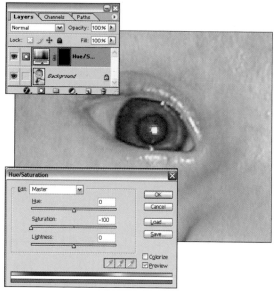

figure 9.124

Desaturate the redeye with a Hue/Saturation layer set to –100 saturation.

Select and Substitute

The following method maintains both pupil texture and catchlights.

1. Open the Channels palette and go to the channel with the best (darkest) pupil. It will most likely be the green channel—it will definitely not be the red channel.

2. Use the Elliptical Marquee tool to select one of the pupils. Hold down the Shift key to select the second pupil, as shown in figure 9.125.

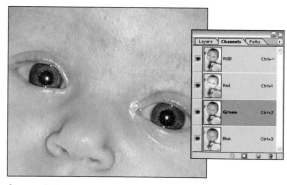

figure 9.125

Find the channel with the best information and select both pupils.

T i p

Saving the selection (by clicking the Save Selection icon on the Channels palette) saves the selection to an alpha channel. You can then activate the selection at any time.

3. Choose Select > Feather and use a setting of 1 to slightly soften the edge of the selection.

4. Copy the selected pupils. With the selection active, click the red channel and choose Edit > Paste Into. This will paste the good green pupil into the bad red pupil.

5. Make the blue channel active and repeat the Paste Into command, as shown in figure 9.126.

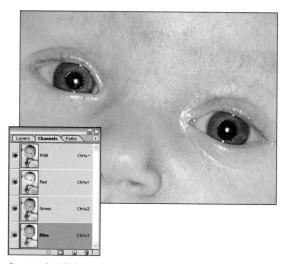

figure 9.126

Repeat the Paste Into in the blue channel.

IMPROVING FACIAL FEATURES

Now that you've improved the portrait's contours, skin, and eyes, it's time to move on to the teeth and hair.

You Have a Lovely Smile

Lightening a person's teeth and reducing discolorization or staining is much more pleasant with Photoshop than in the dentist's chair, as you see in figures 9.127 and 9.128. Keep in mind that a 20-year–old's teeth will be brighter than a senior citizen's, and it is appropriate to maintain some tone and color in the teeth and not make them so bright that they just shout, "Look at me—I'm fake."

figure 9.127

figure 9.128

1. Select the teeth with a one-pixel feathered lasso, as shown in figure 9.129.

figure 9.129

Use the Lasso tool to select the teeth.

2. Add a Levels Adjustment Layer and move the midtone slider to the left (see figure 9.130).

3. If needed, use the Clone Stamp tool (not set to Use All Layers) to clean up any remaining stains, chips, or marks.

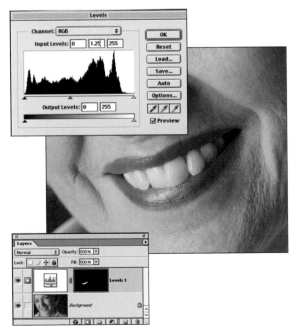

figure 9.130

Use Levels to whiten the teeth (but not too much).

Teeth naturally have a wide variety of colors, and the teeth of smokers or coffee and red wine drinkers can be unpleasantly discolored. In these cases, it is necessary both to reduce the color and brighten the teeth, as shown here in **figures 9.131** and **9.132**.

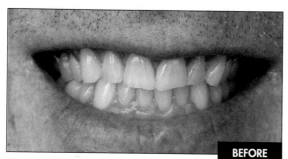

figure 9.131

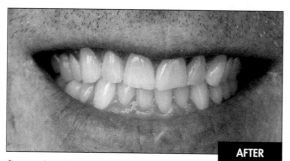

figure 9.132

1. Select the teeth with a one-pixel lasso tool, as shown in **figure 9.133**.

2. Add a Hue/Saturation Adjustment Layer.

3. Select Yellows from the Edit menu. To define the person's tooth color, drag over the person's teeth. You'll notice that the split sliders in the color sliders will change to reflect the colors in the teeth.

4. Move the saturation slider to the left, as shown in **figure 9.134**. Don't move it all the way to the left, because that will make the teeth too gray.

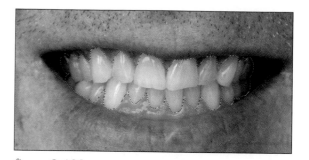

figure 9.133

Select only the teeth using the Lasso tool.

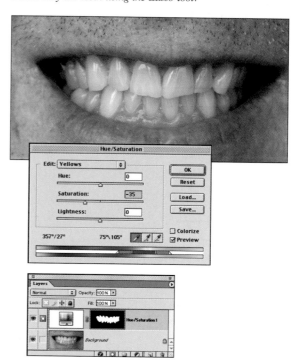

figure 9.134

Use a Hue/Saturation Adjustment layer to desaturate only the yellows.

5. Return to the Master and move the Lightness slider to the right. Once again, don't overdo it. You're not trying to make the person's teeth glow; you just want to make them look a bit whiter and lighter, as shown in **figure 9.135**.

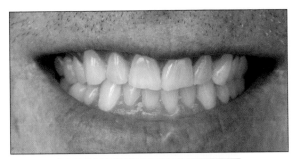

figure 9.135

Adding a bit of lightness to all channels adds the finishing touch.

Removing Braces

Having orthodontic work done is unpleasant enough without having to suffer the reminder of the procedure in an important portrait. Your first inclination may be to grab the Clone Stamp tool to clone away the braces, but believe me, that can be a futile effort because often there just isn't enough good tooth information to create realistic teeth. So step away from the Clone Stamp and look through your image archives or stock photos for an appropriate smile without braces. In figure 9.136, you see a portrait of an attractive young woman, and in figure 9.137, you see the retouching and braces removal done by H & H Color labs.

1. Find an appropriate smile from a different portrait, select it, and Edit > Copy.

2. Select the mouth of the portrait with the braces, using a one-pixel feathered lasso (see figure 9.138).

figure 9.136

figure 9.137

figure 9.138

Select the mouth using the Lasso tool with a one-pixel feathered lasso.

3. Edit > Paste Into and use the Free Transform tool to position and size the teeth, as shown in figure 9.139.

4. (Option + click) [Alt + click] the Create New Adjustment Layer button and drag to Levels. Check Group with Previous to create a clipping group so that the Levels adjustment impacts only the teeth. Adjust the tone of the teeth as needed, as I did in figure 9.140.

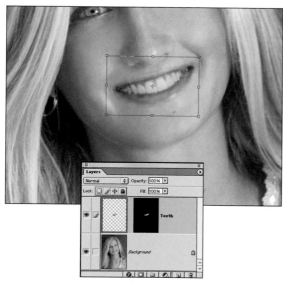

figure 9.139

Paste Into pastes the new smile into the selection where Free Transform can be used to size and position it.

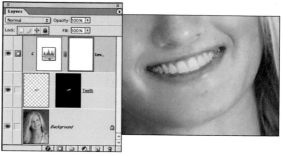

figure 9.140

Grouping the Adjustment Layer limits its effect to only the layer it is grouped with.

5. Add a new layer to the top of the layer stack and select (Option) [Alt] Layer > Merge Visible to create a new working surface. Use the Clone Stamp tool to clean up details that may be showing to create the final smile in figure 9.141.

figure 9.141

On a merged layer, use the Clone Stamp tool to clean up any artifacts.

Shaping the Hair with Light

After retouching a subject's face, take a few minutes to shape the hair by adding highlights and shadow to the natural form of the hair. Figure 9.142 is yours truly, and figure 9.143 shows my hair with sparkle and life added to it. Enhancing highlights and shadows adds dimension and liveliness to hair. This technique is called *wedging*, and you can use it to add tonal depth to hair or a person's clothing. It only takes a few seconds, but it makes the final portrait look richer.

BEFORE

figure 9.142

AFTER

figure 9.143

🌐➢⟨ **ch9_hairshaping.jpg**

1. To accentuate highlights, add a Color Dodge neutral layer by (Option + clicking) [Alt + clicking] the New Layer icon on the Layers palette. Select the Color Dodge Blending Mode and check Fill with Color-Dodge-neutral color (black).

2. Because you want to work subtly and build up the contouring, use a large, soft, white brush set to 2–5% opacity to trace the contours of the natural hair highlights, as shown in figure 9.144.

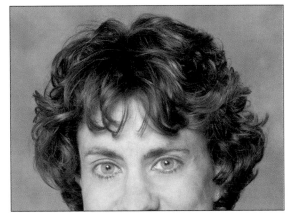

figure 9.144

Painting on a neutral Color Dodge layer with a large soft brush emphasizes the highlights.

3. To accentuate shadows, add a Color Burn neutral layer by (Option + clicking) [Alt + clicking] the New Layer icon on the Layers palette. Select the Color Burn Mode and check Fill with Color-Burn-neutral color (white).

4. Use a large, soft, black brush set to 2–5% opacity to accentuate the contours of the shadows, as shown in figure 9.145.

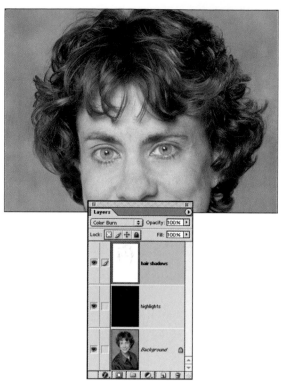

figure 9.145

Painting on a Color Burn neutral layer with a large soft brush emphasizes the shadows.

figure 9.146

© Ablestock

BEFORE

WORKING WITH SOFT AND SELECTIVE FOCUS

Soft-focus effects can be used to soften a portrait or to add a romantic atmospheric effect to an image. Photographers use many types of materials to create soft-focus effects, from nylon stockings and Vaseline over the enlarger lens to taking the picture through a window screen.

Softening a portrait also minimizes skin imperfections and adds a glow to the person's skin. **Figure 9.146** shows the original portrait for this example, which is rather contrasty. Softening the portrait makes the new version more romantic (see **figure 9.147**).

🌐 ⯈⯈⯈ **ch9_model.jpg**

1. Duplicate the background layer and set the Blending Mode to Lighten. Although the image will look too light, this will let you see the true effect of the next step.

figure 9.147

AFTER

2. Select Filter > Blur > Gaussian Blur and use a high setting (see **figure 9.148**). Without the Lighten Blending Mode, the blur would soften the image into oblivion.

figure 9.149

Duplicate blurred layers set to Lighten and Darken mimic an optical blur.

figure 9.148

Duplicating the layer and setting it to Lighten allows you to see the true effect of the Gaussian Blur filter.

3. Adjust the soft layer's opacity between 40–60% to blend the two images.

4. Duplicate the blurred layer and set its Blending Mode to Darken, as shown in **figure 9.149**. The combination of a lightening and a darkening layer mimics an optical blur better than one layer alone can.

5. The last step is to add image grain back into the image. When you use a soft focus filter on a camera lens, the image grain will still be sharp even though the photograph is soft.

   To add noise to the image, select Layer > New > Layer and change the Blending Mode to Overlay and check Fill with Overlay-neutral color (50% gray), as shown in **figure 9.150**. This creates an invisible layer that you can filter to create film grain or add image texture.

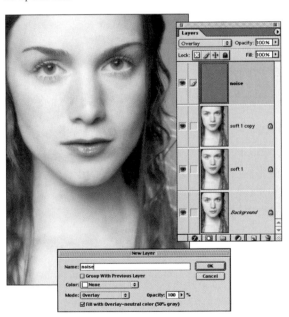

figure 9.150

Check Fill with Overlay-neutral color when making an Overlay layer.

6. Select Filter > Noise > Add Noise and check Monochrome; adjust the noise to your taste, as shown in **figure 9.151**. Use the Gaussian Blur filter with a low setting of 2 to reduce the artificial crispness of the computer-generated noise.

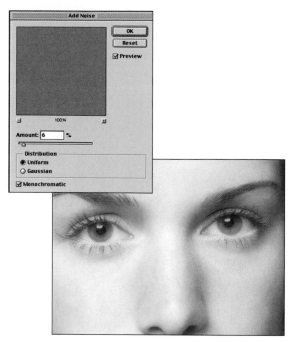

figure 9.151

The Add Noise filter set to Monochrome simulates image grain.

Selective Focus Controls

If you've paged through any fashion magazines recently, you've seen shots in which the model's lower body is thrown out of focus and her face is in focus. In most cases, the photographer has achieved this effect by using a large-format-view camera (4×5" or 8×10") and distorting the plane of focus with the camera's swing and tilt controls.

You can achieve a similar effect with the following technique. **Figure 9.152** is the original version, and **figure 9.153** is the selective focus variation.

1. Duplicate the background layer.

2. Run a high Gaussian Blur filter. (20 pixels is probably a good place to start.)

3. Add a layer mask to the blurred layer and use the Gradient tool set to black to white to control where the focus is placed. In this example, I wanted her face to be in focus and the lower part of the image to be out of focus, as shown in **figure 9.154**.

figure 9.152

BEFORE

figure 9.153

AFTER

ch9_standing_model.jpg

figure 9.154

Use the Gradation Blend tool on the layer mask to control where the image is in focus.

4. If need be, you can strengthen the effect by running the Gaussian Blur filter on the blurred layer again. Or, to add film grain, add an Overlay neutral layer as described in the "Working with Soft and Selective Focus" section to add a hint of image noise to give the soft areas visual tooth.

Refocusing an Image

There is a limit to the magic that Photoshop can do—if an image is so out of focus you can't recognize anything, no amount of sharpening will make it as tack sharp as a properly focused image. Rather than trying to focus out-of-focus areas, consider defocusing unessential image areas even more. This will fool the eye into thinking that the out-of-focus areas are sharp. Our eyes compare image areas and don't linger on less-sharp image areas.

In the example in figure 9.155, the point-and-shoot digital camera had focused on the trees in the background. As Wayne Palmer explains, "I was hired to photograph this wedding and I took along my Nikon CoolPix to capture a few candids for my web site. When I saw the shot on the camera LCD screen, I was thrilled until I saw it on the computer monitor. The camera had focused dead center on the background. I did not want to lose the magic of this moment. I blurred the background and used selective sharpening to accent the couple." (See figure 9.156.)

BEFORE

figure 9.155

AFTER

figure 9.156

1. Wayne duplicated the background layer twice and used a high Gaussian Blur on the lower layer.

2. After activating the topmost layer, which is a duplicate of the original file, he selected the couple with a feathered Lasso tool. After reversing the selection, he created a layer mask to allow the blurred background to show through, as shown in **figure 9.157**.

figure 9.157

Using a layer mask on a copy of the original lets the blurred background show through.

3. Then he duplicated the masked layer again and sharpened slightly (see **figure 9.158**). To bring out fine details, Wayne also selectively sharpened the eyes, necklace and flowers.

The visual difference between the very blurred background and the sharpened couple makes the image look as though it was intentionally composed and photographed to have this attractive soft-focus look.

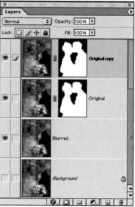

figure 9.158

Sharpening on a duplicate layer gives the option of adjusting it later.

CLOSING THOUGHTS

Retouching a portrait is the most challenging type of retouching you can do. Remember to work with the contrast, color, and detail of the image. Before we move on to Chapter 10, I'd like to give you one last hint. When you are retouching a person's face, keep his or her mother in mind. Try to see the retouching as she would. If the changes were too obvious, she would notice it and, most likely, not like it. If Mom can see the retouching, then she can't see her child; and if her child isn't in the picture, then you've over-worked the portrait.

10

GLAMOUR AND FASHION RETOUCHING

We've all seen pictures of supermodels, actors, and the so-called beautiful people and have been astounded by their blemish-free skin, sparkling eyes, perfectly balanced faces, and cellulite-free thighs. I've always wondered whether those people eat anything, have a bad hair day, or ever get a pimple?

The glamour and fashion business creates an illusion of perfection. It is an ideal that is unachievable without genetic good fortune, a bevy of makeup artists, professional photographers, and highly skilled digital retouchers. The glamour and fashion industry relies on Photoshop to remove the slightest imperfections in makeup, to straighten professionally coifed hair, and to make an already beautiful face perfectly symmetrical.

This chapter shows the techniques used to make the beautiful perfect, and the less-than-perfect beautiful. It is important to me to show you that without extensive help, the ideal is unattainable and shouldn't be chased after by anyone—especially teenage girls and boys. Am I against digital retouching? Of course not, but we do need to learn to recognize, cherish, and appreciate the natural beauty of each individual.

In this chapter, you learn how to

- Develop a retouch strategy
- Perfect skin, eyes, and hair
- Shape bodies
- Add glamour lighting

DEVISING A WORKING STRATEGY

Before you move the mouse to retouch a glamour or fashion photograph, devise a retouching plan with the client to save hours of unnecessary work, haggling, and redos. To be able to talk knowledgeably with the client, research the person or product in the picture before your first meeting. For example, a portrait of a gritty blues musician requires a completely different approach than a picture of the latest teenage pop singer. By knowing about the person or product in the picture, you can emphasize the important, positive aspects while minimizing the less-important or less-flattering aspects. Research helps you communicate with the client and, in the end, deliver the best results.

The Big Picture

The first time you look at a picture, sweep around the image with your eyes. Don't focus on the details, but rather follow the line of the image and notice any distractions. As Helene DeLillo, a photographer, retoucher, and principal of Dancing Icon in New York City, explains, "Listen to your initial feelings and reactions when looking at the image for the first time. What stands out, in both a positive and negative manner?" Some of the issues that Helene keeps in mind when evaluating an image for the first time include these:

- Is the image color balanced?
- Is the lighting working?
- Are the contours of the image smooth?
- Is the environment helping or distracting?
- Is everything correctly in or out of focus?

The closer the retoucher works with the photographer, the more these big-picture issues can be addressed during the initial photo shoot. However, as you can imagine, during a location fashion shoot, some details may slip by the wayside while the photographer rushes to capture the evening light as the sun sinks beneath the horizon.

The Details

Next, look at the details. Zoom in to 100% or 200% view and note all the details that require your attention.

- Does the image need dust removal?
- Is the makeup applied evenly?
- Is the skin texture appealing?
- Do the eyes need cleaning up?
- What blemishes, wrinkles, or shadows need to be removed?
- Are the lips full, round, and attractive?

The longer you retouch and the more images you examine, the faster this process becomes. The goal is for the viewer to be able to get the image's message as quickly as possible. After you remove the distractions, the viewers will get the message as quickly as they can turn the pages of the latest fashion magazines.

Getting It in Writing

After researching and evaluating an image, make sure that you establish what needs to be accomplished. More importantly, make sure that the client agrees with the retouching to be done. Use a combination of Photoshop layers and a work-order form to create a to-do list. **Figure 10.1** shows a file that I'm about to retouch. The blue marks are scribbled onto an empty layer that I named Notes. I can refer to them to keep track with the client's wishes. Additionally, you can use a text layer to make notes on what needs to be done.

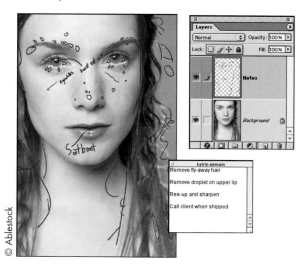

© Ablestock

figure 10.1

Make notes and annotations directly on the file to record what needs to be improved or changed.

In Photoshop 6 and 7, you also can add written or voice annotations to a file with the Notes tool (N). This is incredibly useful when emailing files back and forth; instead of trying to describe something over the phone, a client can just add an annotation right on the file that needs the work.

With each file, you should include a work order or job ticket. This form should list what needs to be done and include the client's initialed approval when the job is complete. As you can see in figure 10.2, the form starts with the usual job tracking information and then addresses the retouching requirements—from global to specific, from color and contrast to blemishes and wrinkles. I've posted a generic order form (orderform.pdf) on the www.digitalretouch.org web site. Use it as a reference when developing your own work-order forms.

🌐⤷✂ **ch10_orderform.pdf**

DIGITAL RESTORATION AND RETOUCH REQUEST

WORK ORDER #: _____

CLIENT INFORMATION

Contact Person: _____
Company: _____
Address: _____
City, ST, Zip: _____
Office Phone: _____
Home Phone: _____
E-mail: _____

DELIVERY INFORMATION

Deliver ____ Hold For Pickup ____ Call When Complete ____
Delivery Address: _____
City, ST, Zip: _____

TURNAROUND INFORMATION

Normal ____ Rush ____ Emergency ____
Date/Time In: _____ Date/Time Out: _____

COPYRIGHT INFORMATION

All that appears on the enclosed medium (including, but not limited to, floppy disk, modem transmission, removable media) is unencumbered by copyrights. We, the customer, have full rights to reproduce and retouch the supplied content.

Signature: _____
Date: _____

ORIGINALS:	TYPE	NUMBER	SIZE

Chrome:

Negative:

Print:

Removeable Media:

Image number:

Image Description:

CLIENT INITIALS	OVERALL RETOUCHING INSTRUCTIONS	CLIENT APPROVAL
_____	Exposure Correction _____	_____
_____	Contrast Correction _____	_____
_____	Color Correction _____	_____
_____	Cleanup _____	_____

RETOUCHING INSTRUCTIONS: FACE AREA

_____	Skin/Blemishes _____	_____
_____	Forehead _____	_____
_____	Eyes _____	_____
_____	Nose _____	_____

figure 10.2

Use a job ticket or order form to ensure that you and the client are in agreement with the work to be done.

THE SUBTLE DIGITAL BEAUTICIAN

The techniques discussed in Chapter 9, "Portrait Retouching," form the foundation for many of the following fashion and glamour retouching techniques. Key techniques for retouching include working on empty layers, using neutral layers to lighten or darken areas, and (of course) never changing the background layer because it is as valuable as your original file. Also make a backup copy of the original scan and store it in a safe place. For additional information on workflow and file organization, please see Chapter 1, "Photoshop Essentials."

In this section, you can work along as I clean up a professional portrait by retouching the hair, removing skin blemishes, refining the eyes, and enriching the lips. **Figure 10.3** shows the original photograph and **figure 10.4** is the retouched portrait.

REMOVING THE DISTRACTIONS

Distractions are all the image elements that take away visual concentration from the subject in the image and include the following: fly-away hair, shiny skin, discolored shadows, blemishes, scars, confusing reflections in the eyes, wrinkles in the clothing, and unappealing body contours often found with thin models whose collar and shoulder bones may protrude at unattractive angles. Distractions also include high-contrast elements, such as single strands of dark hair against light skin, unsightly bulges of clothing, and the folds of skin between a person's arm and torso. To find the distractions, look at the image while squinting—this often shows you which highlights, shadows, and contours are pulling your eye away from the subject.

1. Duplicate the background layer, (Cmd + J) [Ctrl + J] and make it the top layer. Use the Clone Stamp tool and the Healing Brush to remove the fly-away hair on the right side of the image, as shown in **figure 10.5**.

BEFORE

figure 10.3

AFTER

figure 10.4

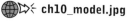 **ch10_model.jpg**

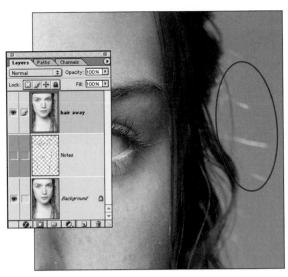

figure 10.7

The exacting nature of glamour retouching means that the tiniest hair out of place must be cleaned up.

 T i p

When retouching hair near the hairline, reduce the opacity of the Clone Stamp tool to 75% to allow some of the skin tone to shimmer through.

figure 10.5

Work on a duplicate layer to clone out or heal distracting elements such as stray hairs.

2. Use the Clone Stamp tool with a soft-edged brush when working on image areas with great tonal differences—for example, where the wider strands of hair fall over her collarbone. Use the Healing Brush to remove the soft-focus strands of hair on the background.

3. Beauty retouching goes down to the individual strands of hair, as **figures 10.6** and **10.7** show. Use the Clone Stamp tool to initially conceal the hair and the Healing Brush to clean up any telltale clone artifacts.

Maintaining Skin Texture

For high-end beauty retouching, both the Clone Stamp tool and the Healing Brush may remove too much characteristic texture from the skin. In fact, beauty retouchers have to work pore by pore—or as I like to say pixel–by-pixel—to create the perfect skin featured in the large format advertisements seen at the cosmetic counters. Chris Tarantino was so kind to create an action that sets up a cleanup layer and a tool preset to maintain the original skin texture.

ch10_cleanups.act

ch10_ cleanup_preset.tpl

1. Either load and run the action or (Option + click) [Alt + click] the New Layer icon on the Layers palette. Change the Mode from Normal to Soft Light and click Fill with Soft-Light-neutral color (50% gray) to create the retouching surface.

2. Either load the tool preset or choose a 5-pixel brush and change its opacity to 15%. Reset the color picker to the default black and white.

figure 10.6

Study the person's hair and look for gaps or distracting hairs that need to be concealed or removed.

3. To conceal dark blemishes (as shown in **figure 10.8**), paint with white to create the results in **figure 10.9**. The advantage to this method is that the original skin texture is not changed one bit.

4. To conceal lighter blemishes, paint with black.

5. To soften visible transitions between the lighter or darker areas, use the Blur tool on the Softlight layer to blur the transitions.

figure 10.8

High-end beauty retouching requires examining the image pore by pore.

figure 10.9

Using a Soft Light layer to conceal individual spots.

As Chris explains, "All retouching can now be done on this one layer that is fully adjustable and undoable. Changing the opacity of the brush will differ for everyone. I find that when using white, I rarely go over 25%. However, when painting with black, I have gone as much as 90%. Sometimes when using black on a very light color, you may see a slight graying affect. If this happens, find and use a dark color that is the same hue as where the fix is being done and use that instead of pure black. You can find these dark colors on the hairline or in the nostril."

Step-by-Step Eye Retouching

When retouching eyes, divide the eye into five areas: eye whites, iris, lashes, brows, and makeup. Lightening the eye whites and darkening the irises draws the viewer to the model's eyes. (For additional eye retouching techniques, please see Chapter 9.)

1. Add a new layer and then select (Option) [Alt] Layer > Merge Visible to create a new working surface of the retouch. Name it *Eyes*. If need be, use the Clone Stamp tool set to 25% Opacity and Lighten to carefully remove bloodshot veins.

2. Select the eye whites with a one-pixel feathered Lasso tool, as shown in **figure 10.10**.

figure 10.10

Holding the Shift key lets you select multiple areas with the Lasso tool.

3. Add a Levels Adjustment Layer and carefully lighten the eye whites, as shown in **figure 10.11**. Don't overdo the lightening because this would make the eyes look unnaturally bright.

4. To increase the intensity of the iris, try this technique, which Greg Gorman uses to make the eyes of the many stars he photographs come to life. Select the iris with a one-pixel feathered Lasso tool, as shown in **figure 10.12**.

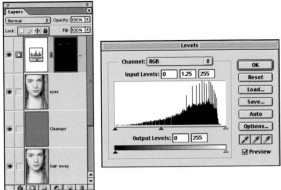

figure 10.11

Giving the eye whites their own adjustment layer allows fine-tuning as the retouch progresses.

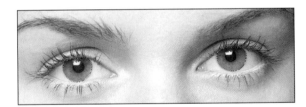

figure 10.12

Trying to select irises with the Elliptical Marquee tool can be maddening. The Lasso tool makes quick work of it.

5. Add a Curves Adjustment Layer and carefully increase the contrast, as shown in **figure 10.13**. This gives the eyes a wonderful depth, saturation, and clarity while maintaining the original characteristics of the eyes. As Greg explains, "I use the Burn tool set to midtones at 10% opacity and draw around the edge of the iris. This rings the iris with darkness, making the eyes richer and intriguing," as shown in **figure 10.14**.

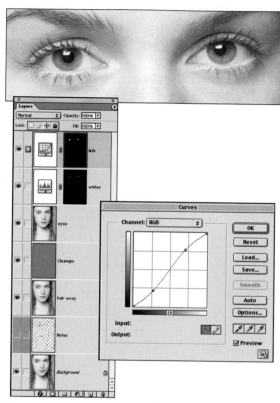

figure 10.13

Using Curves accentuates the irises without changing their character.

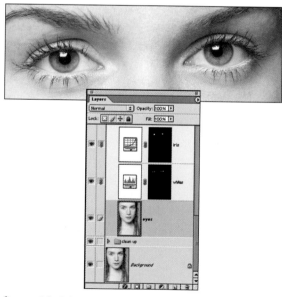

figure 10.14

Darkening the edge of the iris accentuates the eyes beautifully.

6. The model in this image has rather thin eyelashes, which need to be evened out and thickened. Add a new layer and select (Option) [Alt] Layer > Merge Visible to create a new working surface. Select a group of the eyelashes with a one-pixel feathered Lasso tool (see **figure 10.15**) and press (Cmd + J) [Ctrl + J] to copy the selected lashes onto their own layer.

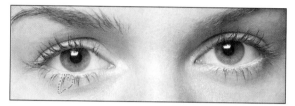

figure 10.15

Don't worry about selecting individual eyelashes. Use the Lasso tool to select groups, skin and all.

7. Nudge the group of lashes into an adjacent position. To eliminate the extraneous skin, change the Blending Mode to Darken. This allows only the eyelashes to be visible and reduces the chance of extraneous skin texture patterns appearing. Use Edit > Free Transform to rotate and scale the eyelashes into a natural position.

8. The copied eyelash will still be on the clipboard, so again press (Cmd + V) [Ctrl + V] to paste the lashes to a new layer. Use Edit > Free Transform to rotate the eyelashes to match the direction of hair flow, as shown in **figure 10.16**.

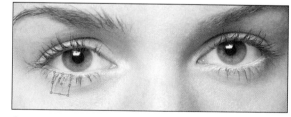

figure 10.16

Thicken the eyelashes by duplicating them and transforming them into place.

9. In this example, I used 14 eyelash layers (see **figure 10.17**) to build them up. Rather than keeping them visible, I placed them into a layer set by linking them all and then selecting New Set From Linked from the Layers palette menu.

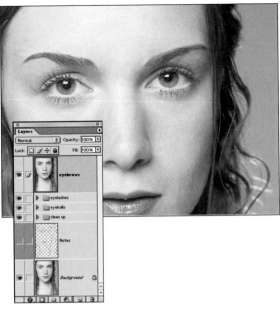

figure 10.18

Fill in the eyebrows using the eyelash technique.

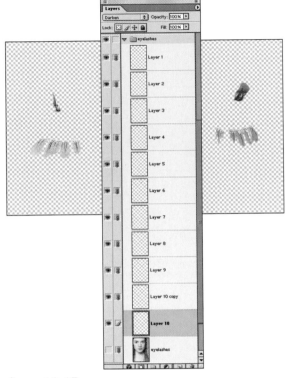

figure 10.17

Using multiple layers to build up and position the eyelashes.

10. To create a surface for the next step, which is to clean up the eyebrows, add a new layer and (Option) [Alt] Layer > Merge Visible. Use a soft-edged Clone Stamp tool set to Lighten to style her eyebrows. Clone over the errant hairs and concentrate on creating soft transitions between the hair and the skin to avoid the harsh chopped-off look.

11. Fill in any missing gaps in a person's eyebrow with the same technique used to fill in eyelashes. **Figure 10.18** shows the cleaned-up eyebrows.

The Lips

A model's lips should be full, symmetrical, and rich in color. In this example, her lips are symmetrical but could use a bit more saturation. Do any required retouching before increasing saturation or changing color. In this example, the droplet needs to be removed. Most people would grab the Clone Stamp tool and try to clone over the droplet, but I've learned that often the Clone Stamp tool can add more problems by changing image texture and adding unwanted softness than it fixes.

1. To remove such critical distractions, zoom in to a 1600% view and work pixel by pixel, as shown in **figure 10.19**. Select a one-pixel Pencil tool (nested under the Brush tool), and (Option + click) [Alt + click] to change the Pencil to the Eyedropper tool to select a darker color. Then release the modifier key to dab in a new darker color one pixel at a time. Keep (Option) [Alt] sampling and dabbing on a variety of colors to carefully hide the water droplet.

2. Carefully sample adjacent pixels and one by one paint away the water droplet, as seen in figure 10.20.

3. To saturate lip color, select the lips with a one-pixel feather lasso and add a Hue/Saturation layer. Increase the saturation by 10 to 20 points. After making the adjustment, you can return to the layer mask to finesse the contours and edges of the color with black or white brushes or the Blur tool.

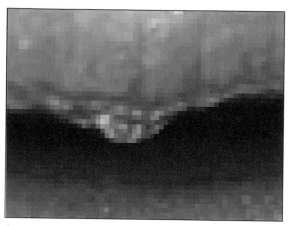
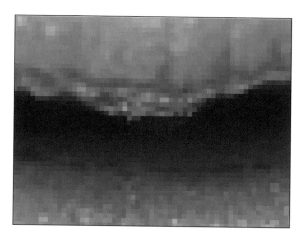

figure 10.19

Use the Pencil tool to work pixel by pixel.

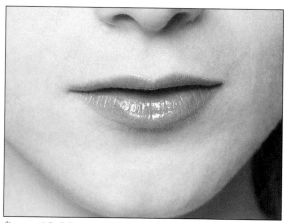
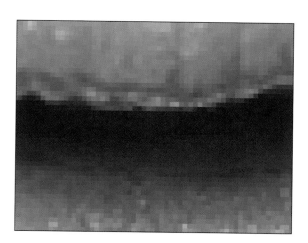

figure 10.20

Changing just a few pixels can make a dramatic difference.

Reviewing and Refining

To check your work, make the Notes layer visible and drag it to the top of the layer stack, as shown in figure 10.21. This enables you to see whether you missed anything. In this example, I can see that I still need to reduce the shadow under the model's neck.

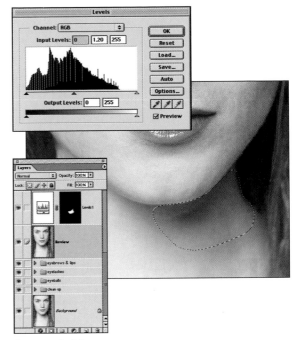

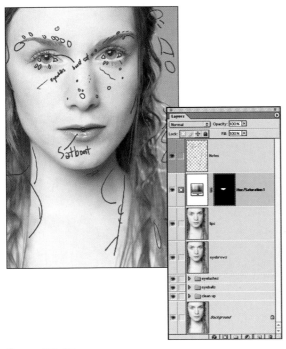

figure 10.21

Drag the strategy layer to the top of the layer stack, and then review your progress by toggling it off and on.

1. You can reduce unwanted shadows like the one under the model's neck by using a variety of methods. Lasso the shadow area and feather the selection 15–25 pixels.

2. Add a Levels Adjustment Layer and move the midtone slider slightly to the left, as shown in figure 10.22.

3. Repeat steps 1 and 2 with a smaller selection to lighten up the center of the shadow again. I used three selections, decreasing in size, and Levels Adjustment Layers to lighten the shadow. To avoid discoloration, change the Blending Mode of each Levels Adjustment Layer to Luminosity, as shown in figure 10.23.

figure 10.22

Adjusting the Levels selectively reduces an unwanted shadow under the chin.

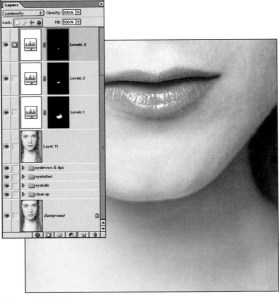

figure 10.23

Gentle gradations, such as shadows, can be subtly adjusted by using multiple selections of decreasing size.

Studying and Reviewing

Before submitting the file or showing the client, I make a high-quality print of the retouched file. I often catch details that need touching up on the print that I didn't notice on the monitor. It also helps to set it aside for a while and come back to it with fresh eyes. When you first come back to it, make a mental note of the first thing that catches your eye. Mark areas needing more work with a photo pen or Sharpie. As Greg Gorman told me, "The most important part of digital retouching is knowing when to stop."

If, for some reason, I can't make a print, I prefer to close the file and reopen it a few hours later to see whether there are any glaring details I overlooked. If you don't have the luxury of a few hours, ask someone you trust to take a look at the final version to see whether they notice anything that needs adjustment.

Flatten the file before submitting it to the client and include a copy of the work order. If the client isn't happy or asks for additional work, refer to the original notes and work order to see whether the newly requested change was on the original work order. If the additional requests were not on the original work order, do the additional work for an additional fee. For example, the client might look at the retouch and say, "Oh, you forgot to change her eyes from blue to green." Referring to the work order enables you to determine whether you forgot to do something or the client is adding extra work.

 Tip

Study the latest fashion and glamour magazines to learn the latest makeup and fashion trends. Issues to look for are the color and amount of makeup used for eyes and lips, shape of eyebrows, and hairstyles.

COMPLEXION, HAIR, AND EYE REFINEMENT

Now that you've seen the strategy and details that go into a complete glamour retouch, here are additional techniques to make the beautiful even more beautiful or as Greg Gorman sees it, "Capitalize on the positive."

Golden Tan

Many fashion models seem to have a perfect golden tan and glowing complexion. Try this technique to give a model creamy golden skin—compare **figures 10.24** and **10.25**.

figure 10.24

figure 10.25

1. Add a Hue/Saturation Adjustment Layer and select Yellows from the Edit drop-down menu. Hold Shift and drag over the model's skin to widen the range of selected Yellows. Add 20 points of saturation to the yellow, as shown in **figure 10.26**. Select Reds from the Edit drop-down menu and add 5 points of saturation to the Reds. Toggle the Adjustment Layer off and on to see whether any non-skin areas need to be masked out.

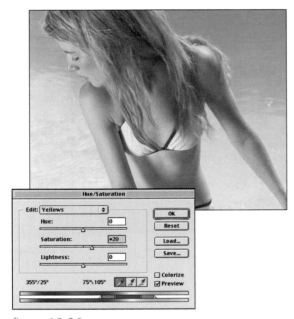

figure 10.26

Increase the yellow and red saturation to add a golden tan.

2. To give the model the glowing complexion, duplicate the background layer twice and change the Blending Mode of one layer to Lighten and one to Darken.

3. Select Filter > Blur > Gaussian Blur and use a high setting on each layer. In this example, I used a 20-pixel radius (see **figure 10.27**) on each layer and adjusted the lighten layer to 35% opacity and the darken layer to 20% opacity. Using separate lighten and darken layers mimics traditional soft-focus filters.

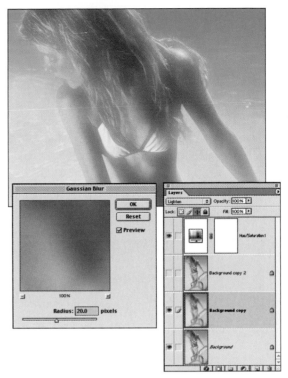

figure 10.27

After blurring the layers, adjust the opacity to soften the skin as desired.

4. In this example, I opted not to soften the water. After adding a new layer and choosing (Option) [Alt] Layer > Merge Visible, I selected the water and the edge of the pool and added a layer mask to control the softening effect (see **figure 10.28**).

figure 10.28

On the merged layer, mask out the areas that need to remain sharp.

5. To add visual tooth back to the image, (Option + click) [Alt + click] the New Layer icon in the Layers palette, choose Soft Light, and check Fill with Softlight neutral 50% gray.

6. Choose Filter > Noise > Add Noise, check Monochrome, and add noise to the Softlight layer. This adds grain texture, which you can adjust as needed by varying the opacity of the layer. As Wayne Palmer mentioned to me, "Sometimes I run a slight blur on the noise layer to reduce the sharp edge of the grain."

Beauty Is in the Details

The folds of skin where the arms meet the torso are areas that all beauty retouchers are requested to remove, as seen in the before and after figures in 10.29 and 10.30. Use the Patch tool and Healing brush to carefully reduce or remove the folds of skin.

figure 10.29

figure 10.30

Perfect Makeup

Lee Varis photographed the young woman shown in figure 10.31 and as Lee explains, "She is already very pretty but, on close examination, her skin is less than perfect. My main effort will be to smooth the skin and give it the perfect glow (see figure 10.32) found on the covers of fashion magazines."

© Lee Varis

figure 10.31

figure 10.32

N o t e

The values Lee used are appropriate for this specific file; you may need to adjust the filter settings to achieve optimal results on your own images.

ch10_varis_model.jpg

1. Duplicate the background layer and select Filter > Noise > Median. Median is a unique blurring filter that smoothes textures while maintaining image sharpness and edge transitions. Use a setting of 9, as shown in figure 10.33.

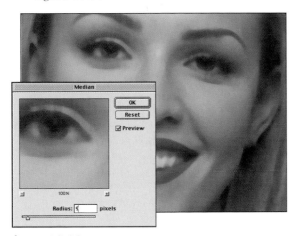

figure 10.33

The Median filter smoothes texture while defining edges, much like real makeup.

2. To offset the faceted look that the Median filter adds, select Filter > Blur > Gaussian Blur and enter a radius of 2 to smooth out the file even more.

3. Select Layer > Add Layer Mask > Hide All to add a black layer mask to the blurred layer. Use a soft white brush to paint back the soft skin, as shown in figure 10.34. Avoid areas with sharp details, such as her eyes and lips. Figure 10.35 shows the painted mask. Wherever it is white, the softened skin is revealed, and wherever it is black, the blurred information is concealed.

The skin looks too smooth, too plastic; we need to add texture back into it.

figure 10.34

Hide All is the same as filling the mask with black, and it saves time when most of the image will be masked.

figure 10.35

(Option + clicking) [Alt + clicking] the layer mask displays it in the editing window.

4. (Option + click) [Alt + click] the New Layer icon in the Layers palette; check Group with Previous, select Overlay, and check Fill with Overlay neutral 50% gray.

5. Choose Filter > Noise > Add Noise and use 4%, Gaussian distribution, and Monochrome.

6. Filter > Blur > Gaussian Blur with a radius of 1.3.

7. Now comes the Lee Varis magic: Apply Filter > Stylize > Emboss and use a Height of 1 and a high amount—between 300 to 500%. This will simulate skin texture as shown in figure 10.36.

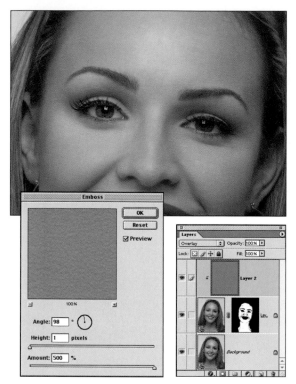

figure 10.36

Using Emboss on a noise layer simulates skin texture. Grouping and using Overlay mode alters the actual skin, rather than painting a texture on top.

figure 10.37

Glamour retouching aims to idealize the model, but making her too perfect can remove the human quality.

8. Now her skin is too uniformly textured. A person has less texture (fewer pores) on slightly stretched areas such as the cheeks and forehead.

9. Add a layer mask to the textured layer and paint on the mask with a 25% opacity black brush to gradually smooth the stretched skin on the nose, cheeks, forehead, and chin (see figure 10.37). Be careful not to remove all the texture.

10. To balance the textured with the less textured areas, select Filter > Noise > Add Noise and use 3% or less with Monochrome checked on the texture layer.

Lee then dodged her eyes and added a subtle burn to the edge of the image (as described in the "Glamour Lighting" section later in this chapter).

Hair Touch-Up

You may be asked to adjust hair color or color roots to match the rest of the hair, as shown in figures 10.38 and 10.39. Shan Canfield developed the following technique that is both easy and effective.

ch10_darkroots.jpg

1. Add a new layer and change its Blending Mode to Soft Light.

2. Select a soft-edged brush and (Option + click) [Alt + click] the hair to sample a lighter shade of blonde.

3. Paint over the dark roots. Adjust the layer opacity to blend in the new hair color. In this example, I used 70%, as shown in figure 10.40. For the best results, sample a new shade of hair color after a few strokes and follow the natural flow of the hair.

© Ablestock

BEFORE

figure 10.38

AFTER

figure 10.39

figure 10.40

Soft Light mode lightens the roots while also adding the desired hair color.

4. To lighten the roots even more, select the darker areas with a 10-pixel lasso and add a Curves Adjustment Layer. Raise the midtones to lighten the selected area, as shown in figure 10.41.

figure 10.41

Fine-tune only the darker areas using Curves.

5. If you need to remove fly-away hair, add a new layer and select (Option) [Alt] Layer > Merge Visible. Use the Clone Stamp and Healing Brush tools to clean up distracting hair, as shown in **figure 10.42**.

figure 10.42

After adding a merged layer, remove the fly-away hair.

As shown in Chapter 9, you also can use Color Dodge and Color Burn layers to add shape and definition to hair highlights and contours. I highly recommend that technique for glamour retouching.

Hollywood Eyes

Since the time of the ancient Egyptians and widely practiced in the Renaissance, artists made eyes larger to be more attractive, sensuous, and interesting. You can achieve a similar effect called "Hollywood Eyes" with Photoshop (see **figures 10.43** and **10.44**).

ch10_blueeyes.jpg

1. Select the eyes with a 15–20 pixel feathered Lasso tool, as shown in **figure 10.45**.

figure 10.43

figure 10.44

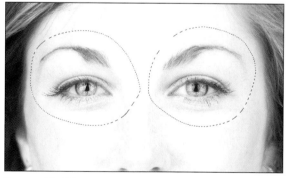

figure 10.45

Roughly select the overall eye areas with a very soft lasso.

2. (Cmd + J) [Ctrl + J] the selected eyes onto their own layer. Choose Edit > Free Transform and increase the size of the eyes by 103–108%. Often, I use a slightly larger height transformation to open the eyes while enlarging them. In this example, I transformed the width by 104% and the height by 105%, as shown in **figure 10.46**.

© Ablestock

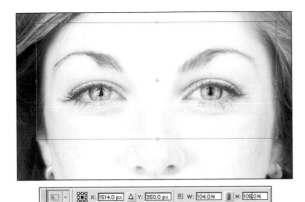

figure 10.46

Enlarge the eyes to make them more interesting and attractive.

3. To avoid changes in skin texture caused by the enlarged eyes, add a layer mask, and, with a soft-edged black brush, paint on the layer mask to cover any extra skin and to blend the two layers together.

4. Change the eyes layer's Blending Mode to Difference, add a layer mask, and, with a soft-edged black brush, paint on the layer mask to cover any extra skin and to blend the two sizes of eyes together (see figure 10.47).

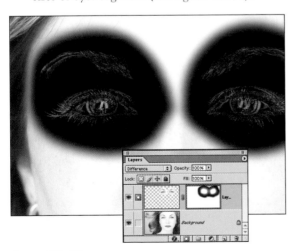

figure 10.47

Temporarily changing the layer's Blending Mode to Difference reveals the extraneous skin that can be masked out to avoid changing the texture of the skin.

5. Make sure to change the Blending Mode back to Normal to create the final image shown in figure 10.44.

T i p

If one of your model's eyes is smaller than the other, make sure that the smaller eye is closer to the camera lens when taking the photograph. Having the larger eye farther away from the camera will make it appear smaller and balance your face.

THE DIGITAL DIET

In the commercial world of cosmetic, swimwear, and beauty advertising, many models need a nip or a tuck here or there to insinuate that the product shown will make the buyer just as perfect as the imaged model. Thighs, bellies, folds of fat under bra straps, and breasts are reshaped to perfection on the computer on a daily basis. For example, every bathing suit or lingerie model needs to be a C cup—something not all of them are. Photoshop is used to add additional fullness with cloning and shadow play to create what isn't there naturally. You can use the slimming techniques shown in Chapter 9, as well as the ones described here.

Photographic Slimming Techniques

When you're taking the picture, use the following photographic techniques to flatter people and make them look slimmer:

- Use a moderate telephoto lens (85–105mm on a 35mm camera) to flatten features and avoid the unflattering distortion that a wide-angle or normal lens can create.

- Position the camera lens at the level of the model's chest or waist. Shooting up elongates and flatters the body.

- Position the person in a three-quarter view to minimize their width.

- Pay attention to the lighting. Use a short or narrow lighting technique to slim down a heftier person with light and shadow.

Tip

The human mind responds to many visual cues we're not consciously aware of. Tests have proven that we see larger eyes and lips as more attractive, but nothing triggers the attraction response more than symmetry. Keep this in mind when planning your glamour retouching.

Digital Tummy Tuck

There are a myriad of Photoshop techniques to slim a person—from cloning, to stretching, to distorting, to painting with light to accentuate the positive and minimize the less attractive lumps and bumps. I learned this technique from Jeff Schewe (www.schewephotography.com) and simply love how easy it is and how well it works. Figure 10.48 shows the before tummy tucked angel and figure 10.49 is a slightly lighter angel.

ch10_angel.jpg

1. Generously select the area to be tucked and feather the selection with a setting of 50–75 pixels, as shown in figure 10.50.

2. Choose Filter > Distort > Pinch and use the preview to judge how much to pinch the waist, as shown in figure 10.51. I usually use between 10%–20%—any higher and the person will look as thought she is wearing a whalebone corset.

Slimming thighs, reducing waistlines, narrowing arms, and removing love handles can be achieved by going to the gym and eating fewer sweets or by using Photoshop to hide the extra pounds. I'm not promoting poor eating habits or avoiding exercise, but sometimes those last pounds just refuse to melt away. In those cases, a bit of Photoshop reshaping with the Pinch and Liquify filters can work wonders (see Chapter 9 for more information).

BEFORE

figure 10.48

AFTER

figure 10.49

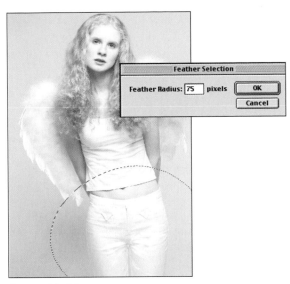

figure 10.50

The secret to making this technique work realistically is an incredibly high feather setting.

figure 10.51

The Pinch filter does not provide a live preview in the main work window, so examine the preview window carefully for unwanted distortions.

Contouring the Body with Light

You can use shading both to draw attention away from the less flattering aspects of a person and to sculpt a person's legs and arms to look more three-dimensional. By darkening these contours, you are making them visually less interesting in addition to making legs look more toned, as shown in **figures 10.52** and **10.53**.

figure 10.52

figure 10.53

1. I made a full body path, as shown in figure 10.54.

2. I made sure that the path was not active and added a Curves Adjustment Layer, pulling the curve down to darken the entire image, as shown in figure 10.55.

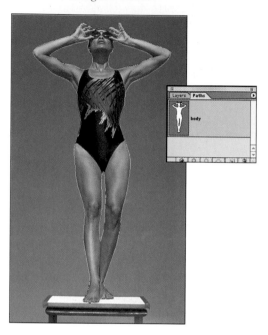

figure 10.54

The full body path.

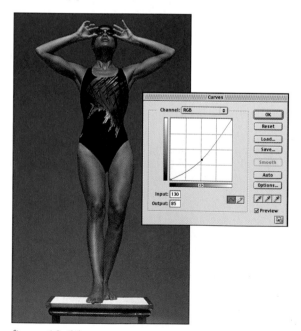

figure 10.55

Darkening the entire image.

3. I clicked the Curves Mask and pressed (Cmd + I) [Ctrl + I] to invert the mask. This turns off the entire darkening.

4. I repeated step 2, but this time I pulled the Curve up to lighten the entire image (see figure 10.56) and then inverted the Curves layer mask.

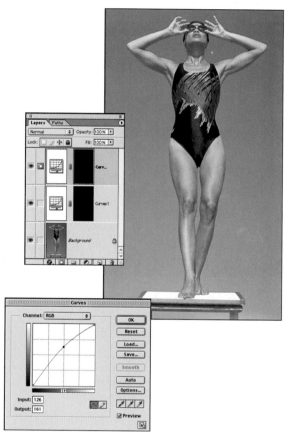

figure 10.56

Repeating the procedure, but this time lightening the entire image.

5. I turned the path into a selection by holding down (Cmd) [Ctrl] and clicking the workpath in the Paths palette. Returning to the Layers palette, I clicked the lower curves layer, which had a darkening Adjustment Layer curve in step 2.

6. With a very large soft-edged white brush, I painted along the edges of the subject's thighs and arms, as shown in figure 10.57. This contours her body shape with slightly darker tones along the edges. For illustration purposes, figure 10.58 shows the Curves Adjustment Layer layer mask by itself. Choose a very large brush and use only the outer edges of the brush to barely touch the edges of the figure, gently caressing the contours with tone.

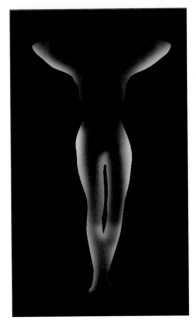

figure 10.58

Use the outer edges of a very large brush to add gentle gradations of tone.

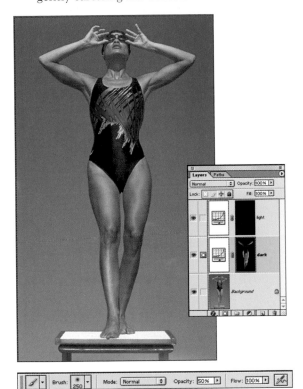

figure 10.57

Painting with white on the black layer mask enables you to selectively paint the darker tone onto the model's outer contours.

7. I used a smaller brush on the light Curves layer to draw down the center of her legs, contrasting dark with light, as shown in figure 10.59.

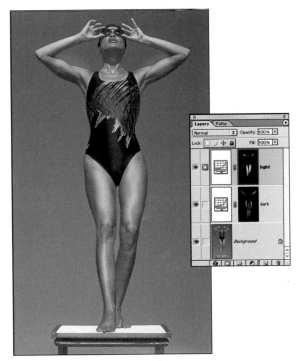

figure 10.59

Painting with white on the layer mask enhances the contours of the model's legs.

GLAMOUR LIGHTING

Of course, photographers pay a lot of attention to lighting while taking pictures, but you can use Photoshop to fine-tune lighting to add a drama that draws the viewer's eyes deeper into the photograph.

Edge Burn

Figures 10.60 and 10.61 show the same retouched portrait of the young woman. Can you see how the image with the darker frame effectively focuses your attention on her face?

1. Add a new layer and make sure that you are working in full-screen mode, as shown in figure 10.62.

2. Press D to reset the color picker to the default settings of black and white. Select the Gradient tool, choose the Black to Transparent gradient, and reduce the opacity to 30%, as shown in figure 10.63.

3. Zoom out so that you can start the gradient well outside of the image. Draw a number of gradients from the outside in toward the image edge. It is better to build up the darkening effect with numerous gradients instead of trying to get it right with one perfect gradient pull.

4. Adjust the final strength of the edge burn by adjusting the layer opacity, as shown in figure 10.63.

figure 10.60

figure 10.61

figure 10.62

Using full-screen mode to work outside the image area.

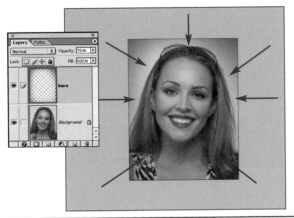

figure 10.63

Start the gradients outside the image area and fine-tune the final appearance by adjusting the layer opacity.

Dramatic Lighting

To add hints of drama or mystery to a portrait, intensify the lighting, as described in the following two techniques. In this first technique, Eddie Tapp uses a darkening Curve with a highly feathered selection to add drama to the portrait, as seen in figures 10.64 and 10.65.

🌐▷< **ch10_tapplight.jpg**

1. Add a Curves Adjustment Layer and drag the highlight point more than halfway straight down the right side of the curve, as you see in figure 10.66.

figure 10.64

figure 10.65

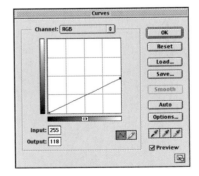

figure 10.66

Eddie begins with a radical Curves adjustment to darken the entire image.

2. Make a rough selection with the Lasso tool (see figure 10.67) and then Select > Feather and use a very high radius, such as 125 pixels.

3. Click the Curves Adjustment Layer layer mask and choose Edit > Fill > Use Black and, voilá—you have dramatic lighting that you can adjust with the layer opacity or Blending Modes (see figure 10.68).

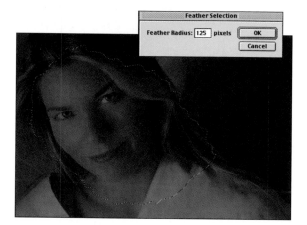

figure 10.67

Notice that Eddie's selection has a wavy pattern.

figure 10.68

Eddie's technique is simple yet effective and offers a great deal of flexibility.

In the second technique, Greg Gorman deepened the shadows of the natural light portrait to emphasize the luminous skin and green eyes of the model, as shown in figures 10.69 and 10.70.

© Greg Gorman

BEFORE

figure 10.69

AFTER

figure 10.70

⊕▷⊱ch10_burn.atn

⊕▷⊱ch10_dodge.atn

1. Greg started by adding a Curves Adjustment Layer, changing the Blending Mode to Multiply, and adjusting the layer opacity to 60%, as shown in **figure 10.71**. When using Multiply, 40% opacity is approximately one *f*-stop in camera exposure, meaning that in this example, Greg is darkening down the portrait by approximately one and a half stops.

> **N o t e**
>
> Download the two actions ch10_burn.atn and ch10_dodge.atn to automatically add lightening and darkening exposure layers.

figure 10.71

Notice Greg does not actually change the curve.

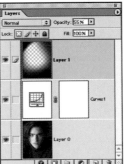

figure 10.72

Greg uses Normal Blending Mode for the gradient layer, but he turns down the opacity.

2. He then added a new layer and used a Black to Transparent gradient to further burn down the corners, as shown in **figure 10.72**.

Because Greg is working with layers, he can adjust the intensity of the lighting to suit the subject without ruining the image.

CLOSING THOUGHTS

I hope that the techniques you've seen here help you in a Photoshop sense, but also in a dose-of-reality sense. To maintain a healthy body and self-image, it is important to separate the reality from the illusion. More often than not, the perfect bodies and faces in the fashion magazines, cosmetic advertising, and swimwear calendars just don't exist—except as a collection of finely tuned pixels on a professional retoucher's hard drive.

APPENDIX

CONTRIBUTORS

This book would never have come to fruition without the generous sharing of Photoshop knowledge and techniques by these very talented professionals. I thank them all for their time and help.

MARK BECKELMAN

Beckelman Photo Illustration
Digital imaging, conceptual and editorial illustration
Springfield, NJ
973-467-3456
www.beckelman.com • mark@beckelman.com

JOEL BECKER

Joel Becker Digital Photography
High-resolution digital capture for advertising
and marketing
Virginia Beach, VA
757-270-1235
www.joelbecker.com • pix@joelbecker.com

CARRIE BEENE

Digital retouching, color correction, and colorization
Kansas City, MO
816-221-3862
cbeene@kc.rr.com

RICK BILLINGS

Photowave
Digital portraiture, digital sports, and digital training
Orlando, FL
407-905-5782
Rick.Billings@aspn.com
www.PhotoWave.com • www.ASPN.com

CHARLES BRYANT

Sports photography
Hampton, VA
csbryant@infionline.net

DAVID R. BRYANT

IPAT, Inc.
Restoration and retouching, nature photography
South Charleston, WV
304-768-2336
drbryant@charter.net

MAGGIEBEE BURNETT

Touching Memories
Photo restoration and retouching, color to black
and white conversions, and hand coloring
Auckland, New Zealand
(+) 64 9 444 3677
www.touchingmemories.co.nz
maggiebee@touchingmemories.co.nz

SHAN CANFIELD

MOI Design Studio
Digital photography, glamour retouching, digital
restoration, digital collage, and compositing
Nashville, TN
615-228-5935
www.shanzcan.com • mama@shanzcan.com

DAN CAYLOR

Image restoration and manipulation
Harwich, Essex, United Kingdom
(+) 01255243182
www.thinkdan.com • dc@thinkdan.com

RICK CHASTAIN

Chastain Photography
Wedding and portrait photography, restoration
828-648-6761
chastain@brinet.com
chastr@BlueRidgePaper.com

KEN CROST

Before and After
Digital photo restoration and digital imaging
Littleton, CO
720-260-5582
www.beforeafter.biz
kcrost@beforeafter.biz

COLIN M. DEARING

CD Imaging
Photo restoration and manipulation,
military montages
Cheltenham, United Kingdom
www.cdimaging.net
colin.dearing@ntlworld.com

HELENE DELILLO

Digital retouching, digital capture, and
workflow consulting
Toll Free: 800-626-0817, 212-334-6705
New York, NY
www.dancingicon.com • info@dancingicon.com

FRANK EIRUND

Digital photography
(+) 49-89-6807 12 81
Munich, Germany
www.dat-ei.de • frank.eirund@dat-ei.de

FABRIZIO FIORBIANCO

studiociotola s.a.s.
Digital imaging and video presentations
Naples, Italy
(+) 39-0815467746
www.studiociotola.it • info@studiociotola.it

FORREST FRIELDS

Photography by Forrest
Portrait photography
Thousand Oaks, CA
805-496-2255
forrestphoto1414@yahoo.com

GREG GORMAN

Celebrity portraiture, digital capture and print
Los Angeles, CA
www.greggormanphotography.com

H AND H COLOR LAB

Full-service professional photo lab specializing in
optical and digital services, digital and traditional
retouching/enhancement, and finishing services
Toll Free: 800-821-1305, 816-358-6677
Kansas City, MO
www.hhcolorlab.com
customerservice@hhcolorlab.com

RONALD B. HIRSCH

Passionate photographer and Photoshop user
Boca Raton, FL
561-241-4424
ronhirsch@adelphia.net

ART JOHNSON

Memories in Minutes, Inc.
Portrait and aerial photography, retouching
and restoration
Albany, GA
www.artphotog.com • artphotg@bellsouth.net

ELLIE KENNARD

Fine art reproduction, digital photographic studio,
web site design, restoration and retouching
Canning, Nova Scotia, Canada
902-582-3795
www.iiStudio.com • Ellie@iiStudio.com

ERIC KUAIMOKU

Digital photography and retouching
ericmailbox2000@yahoo.com

PJ LEFFINGWELL

Photos by PJ
Digital imaging and wedding photography
Melbourne, FL
321-255-5095
www.PhotosByPJ.com • ninjapj@earthlink.com

ELLIOT LINCIS

Editorial and commercial photography
Scottsdale, AZ
602-290-0884
www.elliotlincus.com

MATT MATHERNE

Black and white photo restoration
Biddeford, ME
207-282-1731
lmathern@maine.rr.com

JOHN MCINTOSH

Chair, Computer Art
School of VISUAL ARTS
New York, NY
212-592-2526
jmcintosh@sva.edu

SEAN E. MELNICK

S.E. Melnick Digital Imaging
Digital imaging, color correction, restoration
and retouching
Rockville Centre, NY 11570
www.semdi.com • sean@semdi.com

MICHAEL NINNESS

Training, design, and retouching
Seattle, WA
myke@microsoft.com

RICHARD L. OASEN

Naval Media Center
Portrait photography
www.fotoace.com • fotoace@adelphia.net

PATRICK O'CONNELL

poconnell@snowcrest.net

WAYNE R. PALMER

Palmer Multimedia Imaging
Restoration, photography, video and
multimedia projects
Williamsport, PA
Toll Free: 877-321-9660
www.palmermultimedia.com
pmi@palmermultimedia.com

HERB PAYNTER

IXSoftware
Digital photo reconstruction and reproduction
Blue Ridge, GA
706-492-4542
ixsoftware.com • hpaynter@mac.com

PHIL POOL

Digital portraiture and enhancement
San Pedro, CA
310-748-9918
pep9454@yahoo.com

DARYL-ANN SAUNDERS

Commercial and fine-art photography:
Interiors, events, corporate and private portraiture,
nudes, landscapes, and conceptual ideas utilizing
alternative processes, silver gelatin and color
www.dasaunders.com • dastudio@pobox.com
www.ExecutivePortraits.com

SAL SESSA

Wedding and event photography
Dallas, TX
214-683-6363
www.salsessa.com • sal@salsessa.com

EDDIE TAPP

Photographer, consultant, educator in digital
photography and media
Atlanta, GA
770-414-1452
www.eddietapp.com • etapp@aol.com

CHRISTOPHER TARANTINO

High-end glamour and fashion retouching and
color correction, Photoshop consultant
New York, NY and Milford, CT
203-877-1507
christoperedmund@mac.com

LAURIE THOMPSON

Digital photo restoration, retouching, composites
New Orleans, LA
504-524-4257
www.imaginationstudio.com
Laurie@imaginationstudio.com

LEIGH-ANNE TOMPKINS

Graphics Afoot Studio Design
Design, multimedia, restoration and retouching
Jacksonville, FL
904-641-0192
www.graphicsafoot.com • madtoe@attbi.com

DIANE TREMBLAY

Multimedia-Designs
Web and CD-ROM design and development,
video editing, photo restoration and retouching
Corel Springs, FL
www.multimedia-designs.com
dtremblay@multimedia-designs.com

LEE VARIS

Digital image capture, enhancement,
and compositing
Los Angeles, CA
Toll Free: 888-964-0024
www.varis.com • varis@varis.com

THOMAS VON LIPTAK

Turnpike Production
Photography, digital retouching, color correction,
and motion graphics
Copenhagen, Denmark
(+) 45 - 20 66 81 07
(+) 45 - 88 330 339
www.turnpike.dk • tvl@turnpike.dk

ROBERT WALDEN

targa912@aol.com

JOHN WARNER

Warner Photography, Inc.
Advertising, architecture, annual reports, digital
and new media
Asheville, NC
828-254-0346
www.warnerphotography.com
john@warnerphotography.com

LLOYD WELLER

Instructor of photography/digital photography
and musician
Everett Community College
Everett, WA
lweller@evcc.ctc.edu
elleray@mindspring.com

LORIE ZIRBES

Retouching by Lorie
Retouching, restoration, color tinting, and
photo composition
San Francisco, CA and Las Vegas, NV
415-753-6674
www.RetouchingByLorie.com
ArtistLZ@aol.com

Symbols

0%-100% scale, 46
0-255 scale, 46
100% view, 17
16-bit-per-channel images. *See*
  high-bit data

A

accentuating eyes, 301-302
    cleaning up, 304-306
    creating contrast with Dodge and
        Burn tools, 302-304
    painterly approach, 306-309
accessing channels with keyboard
    shortcuts, 159
activating tools in Photoshop
    toolbar, 11
Adams, Ansel, 34
adding. *See also* increasing
    color to black and white
        images, 236-238
    contrast with Hard Light, 52
    creative edges, 258-259
    fill-flash, 75-79
    frames, 258
additive colors, 92-93
adjusting
    posture, 282-284
    screens, 18
    shadows, 335
Adjustment Layers, 19
    Channel Mixer, 54, 238
    combining tonal corrections,
        56-58
    Curves. *See* Curves
        Adjustment Layers
    importance of, 37-38
    isolating, 70
    layer masks, 70
        multiple masked adjustments, 61
    Levels, *See* Levels
        Adjustment Layers
    loading, 54-55
    moving, 54
    painting, 72-73
    saving, 54-56

aged photos, removing stains, 175-177

aging, wrinkles. *See* skin, wrinkles

aging process, reversing, 294-296

alpha channels, applying filters to, 191

Annotation tool, 11

Apply Image, 131
rebuilding color channels, 218-222

applying filters to alpha channels, 191

archive systems, 26

assessing. *See* evaluating

assigning false color profiles, 120

Auto Color Correction, 99-100
cropping images, 102-103
details, 100-101

Auto Color Correction Options Interface, 100

avoiding
banding, 257
demarcation lines, 203
moiré patterns when shooting digital pictures, 161
posterization, 70

B

back-up systems, 26

background layers, 18

backgrounds
creating digital background collections, 196-197
re-creating, 184, 188-189
concentrating on the essentials, 184
drop shadows, 192-193
lifting subjects off photographs, 190-192
Quick Mask technique, 184-188
replacing, 192

balancing
exposure and fading, 86-88
highlights, 112
midtones, 112
neutral tones with Levels, 112-114
shadows, 112
stains, 178-180

banding, avoiding, 257

Beard, Bruce (skin and hair color reference charts), 115

Beckelman, Mark, 254

Beene, Carrie, 209, 278, 309

Billings, Rick, 274

black-and-white images
adding color, 236, 238
converting from color images, 224
Blending Modes, 232-234
Channel Mixer, 226-229
color channels, 225
Grayscale mode, 224-225
luminance channels, 226
mimicking photographic film and filters, 230-231
using Calculation functions, 235-236
hand-coloring, 245-249
traditional versus digital, 250-251

black point sliders, improving tones, 39-40

black points, 38
finding, 41-43

blemishes
correcting with History Brush and Blending Modes, 290-292
healing good over bad, 288-289
patching good over bad, 289-290

Blending Modes, 49
adding contrast with Hard Light, 52
Color, 243
contrast, 70
converting color images to black and white, 232-234
fixing blemishes, 290-292
images, 50
Linear Dodge, 70
Luminosity, using with Curves Adjustment Layers, 111
Multiply, 50-51
overexposed images, 80-81
Overlay, 243
Pin Light, 243
Screen, 53-54
lightening dark images, 68-70

Blur filters, 252

blurring in Lab Color mode, 160-161

bodies, contouring with light, 345-347

body parts
chins, reducing double chins, 298-300
eyes. *See* eyes
lips, 288, 333-334
skin. *See* skin
working with substitutes, 198-199

borders. *See* edges

borrowing image information, 200

braces, removing from teeth, 317-318

Brown, Russell, 230

Brush, 11

brushes
context-sensitive menus, 16
hardness, changing, 13
sizes, 13
for removing dust, 140

Bryant, David (fill-flash), 78

Burn tool
exposure, 303
eyes, accentuating contrast, 302-304

Burnett, Maggie, 201

C

cables, removing, 168-169

Calculation functions, converting color images to black and white, 235-236

cameras, digital cameras. *See* digital cameras

Canfield, Shan, 205, 340

capturing high-bit data, 64-66

CD-ROM, 26

chairs, 24

changing brush attributes, 13

Channel Mixer Adjustment Layer, 54, 178, 238
converting color images to black and white, 226-229

channels, 53
accessing with keyboard shortcuts, 159
alpha channels, applying filters to, 191
Channel Mixer, converting color images to black and white, 226-229
color channels, 211
converting color images to black and white, 225
rebuilding with Apply Image, 218-222
replacing damaged channels, 215-217
luminance channels, converting color images to black and white, 226
replacing, 220
thumbnails, increasing size of, 212

Channels palette, 53
charts, skin and hair color reference charts, 115
chins, reducing double chins, 298-300
cleaning up eyes, 304-306
clients, working with, 274
Clone Stamp tool, 11, 169
    removing
        mold, mildew, and fungus, 141
        scratches, 166-168
    repairing images, 142-143
clothing, smoothing folds in, 279-280
clutter, hiding, 169-170
CMYK (cyan, magenta, yellow, and black), 92
    skin tones, 118-120
collecting payments, 22
collections, backgrounds. See backgrounds
Color Balance Adjustment Layers, 98-99
Color Blending Mode, 243
color casts, 93
    identifying, 94
    magenta, 99
    red, 99
color channels
    converting color images to black and white, 225
    rebuilding with Apply Image, 218-222
color correction
    alleviating extreme color problems, 124-125
        with Levels, 125-126
    Auto Color Correction, 99-100
        cropping images, 102-103
        details, 100-101
    Auto Color Correction Options Interface, 100
    balancing neutral tones with Levels, 112-114
    by numbers, 112
        skin tones, 114
    Curves, 108-110
        Luminosity Blending Mode, 111
    interchannel color correction, 131-133
    Levels, multiple color corrections, 106-108
    Levels or Curves eyedroppers, 104-106
    RGB, skin tones, 115-116

selective color correction, 121
    targeting the problem color, 121-123
skin tones
    balancing with Curves, 114-118
    CMYK, 118-120
    RGB, 115-116
temperature problems
    correcting, 126-128
    correcting mixed color temperature, 128-130
    Macbeth targets, 130-131
with Variations, 94-97
    undoing, 97
Color Fill layers, 247
color images, histograms, 35
color profiles, assigning, 120
Color Range command, 217
Color Sampler tool, 11, 35
Color Samplers, 36
coloring, hand-coloring. See hand-coloring, 245
ColorMatch RGB, 115
colors
    additive colors, 92-93
    channels, 211
        replacing damaged channels, 215-217
    CMYK, 92
        skin tones, 118-120
    Color Balance Adjustment Layers, 98-99
    combining
        with sepia, 239-240
        with black and white images, 236-238
    correcting color temperature problems, 126-128
        Macbeth targets, 130-131
        mixed color temperature, 128-130
    extreme color damage, alleviating, 215
    fine-tuning individual colors, 217-218
    HSB, 93
    images, converting to black and white. See converting, color images to black and white
    Lab, 92
    Magenta, color casts, 99
    matching, 210
    problems, alleviating extreme color problems, 124-126
    reconstructing, 210-214

red color casts, 99
RGB, 92
    ColorMatch RGB, 115
    skin tones, 118-120
subtractive colors, 92-93
of teeth, 316
toning images, 241-242
    monocolor toning, 242-243
    multicolor toning, 244-245
    Variations, 241-242
combining
    color with black-and-white images, 236-238
    filters, 197
    images, 254-255
    sepia with color, 239-240
commands
    Apply Image, 131, 218-222
    Color Range, 217
complexions, retouching, 336-338
computer equipment, 24
    back-up systems, 26
    CD- or DVD-ROM, 26
    copy work, 27
    CPU speed, 25
    hard drive space, 25
    monitors, 25
    pressure sensitive tablets, 26
    printers, 28
    professional digital cameras, 27
    prosumer digital cameras, 28
    RAM, 25
    scanners, 26
    scratch disks, 25
    software, 28
    switchers, 25
combining tonal corrections, 56-58
context-sensitive menus, 16-17
continuity mistakes, 196
contouring bodies with light, 345-347
contours, smoothing, 279
    adjusting posture, 282-284
    folds in clothing, 279-280
    narrowing faces, 280-282
    slimming techniques, 285-286
contrast
    accentuating in eyes, 302-304
    adding with Hard Light, 52
    Blending Modes, 70
    correcting, 221
    increasing
        with Blending Modes, 50
        with Curves, 46-47
    tonal changes, 70

converting
  color images to black and
    white, 224
      Blending Modes, 232-234
      Channel Mixer, 226-229
      color channels, 225
      Grayscale mode, 224-225
      luminance channels, 226
      mimicking photographic film and
      filters, 230-231
      using Calculation functions,
      235-236
  files to grayscale, 175
copied layers, 19
copy negatives, reducing reflections
  and print texture, 152
copy work, 27
correcting
  color temperature problems,
    126-128
    Macbeth targets, 130-131
    mixed color temperature,
    128-130
  colors, 210-214
    extreme color damage, 215
  contrast, 221
  high-bit scans, 65-66
  overexposed images from digital
    cameras, 82-83
  tones based on selections, 59-60
CPU speed, 25
cracks, repairing, 171-174
creative edges, adding, 258-259
Crop tool presets, creating, 12
cropping images, Auto Color
  Correction, 102-103
Curves Adjustment Layers, 46
  balancing skin tones, 114-118
  bringing out details, 48-49
  color correction, 108-110
  eyedroppers, color correction,
    104-106
  increasing contrast, 46-47
  Luminosity Blending Mode, 111
Custom filter, 268
custom workspaces, creating, 15

D

dark images, 68. *See also* **lightening**
  painting with Adjustment
    Layers, 72-73
  Screen Blending Mode, 68-70
  tonal correction, transitioning,
    70-72

darkening images with Blending
  Modes, 50
Delete Workspace, 15
deleting layers, 21. *See also*
  removing
DeLillo, Helene, 326
demarcation lines, avoiding, 203
densitometer, 35
density, creating with Multiply
  Blending Mode, 50-51
descreen function, 154
destination, patching from, 149
details
  Auto Color Correction, 100-101
  bringing out
    with Screen, 53-54
    with Curves, 48-49
digital background collections,
  196-197
digital cameras, 27-28
  overexposed images, correcting,
    82-83
  reducing noise, 159
digital flash techniques, 74-75
digital pictures, avoiding moiré
  patterns when shooting, 161
disadvantages of Variations, 94
discarding layers, 21
discoloration. *See* **stains**
distractions
  hiding, 169-170
  removing, 328-329
    portrait retouching, 278
docking palettes, 14
Dodge tool, 294
  exposure, 303
  eyes, accentuating contrast,
    302-304
  shortcut keys, 306
double chins, reducing, 298-300
dramatic lighting, 349-351
drop shadows, creating, 192-193
duplicate layers, 19
dust, 138
  removing
    brush sizes, 140
    with float and move technique,
    138-140
Dust & Scratches filter, 157, 164
DVD-ROM, 26
dynamic range, enhancing with
  selections, 62-63

E

edge burns, 348-349
edges, 256
  creative edges, adding, 258-259
  image edges, removing, 187
  vignetting portraits, 256-258
eliminating. *See* **removing**
Emboss filter, 267, 340
empty layers, 19
enhancing high-bit data, 64-66
environments, workspaces, 23
Eraser, 11
erasing pen marks, 180-182
ethnicity, skin tones, 115
evaluating image tones, 34-35
  with measuring tools, 35
  with stepwedges, 37
exposure
  balancing with fading, 86-88
  Burn tool, 303
  dark images. *See* dark images
  Dodge tool, 303
  filters, 252-255
  flashes, 74-75
  overexposed images. *See*
    overexposed images
extensions, 21
Eyedropper, 11, 35
eyedroppers
  Levels, improving tone, 43-44
  Levels or Curves, color
    correction, 104-106
eyes
  accentuating, 301-302
    cleaning up, 304-306
    contrast with Dodge and Burn
    tools, 302-304
    painterly approach, 306-309
  glasses, removing reflections,
    309-312
  redeye, removing, 312-314
  retouching, 331-333, 342-344
  tear ducts, 308

F

F keys. *See* **function keys, 13**
faces
  eyes. *See* eyes
  lips, 333-334, 344
  narrowing, 280-282
  symmetry, 344

facial features, 301
  eyes. *See* eyes
  hair. *See* hair
  teeth. *See* teeth
fading, balancing with exposure, 86-88
fashion and glamour
  retouching, 328
    eyes, 331-333, 342-344
    hair, 329, 340-342
    lighting, 348
      dramatic lighting, 349-351
      edge burns, 348-349
    lips, 333-334
    makeup, 338-340
    removing distractions, 328-329
      eyes, 331-333
      lips, 333-334
      maintaining skin texture, 329-331
    reviewing your work, 335
    skin
      complexions, 336-338
      maintaining texture, 329-331
      removing folds of skin, 338
    slimming techniques. *See* slimming techniques
    studying your work, 336
ferric oxide toners, 241
File Browser, 15
files
  converting to grayscale, 175
  extensions, 21
  organizing, 21
fill layers, 19
fill-flash, adding, 75-79
filters, 251
  applying to alpha channels, 191
  Blur, 252
  combining, 197
  Custom, 268
  Dust & Scratches, 157, 164
  Emboss, 267, 340
  focus and exposure, 252-255
  Gaussian Blur, 160, 259
    softening portraits, 291
  High Pass filter, 265-266
  Liquify
    Pucker tool, 287
    Warp tool, 299
  Median, 339
  photographic filters, mimicking to convert color images to black and white, 230-231
  Pinch, 345

sharpening, 259
  Custom filter, 268
  Emboss filter, 267
  High Pass filter, 265-266
  smart sharpening, 264-265
  Unsharp Mask filter, 260-261
  when to sharpen, 259-260
  Unsharp Mask, 260-261
    workflow of, 261-263
finding
  black and white points, 41-43
  highlights, 105
  replacement materials, 194-195
fine-tuning individual colors, 217-218
Fiorbianco, Fabrizio, 144, 168
flashes
  digital flashes, 74-75
  fill-flash, adding, 75-79
flatbed scanners, 152
flattening
  images, 205
  layers, 21
flesh tones. *See* skin tones
float and move technique, removing dust, 138-140
focus
  matching, 209
  refocusing images, 323-324
  selective focus, 252-255
  selective focus controls, portrait retouching, 322-323
frames, adding, 258
function keys, palettes, 13-14
fungus, removing, 141-144
furniture for workspaces, 24

G

Gaussian Blur, 160, 259
  softening portraits, 291
glasses
  photographing people with glasses, 312
  removing reflections from, 309-312
Gorman, Greg, 350
Gradient tool, creating stepwedges, 37
Graphics Afoot, 207
grayscale. *See also* black-and-white images
  converting files to, 175
  images, histograms, 35
Grayscale mode, converting to, 224-225

H

H&H Color Labs, 209, 278
hair
  retouching, 329, 340-342
  shaping with light, 318-320
hand-coloring black-and-white images, 245-249
  traditional versus digital, 250-251
hard drive space, 25
Hard Light Blending Mode, adding contrast, 52
healing skin, 288-289
Healing Brush, 11, 17
  controlling coverage of, 143
  healing from patterns, 144-146
  removing
    mold, mildew, and fungus, 141
    scratches, 166-168
  troubleshooting, 289
hiding
  clutter and distractions, 169-170
  palettes, 13
High Pass filter, 265-266
high-bit data
  benefits of, 63-64
  capturing, 64-66
  enhancing, 64-66
high-bit scans, correcting, 65-66
high-key images, 34
highlight exposure of red channel, improving, 82
highlights
  balancing, 112
  revealing true highlights, 105
  specular highlights, reducing, 84-85
Hirsch, Ron, 97
histograms, 34-35
History Brush, 11
  fixing blemishes, 290-292
hot spots, reducing, 300-301
HSB (hue, saturation, and brightness), 93
Hue/Saturation, 202
humidity, 141

I

identifying color casts, 94
image edges, removing, 187
image luminosity, loading, 89
Image Variations. *See* Variations

images. *See also* photographs;
  portraits
    borrowing image
      information, 200
    combining, 254-255
    cropping before using Auto
      Color Correction, 102-103
    dark images. *See* dark images
    darkening with Blending
      Modes, 50
    erasing pen marks, 180-182
    evaluating tones, 34-35
      with measuring tools, 35
    flattening, 205
    histograms, 35
    increasing contrast with
      Blending Modes, 50
    lightening with Blending
      Modes, 50
    maintaining structure, 162-164
    navigating, 17-18
    overexposed images. *See*
      overexposed images
    panning through, 18
    refocusing, 323-324
    repairing
      healing from patterns, 144-146
      with Clone Stamp, 142-143
    scanning, 152
    softening, 252
    tips for starting restoration, 29
    tones. *See* tones
    toning with color, 241-242
      monocolor toning, 242-243
      multicolor toning, 244-245
      Variations, 241-242
  improving
    dark images. *See* dark images
    highlight exposure of red
      channel, 82
    image tones with Levels, 39
    skin tones, 213
    teeth, 315-317
      removing braces, 317-318
    tones
      with Levels' eyedroppers, 43-44
      with Output levels, 45
  increasing. *See also* adding
    contrast with Blending
      Modes, 50
    size of thumbnails, 212
Info palette, 36
  identifying color casts, 94
interchannel color correction,
  131-133
IOGEAR, switchers, 25
isolating Adjustment Layers, 70

J

Johnson, Art, 178, 198
Johnson, Stephen (float and move
  technique), 138
jowls, reducing, 298-300

K

keyboard shortcuts, 10
  for accessing channels, 159
  for changing brush size or
    hardness, 13
  Dodge tool, 306
keys
  Macintosh Command (Cmd), 10
  PC Control (Ctrl), 10
Kuaimoku, Eric, 285

L

Lab Color mode, 92, 216
  blurring and sharpening, 160-161
Lasso, 11
layer masks, 70. *See also* masks
  multiple masked adjustments, 61
layer sets, 20-21
layers, 19
  Adjustment Layers. *See*
    Adjustment Layers
  background layers, 18
  Channel Mixer Adjustment
    Layers, 178
  Color Balance Adjustment
    Layers, 98-99
  Color Fill layers, 247
  copied layers, 19
  Curves Adjustment Layers, color
    correction, 108-110
  Curves Adjustment Layers. *See*
    Curves Adjustment Layers
  deleting, 21
  duplicate layers, 19
    *working on to reduce
      wrinkles, 294*
  empty layers, 19
  fill layers, 19
  flattening, 21
  Levels Adjustment Layers. *See*
    Levels Adjustment Layers
  merged layers, creating, 19
  naming, 19-21, 248
  navigating, 19-20
  neutral layers, 19
  Soft Light neutral layers, working
    on to reduce wrinkles, 294

learning tool tips, 11
Leffingwell, PJ, 238
Levels Adjustment Layers
  balancing neutral tones, 112-114
  color correction, multiple color
    corrections, 106-108
  correcting extreme color
    problems, 125-126
  eyedroppers, color correction,
    104-106
  finding black and white points,
    41-43
  histogram, 34
  improving tones, 39
    *black and white point sliders,
      39-40*
    with eyedroppers, 43-44
    midtone sliders, 40-41
    with Output levels, 45
  tones, 38-39
levels of retouching, 274-275
libraries, 196. *See also* collections
lifting subjects off of photographs,
  190-192
light
  contouring bodies, 345-347
  painting with, 88-89
  shaping hair, 318-320
lightening. *See also* dark images
  details with Screen and Channel
    Mixer Adjustment Layer, 54
  images with Blending Modes, 50
lighting
  for glamour, 348
    dramatic lighting, 349-351
    edge burns, 348-349
  in workspaces, 23
Linear Dodge Blending Mode, 70
lines, avoiding demarcation
  lines, 203
lips, retouching, 333-334
Liquify filter
  Pucker tool, 287
  Warp tool, 299
loading
  Adjustment Layers, 54-55
  image luminosity, 89
low-key images, 34
luminance channels, converting
  color images to black and
  white, 226
luminosity, loading image
  luminosity, 89
Luminosity Blending mode,
  using with Curves Adjustment
  Layers, 111

M

Macbeth ColorChecker, 130-131

Macbeth targets, 130-131

Macintosh Command (Cmd)
key, 10

magenta, color casts, 99

Magnifying tools, context-sensitive
menus, 17

maintaining image structure,
162-164

makeup, retouching, 338-340

Margulis, Dan, 115

Marquee, 11

Marshall Oils, 245

masks, Gradient tool, 70

matching
colors, 210
sharpness of elements, 209

Measure tool, 11

measuring tools, evaluating
tones, 35

Median filter, 339

medium-key images, 34

Melnick, Sean, 188

menus, context-sensitive
menus, 16-17

merged layers, creating, 19

midtone gamma slider, 38

midtone sliders, improving
tones, 40-41

midtones, balancing, 112

mildew, removing, 141

mistakes, continuity mistakes, 196

mixed color temperature problems,
correcting, 128-130

moiré from digital cameras,
reducing, 159

moiré artifacts, reducing, 151

moiré patterns, avoiding when
shooting digital pictures, 161

moiré problems, reducing, 158-159

mold, removing, 141-144

monitors, 25
workspace, 15

monocolor toning, 242-243

moving
Adjustment Layers, 54
objects, closer together, 207-209

multicolor toning, 244-245

Multiply Blending Mode, 50-51
overexposed images, 80-81

N

naming
layers, 19-21, 248
Tool presets, 12

navigating
images, 17-18
layers, 19-20

nested retouching tools, 11

neutral layers, 19

new features, File Browser, 15

noise, reducing digital camera
noise, 159

Notes tool, 327

numbers, color correction, 112
skin tones, 114

O

O'Connell, Patrick, 24, 200

objects, moving closer together,
207-209

options bar, 13

organizing files, 21

Output levels, improving tone, 45

overexposed images, 80
from digital cameras, correcting,
82-83
Multiply Blending Mode, 80-81

overexposure
balancing exposure and fading,
86-88
specular highlights, reducing,
84-85

Overlay Blending Mode, 243

P

painterly approach to accentuating
eyes, 306-309

painting
with Adjustment Layers, 72-73
with light, 88-89

palette wells, 13

palettes
Channels, 53
docking, 14
function keys, 13-14
hiding, 13
Info, 36
identifying color casts, 94
revealing, 13
tips for working with, 14

Palmer Multimedia Imaging, 207

Palmer, Wayne, 152, 171,
207, 249

panning through images, 18

paper texture, reducing, 154-156

Patch tool, 147-150, 167
patching, 148-150

patching
from destination, 149
from patterns, 149-150
from source, 148
skin, 289-290

Path Selection tools, 11

Path tool, tips for using, 290

paths, creating with Pen tool, 169

patience when rebuilding
portraits, 206-207

Pattern Maker, 145

patterns
healing from, 144-146
patching from, 149-150
print patterns, removing,
156-158

payments, collecting, 22

PC Control (Ctrl) key, 10

Pen tool, 11, 168
paths, creating, 169

Pencil, 11

pens, erasing marks from, 180-182

perseverance, rebuilding portraits,
206-207

photographic film and filters, mimicking to convert color images to
black and white, 230-231

photographing people with
glasses, 312

photographs. *See also* images;
portraits
lifting subjects off of, 190-192
replacement materials, finding,
194-195
storing, 141

Pin Light Blending Mode, 243

Pinch filter, 345

Pool, Phil, 257

portrait retouchers, role of, 273

portrait retouching
accentuating facial features. *See*
facial features
contours, 279
adjusting posture, 282-284
folds in clothing, 279-280
narrowing faces, 280-282
slimming techniques, 285-286

eyes. *See* eyes
levels of, 274-275
refocusing images, 323-324
removing distractions, 278
selective focus controls, 322-323
skin. *See* skin
soft-focus effects, 320-322
strategies for, 276-278
portraits. *See also* **images;**
photographs
rebuilding, 201-204
with patience and perseverance,
206-207
softening
with selective focus controls,
322-323
soft portrait effects, 320-322
vignetting, 256-258
posterization, 70
posture, adjusting, 282-284
Preset manager, 249
presets, Tool presets, 12-13
pressure-sensitive tablets, 26
preventing redeye, 312
previsualization, 34
print patterns, removing, 156-158
print texture, reducing, 151
before retouching, 151-154
printers, 28
prints, scanning, 172
problems, targeting color problems,
121-123
professional digital cameras, 27
prosumer digital cameras, 28
Pucker tool, 287

Q

Quantum Mechanic Lite, 161
Quantum Mechanic Pro, 161
Quick Mask, 259
Quick Mask technique, 184-188

R

RAM, 25
re-creating
backgrounds. *See* backgrounds
colors, 210-214
rebuilding portraits. *See* **portraits**
red, color casts, 99
red channel, improving highlight
exposure, 82
redeye, 312-314

reducing
digital camera noise, 159
double chins, 298-300
moiré from digital cameras, 159
moiré artifacts, 151
moiré problems, 158-159
paper texture, 154-156
print texture, 151
before retouching, 151-154
reflections before
retouching, 152
shiny spots on skin, 300-301
specular highlights, 84-85
wrinkles, 293
by working on duplicate
layers, 294
by working on Soft Light
neutral layers, 294
reversing the aging process,
294-296
refining your work, 335
reflections
reducing before retouching, 152
removing from glasses, 309-312
refocusing images, 323-324
removing
braces from teeth, 317-318
Color Samplers, 36
discoloration. *See* stains
distractions, 328-329
portrait retouching, 278
dust
brush sizes, 140
float and move technique,
138-140
five o'clock shadows, 296-298
fungus, 143-144
image edges, 187
mold, mildew, and fungus, 141
print patterns, 156-158
redeye, 312-314
reflections from glasses, 309-312
scratches, 166
with Clone Stamp and Healing
Brush, 166-168
stains, 174
aged photos, 175-177
unwanted elements, 168
hiding clutter and distractions,
169-170
wires or cables, 168-169
repairing
images
with Clone Stamp, 142-143
healing from patterns, 144-146
tears, rips, and cracks, 171-174

replacement materials, finding,
194-195
replacing
backgrounds, 192
channels, 220
color channels, 215-217
Reset Palette Locations, 15
retouching, 274
eyes, 331-333, 342-344
fashion and glamour retouching
techniques. *See* fashion and
glamour retouching
hair, 329, 340-342
lips, 333-334
portraits. *See* portrait retouching
reducing print texture before
retouching, 151-154
reducing reflections before
retouching, 152
skin. *See* skin
strategies
looking at the big picture, 326
looking at the details, 326
written confirmation of what
needs to be done, 326-327
strategies for, 326
retouching workflow, 22
revealing
palettes, 13
true highlights, 105
reviewing your work, 335-336
RGB (red, green, blue), 92
ColorMatch RGB, 115
skin tones, 115-120
rips, repairing, 171-174
roles of portrait retouchers, 273

S

saving
Adjustment Layers, 54-56
Tool presets, 12-13
workspaces, 14-15
scales, tonal values, 46
scanners, 26
descreen function, 154
flatbed scanners, 152
scanning
images, 152
large print pieces, 172
scans, correcting high-bit
scans, 65-66
Schewe, Jeff, 344
scratch disks, 25

scratches, removing, 166
with Clone Stamp and Healing Brush, 166-168
Screen Blending Mode, 53-54
lightening dark images, 68-70
screens, adjusting width and height, 18
select and desaturate technique, removing redeye, 313
select and substitute technique, removing redeye, 314
selections
basing tonal corrections on, 59-60
enhancing dynamic range, 62-63
making, 190
selective color correction, 121
targeting the problem color, 121-123
selective focus, 252-255
selective focus controls, portrait retouching, 322-323
selenium toners, 241
sepia, combining with color, 239-240
shades. See color casts
shadows, 193
adjusting, 335
balancing, 112
drop shadows, creating, 192-193
five o'clock shadows, removing, 296-298
shaping hair with light, 318-320
sharpening
filters, 259
Custom filter, 268
Emboss filter, 267
High Pass filter, 265-266
smart sharpening, 264-265
Unsharp Mask filter, 260-261
when to sharpen, 259-260
in Lab Color mode, 160-161
Sharpening tools, 11
sharpness of image elements, matching, 209
shortcuts, keyboard shortcuts. See keyboard shortcuts
showing palettes, 13
skin, 288
blemishes, 288
healing good over bad, 288-289
patching good over bad, 289-290
using History Brush and Blending Modes, 290-292

complexions, 336-338
double chins, reducing, 298-300
five o'clock shadows, removing, 296-298
hot spots, reducing, 300-301
maintaining texture, 329-331
makeup, 338-340
removing folds of skin, 338
shiny spots, reducing, 300-301
tones. See skin tones
wrinkles, 292-293
reducing, 293-296
skin and hair color reference charts, 115
skin tones, 112
balancing with Curves, 114-118
CMYK, 118-120
ethnicity, 115
improving, 213
RGB, 118-120
sliders
black and white point sliders, improving tones, 39-40
midtone gamma slider, 38
midtone sliders, improving tones, 40-41
splitting, 263
slimming techniques, 343
contouring bodies with light, 345-347
portrait retouching, 285-286
tummy tucks, 344
smart sharpening, 264-265
smoothing contours, 279
adjusting posture, 282-284
folds in clothing, 279-280
narrowing faces, 280-282
slimming techniques, 285-286
Soft Light mode, 341
Soft Light neutral layers, reducing wrinkles, 294
soft-focus effects, portrait retouching, 320-322
softening
images, 252
portraits
Gaussian Blur, 291
selective focus controls, 322-323
soft-focus effects, 320-322
software, 28
source, patching from, 148
specular highlights, reducing, 84-85
splitting sliders, 263
Sponge tool, 306

stains
balancing, 178-180
removing, 174
stain of age, 175-177
stealing image information, 200
stepwedges, 37
stomachs, slimming, 344
storing photographs, 141
strategies
for portrait retouching, 276-278
for retouching, 326-327
structure of images, maintaining, 162-164
studying your work, 336
subjects. See also objects
lifting off of photographs, 190-192
moving, 207
substitute body parts, working with, 198-199
subtractive colors, 92-93
switchers, 25
symmetry, 344

T

tans, retouching complexions, 336-338
Tapp, Eddie, 349
Tarantino, Chris, 131, 268
targeting, 38
targets, Macbeth targets, 130-131
tear ducts, 308
tears, repairing, 171-174
techniques
Quick Mask, 184-188
select and desaturate, removing redeye, 313
select and substitute, removing redeye, 314
teeth
color of, 316
improving, 315-317
removing braces, 317-318
temperature, color temperature problems
correcting, 126-130
Macbeth targets, 130-131
texture
of skin, maintaining, 329-331. See also skin
paper texture, reducing, 154-156
print texture. See print texture
Thompson, Laurie, 184, 190
thumbnails, increasing size of, 212

tinges. *See* color casts

tintypes, 68

Tompkins, Leigh-Anne, 206-207

tonal changes, contrast, 70

tonal correcting, transitioning in dark images, 70-72

Tonal tools, 11

tonal values, 63

toners, 241

tones

  basing corrections on selecting, 59-60

  Blending Modes. *See* Blending Modes

  combining tonal corrections, 56-58

  correcting with multiple masked adjustments, 61

  details, bringing out with Curves, 48-49

  enhancing dynamic range with selections, 62-63

  evaluating image tones, 34-35

    with measuring tools, 35

  finding black and white points, 41-43

  improving with Output levels, 45

  improving with Levels, 39

    black and white point sliders, 39-40

    eyedroppers, 43-44

    midtone sliders, 40-41

  increasing contrast with Curves, 46-47

  Levels, 38-39

  neutral tones, balancing with Levels, 112-114

  skin tones, balancing with Curves, 114-118

  stepwedges, 37

  tracking changes with Color Samplers, 36

toning

  images with color, 241-242

    monocolor toning, 242-243

    multicolor toning, 244-245

    Variations, 241-242

  monocolor toning, 242-243

  multicolor toning, 244-245

toning tools, context-sensitive menus, 17

Tool presets, 12-13

tool tips, learning, 11

toolbars, activating tools, 11

tools

  activating in Photoshop toolbar, 11

  Annotation, 11

  Brush, 11

  Burn, accentuating contrast in eyes, 302-304

  Clone Stamp. *See* Clone Stamp tool

  Color Sampler, 11, 35

  Dodge

    accentuating contrast in eyes, 302-304

    reducing wrinkles, 294

  Eraser, 11

  Eyedropper, 11, 35

  Gradient

    creating stepwedges, 37

    masks, 70

  Healing Brush. *See* Healing Brush

  History Brush, 11

    fixing blemishes, 290-292

  Lasso, 11

  Magnifying tools, context-sensitive menus, 17

  Marquee, 11

  Measure, 11

  nested retouching tools, 11

  nested tools, 11

  Notes, 327

  Patch. *See* Patch tool

  Path, tips for using, 290

  Path Selection tools, 11

  Pen, 11, 168

    creating paths, 169

  Pencil, 11

  Pucker, 287

  Sharpening tools, 11

  Sponge, 306

  Tonal tools, 11

  toning tools, context-sensitive menus, 17

  Variations. *See* Variations

  Warp, 299

  Zoom, 17

tracking tonal changes with Color Samplers, 36

transitioning tonal correction in dark images, 70-72

Trembley, Diane, 248

troubleshooting Healing Brush, 289

tummy tucks, 344

U-V

undoing changes of Variations, 97

Unsharp Mask filter, 260-261

  tips for using, 263

  workflow of, 261-263

unwanted elements

  hiding clutter and distractions, 169-170

  removing, 168

    wires or cables, 168-169

Vander Houwen, Greg, 267

Variations, 94

  color correction, 94-97

  disadvantages of, 94

  toning, 241-242

  undoing changes, 97

Varis, Lee, 261, 338

viewing tool tips, 11

vignetting portraits, 256-258

Volk, Carl, 158

W-X-Y-Z

Walden, Bob, 180

Warner, John, 162

Warp tool, 299

wedging hair, 318-320

Weller, Lloyd, 218

Weston, Edward, 34

white point sliders, improving tones, 39-40

white points, 38

  finding, 41-43

wires, removing, 168-169

workflow

  retouching workflow, 22

  of Unsharp Mask filter, 261-263

workspaces, 22

  computer equipment. *See* computer equipment

  creating custom workspaces, 15

  environments, 23

  furniture, 24

  lighting, 23

  monitors, 15

  saving, 14-15

  setting up, 14-15

wrinkles in skin. *See* skin, wrinkles

Zirbes, Lori, 250

Zoom tool, 17

zooming in, 17-1

informIT

www.informit.com

VOICES THAT MATTER

VISIT OUR WEB SITE

WWW.NEWRIDERS.COM

On our web site, you'll find information about our other books, authors, tables of contents, and book errata. You will also find information about book registration and how to purchase our books, both domestically and internationally.

EMAIL US

Contact us at: **nrfeedback@newriders.com**

- If you have comments or questions about this book
- To report errors that you have found in this book
- If you have a book proposal to submit or are interested in writing for New Riders
- If you are an expert in a computer topic or technology and are interested in being a technical editor who reviews manuscripts for technical accuracy

Contact us at: **nreducation@newriders.com**

- If you are an instructor from an educational institution who wants to preview New Riders books for classroom use. Email should include your name, title, school, department, address, phone number, office days/hours, text in use, and enrollment, along with your request for desk/examination copies and/or additional information.

Contact us at: **nrmedia@newriders.com**

- If you are a member of the media who is interested in reviewing copies of New Riders books. Send your name, mailing address, and email address, along with the name of the publication or web site you work for.

BULK PURCHASES/CORPORATE SALES

The publisher offers discounts on this book when ordered in quantity for bulk purchases and special sales. For sales within the U.S., please contact: Corporate and Government Sales (800) 382-3419 or **corpsales@pearsontechgroup.com**. Outside of the U.S., please contact: International Sales (317) 581-3793 or **international@pearsontechgroup.com**.

WRITE TO US

New Riders Publishing
201 W. 103rd St.
Indianapolis, IN 46290-1097

CALL/FAX US

Toll-free (800) 571-5840
If outside U.S. (317) 581-3500
Ask for New Riders
FAX: (317) 581-4663

Publishing
the Voices
that Matter

OUR AUTHORS

PRESS ROOM

| web development | design | photoshop | new media | 3-D | server technologies |

EDUCATORS

ABOUT US

CONTACT US

You already know that New Riders brings you the **Voices that Matter**.

But what does that mean? It means that New Riders brings you the

Voices that challenge your assumptions, take your talents to the next

level, or simply help you better understand the complex technical world

we're all navigating.

Visit **www.newriders.com** to find:

▸ **10% discount** and **free shipping** on specific book purchases

▸ Never-before-published chapters

▸ Sample chapters and excerpts

▸ Author bios and interviews

▸ Contests and enter-to-wins

▸ Up-to-date industry event information

▸ Book reviews

▸ Special offers from our friends and partners

▸ Info on how to join our User Group program

▸ Ways to have your Voice heard

New
Riders

W W W . N E W R I D E R S . C O M

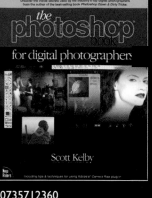

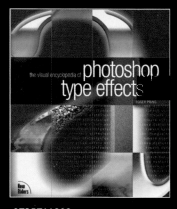
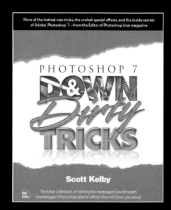